Effective Implementation of ISO 14001

Also available from ASQ Quality Press:

ANSI/ISO/ASQ E14001-2004: Environmental management systems—
Requirements with guidance for use
ANSI/ISO/ASQ

Integrating ISO 14001 into a Quality Management System, Second
Edition
Marilyn R. Block and I. Robert Marash

The ASQ Auditing Handbook, Third Edition
J.P. Russell, editing director

The Management System Auditor's Handbook
Joe Kausek

Clean, Green, and Read All Over: Ten Rules for Effective Corporate
Environmental and Sustainability Reporting
J. Emil Morhardt

The Certified Manager of Quality/Organizational Excellence Handbook:
Third Edition
Russell T. Westcott, editor

Enterprise Process Mapping: Integrating Systems for Compliance and
Business Excellence
Charles G. Cobb

Bringing Business Ethics to Life: Achieving Corporate Social
Responsibility
Bjørn Andersen

5S for Service Organizations and Offices: A Lean Look at Improvements
Debashis Sarkar

Lean Kaizen: A Simplified Approach to Process Improvements
George Alukal and Anthony Manos

Root Cause Analysis: Simplified Tools and Techniques, Second Edition
Bjørn Andersen and Tom Fagerhaug

To request a complimentary catalog of ASQ Quality Press publications,
call 800-248-1946, or visit our Web site at http://qualitypress.asq.org.

Effective Implementation of ISO 14001

Marilyn R. Block

ASQ Quality Press
Milwaukee, Wisconsin

American Society for Quality, Quality Press, Milwaukee 53203
© 2007 by ASQ
All rights reserved. Published 2006
Printed in the United States of America
12 11 10 09 08 07 06   5 4 3 2 1

Library of Congress Cataloging-in-Publication Data

Block, Marilyn R.
  Effective implementation of ISO 14001 / Marilyn R. Block.
    p. cm.
  Includes bibliographical references and index.
  ISBN-13: 978-0-87389-688-7 (alk. paper)
  ISBN-10: 0-87389-688-2 (alk. paper)
  1. ISO 14000 Series Standards. 2. Manufacturing industries—Environmental
aspects. I. Title.

  TS155.7.B554 2006
  658.4'08—dc22   2006018465

ISBN-13: 978-0-87389-688-7
ISBN-10: 0-87389-688-2

Publisher: William A. Tony
Acquisitions Editor: Annemieke Hytinen
Project Editor: Paul O'Mara
Production Administrator: Randall Benson

ASQ Mission: The American Society for Quality advances individual, organizational,
and community excellence worldwide through learning, quality improvement, and
knowledge exchange.

Attention Bookstores, Wholesalers, Schools and Corporations: ASQ Quality Press books,
videotapes, audiotapes, and software are available at quantity discounts with bulk purchases for
business, educational, or instructional use. For information, please contact ASQ Quality Press at
800-248-1946, or write to ASQ Quality Press, P.O. Box 3005, Milwaukee, WI 53201-3005.

To place orders or to request a free copy of the ASQ Quality Press Publications Catalog,
including ASQ membership information, call 800-248-1946. Visit our Web site at www.asq.org
or http://qualitypress.asq.org.

Printed in the United States of America

 Printed on acid-free paper

Quality Press
600 N. Plankinton Avenue
Milwaukee, Wisconsin 53203
Call toll free 800-248-1946
Fax 414-272-1734
www.asq.org
http://qualitypress.asq.org
http://standardsgroup.asq.org
E-mail: authors@asq.org

In memory of Ricky L. Chapman and Kevin S. Hursey, who played significant roles in the development and maintenance of the Gary Works environmental management system.

Table of Contents

List of Tables . . . . *xiii*
Preface . . . . *xv*
Acknowledgments . . . . *xxv*

Chapter 1 Environmental Management **1**
   History of Environmental Management 1
   Purpose of Environmental Management 6
   ISO 14001 Worldwide 8
   Environmental Management in the Private Sector 10
   Environmental Management in the Public Sector 10
   Revision of ISO 14001:1996 12
   Organization of ISO 14001:2004 12
   Supporting Guidelines 16
   References 17

Chapter 2 General Requirements **19**
   ISO 14001:2004 Text 19
   ISO 14001:1996 Text 19
   Significant Changes 19
   Intent of ISO 14001:2004 20

Chapter 3 Environmental Policy **23**
   ISO 14001:2004 Text 23
   ISO 14001:1996 Text 23
   Significant Changes 24
   Intent of ISO 14001:2004 25
   Examples 28

Chapter 4 Environmental Aspects **35**
   ISO 14001:2004 Text 35
   ISO 14001:1996 Text 35

Significant Changes   36
Intent of ISO 14001:2004   37
Examples.   40

Chapter 5   Legal and Other Requirements.   61
ISO 14001:2004 Text   61
ISO 14001:1996 Text.   61
Significant Changes   62
Intent of ISO 14001:2004   62
Examples.   64

Chapter 6   Objectives, Targets, and Programs.   83
ISO 14001:2004 Text   83
ISO 14001:1996 Text.   83
Significant Changes   84
Intent of ISO 14001:2004   85
Examples.   88

Chapter 7   Resources, Roles, Responsibility, and Authority . . .   99
ISO 14001:2004 Text   99
ISO 14001:1996 Text.   99
Significant Changes   100
Intent of ISO 14001:2004   100
Examples.   102

Chapter 8   Competence, Training, and Awareness   123
ISO 14001:2004 Text   123
ISO 14001:1996 Text.   123
Significant Changes   124
Intent of ISO 14001:2004   125
Examples.   127

Chapter 9   Communication.   139
ISO 14001:2004 Text   139
ISO 14001:1996 Text.   139
Significant Changes   140
Intent of ISO 14001:2004   140
    Internal Communication.   140
    External Communication   141
Examples.   154

Chapter 10   System Documentation.   163
ISO 14001:2004 Text   163
ISO 14001:1996 Text.   163

Significant Changes 164
Intent of ISO 14001:2004 164
Examples... 166

Chapter 11   Control of Documents...................... 197
ISO 14001:2004 Text 197
ISO 14001:1996 Text................................. 197
Significant Changes 198
Intent of ISO 14001:2004 199
Examples... 201

Chapter 12   Operational Control....................... 215
ISO 14001:2004 Text 215
ISO 14001:1996 Text................................. 215
Significant Changes 216
Intent of ISO 14001:2004 216
Examples... 218

Chapter 13   Emergency Preparedness and Response 241
ISO 14001:2004 Text 241
ISO 14001:1996 Text................................. 241
Significant Changes 242
Intent of ISO 14001:2004 242
Examples... 244

Chapter 14   Monitoring and Measurement................. 253
ISO 14001:2004 Text 253
ISO 14001:1996 Text................................. 253
Significant Changes 254
Intent of ISO 14001:2004 254
Examples... 257

Chapter 15   Evaluation of Compliance 269
ISO 14001:2004 Text 269
ISO 14001:1996 Text................................. 269
Significant Changes 270
Intent of ISO 14001:2004 270
Examples... 272

Chapter 16   Nonconformity, Corrective Action and
Preventive Action................................... 281
ISO 14001:2004 Text 281
ISO 14001:1996 Text................................. 281
Significant Changes 282

Intent of ISO 14001:2004   283
Examples.   284

Chapter 17   Control of Records **299**
ISO 14001:2004 Text   299
ISO 14001:1996 Text.   299
Significant Changes   300
Intent of ISO 14001:2004   300
Examples.   302

Chapter 18   Internal Environmental Management
System Audit **311**
ISO 14001:2004 Text   311
ISO 14001:1996 Text.   311
Significant Changes   312
Intent of ISO 14001:2004   313
Examples.   315

Chapter 19   Management Review. **323**
ISO 14001:2004 Text   323
ISO 14001:1996 Text.   323
Significant Changes   324
Intent of ISO 14001:2004   325
Examples.   326

Chapter 20   The Future of Environmental Management **335**
The ISO 9001 Model   335
Integration of Management Systems   337
Environmental Management and Occupational
Health and Safety.   338
Environmental Management and Social
Responsibility   340
Implementation by SMEs   341
Experience with ISO 14001:1996   342
Outlook for Medium-Sized Businesses   343
The Challenge Ahead   344

Glossary. *345*
Bibliography *349*
Index. *351*

List of Tables

Table 1.1   Standards in the ISO 14000 series. 5

Table 1.2   ISO 14001 certifications worldwide, 1996–2004. 8

Table 1.3   ISO 14001 certifications by region, 1996–2004. 9

Table 1.4   ISO 14001 certifications in North America, 1996–2004. 9

Table 1.5   Top ten countries with ISO 14001 certifications, 2004. 10

Table 4.1   Examples of environmental aspects and impacts. 37

Table 9.1   Written communications approaches and tools. 143

Table 9.2   Verbal communications approaches and tools. 146

Table 9.3   Other communications approaches and tools. 152

Table 10.1   EMS manual organized by activity. 166

Table 20.1   Comparison of ISO 9001 certificates and ISO 14001
certificates worldwide eight years after publication. 336

Table 20.2   Comparison of ISO 9001 certificates and ISO 14001
certificates in North America eight years after
publication. 337

Table 20.3   ISO 9001 certificates worldwide, 2004. 337

Table 20.4   Comparison of clauses in ISO 14001:2004 and OHSAS
18001:1999. 339

Table 20.5   Definitions of small and medium-sized businesses. 341

Preface

Revision of ISO 14001, *Environmental management systems—Specification with guidance for use*, has generated questions among those responsible for implementing new environmental management systems and those in charge of maintaining mature ones. Some view ISO 14001:2004 as a clarification of previously ambiguous language; others believe it has imposed additional requirements.

Effective Implementation of ISO 14001 provides a clear explanation of each requirement imposed by ISO 14001:2004 and describes how it compares to the comparable requirement in the original standard. It also presents the documentation developed by organizations from three discrete sectors—heavy industry, service, and government. These organizations are described in detail below.

For readers who are designing and implementing an environmental management system for the first time, *Effective Implementation of ISO 14001* goes beyond general description to identify the ways in which ISO 14001:2004 can be implemented within the constraints of business strategies, environmental imperatives, and regulatory requirements. For readers faced with maintaining a mature environmental management system, it assists the process of comparing existing approaches and activities with the revised requirements, identifying weak or missing elements, and modifying the environmental management system to conform to ISO 14001:2004.

The book is organized into 20 chapters. Chapter 1 provides an overview of environmental management and the historical underpinnings of ISO 14001:2004 and is, therefore, a good place to start. Chapter 20 contemplates the future of environmental management.

Chapters 2 through 19 correspond to the 18 numbered clauses and subclauses in ISO 14001:2004 that contain environmental management system requirements. Because each chapter is dedicated to a single clause or subclause, it is not necessary to read them in order. Each of these chapters embodies the following format:

- *ISO 14001:2004 text and ISO 14001:1996 text.* The revised language of the relevant clause or subclause from ISO 14001:2004 and that of the comparable clause or subclause from the original standard are presented. This assists the reader in comparing the two documents.

- *Significant changes.* Discussion of wording changes in the revised standard (2004) and how the new language differs from the wording contained in the original standard (1996).

- *Intent of ISO 14001:2004.* Explanation of the intent of the clause and discussion of acceptable approaches to implementation.

- *Examples of how the clause has been implemented.* When ISO 14001:1996 was published, books dedicated to the purpose and intent of an environmental management system (including one by this author) were long on conjecture and short on experience. Nearly a decade later, however, there has been ample opportunity for organizations across a variety of business sectors to translate theory into practice. Their collective experience confirms that no single approach is appropriate for all organizations.

The procedures presented in each chapter, therefore, are not intended as templates to be copied. Rather, they illustrate three different approaches to fulfilling stated ISO 14001:2004 requirements. Interestingly, none of the procedures employs a flowchart. If an organization prefers to present procedures in the form of flowcharts or other symbols and images, it is acceptable to do so. Some procedures might be most easily understood in the form of a videotape, DVD, or CD.

Although text procedures are not appropriate in all situations, this format enables the reader to clearly understand exactly how each example organization fulfills ISO requirements. Every procedure is presented as written by the implementing organization with the following exceptions:

- Header information such as original issue date, revision level, number of pages, and organizational logo is not reproduced. Each procedure is identified by title and the date on which the current revision went into effect.

- Some accompanying exhibits and appendixes are not provided. Those that are included are identified by reference to the page on which they appear.

- Proper names have been removed. Any reference to individuals is by title only.

- All internal contact information such as telephone numbers and Web addresses used by workers to access documents has been sanitized.

ABOUT THE ORGANIZATIONS

Although the majority of organizations that have implemented ISO 14001 come from manufacturing, registration of companies in the service sector has grown dramatically. Less obvious because they self-declare rather than pursue registration, but no less important, are the many U.S. federal government agencies that have implemented environmental management systems. Examples of the practices employed to fulfill ISO 14001 requirements must, therefore, represent all three of these segments.

Three organizations have generously shared their environmental management system documentation: United States Steel Corporation exemplifies heavy industry while Delaware North Companies Parks & Resorts epitomizes service companies. Government efforts are represented by the United States Coast Guard Air Station Cape Cod.

UNITED STATES STEEL CORPORATION

United States Steel Corporation, founded in 1901 and headquartered in Pittsburgh, Pennsylvania, manufactures a wide variety of steel sheet, tubular, and tin products, coke, and taconite pellets. The company has a worldwide annual raw steel production capability of 26.8 million net tons.

U. S. Steel is the second largest integrated steel producer in North America. Its domestic primary steel operations are:

- Gary Works, Gary, Indiana

  - East Chicago Tin, East Chicago, Indiana (operated as part of Gary Works)

  - Midwest Plant, Portage, Indiana (operated as part of Gary Works)

- Great Lakes Works, Ecorse and River Rouge, Michigan

- Mon Valley Works (including the Edgar Thomson and Irvin plants near Pittsburgh, Pennsylvania, and Fairless Works near Philadelphia, Pennsylvania)

- Granite City Works, Granite City, Illinois

- Fairfield Works, Birmingham, Alabama

U. S. Steel operates a seamless tubular mill, Lorain Pipe Mills, in Lorain, Ohio. The company produces coke at Clairton Works near Pittsburgh, at Gary Works, and Granite City Works. On northern Minnesota's Mesabi Iron Range, U. S. Steel's iron ore mining and taconite pellet operations— Minnesota Taconite (Minntac) and Keewatin Taconite (Keetac)—support the steelmaking effort. A subsidiary, ProCoil Company, provides steel distribution and processing services.

U. S. Steel maintains an environmental management system that applies to the integrated operations of Gary Works, tin and pickling facilities at East Chicago Tin, and the finishing and support operations at the Midwest Plant. Processes within these operations include cokemaking and by-product recovery, ironmaking and sintering, steel slabs, hot and cold rolled steel sheet, galvanized steel, tin plate and tin-free steel, and black plate products.

Gary Works, U. S. Steel's largest manufacturing plant, is situated on approximately 4000 acres on the south shore of Lake Michigan. With both steelmaking and finishing facilities, Gary Works is one of five integrated steelmaking facilities U. S. Steel operates in the United States.

Sheet products, hot strip mill plate products, and tin products are manufactured at Gary Works. Hot rolled, cold rolled, and galvanized sheet products are produced for customers in the automotive, metal building components, home construction, and appliance markets. Gary Works produces tin mill products—electrolytic tin plate and black plate—used in the manufacture of food and beverage containers, aerosol cans, paint cans, and pails.

Gary Works has an annual raw steelmaking capability of 7.5 million tons. It also operates three coke batteries with an annual production capacity of approximately 1.6 million tons.

Production facilities include:

- Four blast furnaces

- Two basic oxygen process shops

- Vacuum degasser

- Four continuous casters

- Ladle metallurgy facility

- 84-inch hot strip mill

- Six-stand, five-stand, and two-stand cold reduction lines

- 84-inch and 80-inch pickle lines

- Anneal and temper line

- Hot dip galvanizing

- Electrogalvanizing lines

- Two electrolytic tinning lines

East Chicago Tin and the Midwest Plant are finishing facilities that operate as part of Gary Works. East Chicago Tin has an annual production capacity of approximately 600,000 tons of tin products—tin plate, black plate, tin-free steel, and coated sheet. These products serve primarily the container market for the manufacture of cans, ends, and closures for the food and beverage industry. Production facilities include:

- 6-stand cold mill

- 2-stand temper mill

- Continuous anneal line

- Batch anneal line

- Pickle line

- Tin line

The Midwest Plant produces sheet and tin products for customers in the automotive, construction, and container markets. Production facilities include:

- Pickle line

- Sheet 80-inch cold reduction mill

- Batch annealing shop

- Two continuous galvanizing lines

- Sheet temper mill

- Combination line

- 52-inch cold reduction tin mill

- Electrolytic cleaning line

- Continuous annealing line

- Tin temper mill

- Double cold reduction mill

- Two coil prep/recoil lines

- Electrolytic tinning line

- Chrome line

Together, Gary Works, East Chicago Tin, and the Midwest Plant employ approximately 6200 people. Gary Works is registered to ISO 14001 by ABS.

DELAWARE NORTH COMPANIES PARKS & RESORTS

Delaware North Companies Parks & Resorts Inc. (DNCP&R), a subsidiary of Delaware North Companies Inc. (DNC), is a leading hospitality provider with significant experience in hotel, retail, food service, recreation, and transportation operations and the first company in the U.S. hospitality industry to achieve ISO 14001 registration. The company's portfolio includes many unique properties in North America, including national parks, U.S. mints, hotels, and resorts.

When DNCP&R assumed management of visitor services at Yosemite National Park in 1993, it quickly became known in the industry for its innovative environmental practices and management style. Its sense of stewardship is embodied in GreenPath,* a formal, documented system that demonstrates the company's commitment to environmental excellence.

Some elements of GreenPath are highly technical, while others are quite basic. Examples of GreenPath initiatives include:

- Installing bulk dispensers for amenities such as shampoo, conditioner, soap, and lotion in guest rooms and for condiments in quick-serve food facilities.

- Replacing toxic cleaning products used in housekeeping, retail outlets, and housing operations with non-toxic, biodegradable products.

---

* Greenpath is a registerd trademark of Delaware North Companies Parks & Resorts.

- Using re-refined oil in its fleet of more than 250 vehicles (tour buses, visitor shuttles, and support vehicles) and arranging for waste oil generated from vehicle maintenance to be processed for re-refinement.

- Converting chain saws and winch cables used in park operations from petroleum-based bar oil (one quart can contaminate one million gallons of water) to canola-based bar oil (one quart is potable in 1000 gallons of water).

- Using zero-emissions vehicles.

- Establishing waste diversion programs to recycle used mattresses, toiletries, uniforms, and office equipment, and to safely dispose of computer monitors, computer disks, and alkaline batteries. At Yosemite National Park, for example, 33 materials are recycled and 13 are diverted, preventing approximately 40 percent (1500 tons) of waste from reaching landfills.

- Replacing environmentally unfriendly products with recycled-content and/or biodegradable products in foodservice facilities, retail outlets, and offices.

According to John Huey, Director of Sustainability and Environmental Affairs, DNCP&R, "GreenPath was born out of a concern for protecting the environment where our company does business. Now, GreenPath has become the business of our company. Business considerations and environmental concerns have joined each other on the GreenPath."

ISO 14001 registration serves as a mechanism for maintaining environmental excellence. It puts the burden on each GreenPath property to implement and maintain strict standards designed to protect the environment.

This comprehensive, award-winning environmental management program has earned ISO 14001 registration for DNC's corporate office (Buffalo, New York), its central reservation system (Fresno, California), and at 13 operating units:

- Asilomar Conference Grounds (Pacific Grove, California)

- Denver Mint (Colorado)

- Geneva on the Lake (Ohio)

- Grand Canyon National Park (Arizona)

- Harrison Hot Springs Spa & Resort (British Columbia, Canada)

- Jones Beach State Park (New York)

- Kennedy Space Center Visitor Complex (Florida)

- Niagara Reservation State Park (New York)

- Philadelphia Mint (Pennsylvania)

- Sequoia National Park (California)

- Tenaya Lodge at Yosemite (California)

- Yellowstone National Park (Montana and Wyoming)

- Yosemite National Park (California)

Registration is anticipated in 2006 for:

- Old Town San Diego State Park (California)

- The Balsams (New Hampshire)

- Wheeling Island (West Virginia)

DNCP&R is registered by NSF International Strategic Registrations.

U.S. COAST GUARD AIR STATION CAPE COD

U.S. Coast Guard Air Station Cape Cod (ASCC) is located on the Massachusetts Military Reservation along with three Department of Defense counterparts. ASCC operates four HU25 Falcon jet aircraft and four HH60 Jayhawk helicopters in support of a wide variety of Coast Guard missions, including homeland security, search and rescue, maritime law enforcement, drug interdiction, and marine environmental protection.

The primary mission of the Coast Guard has always been the protection and safety of life and property at sea. Since it was commissioned in 1970, ASCC has launched more than 6700 missions, saved more than 2500 lives, and prevented the loss of $340 million worth of property. Among its missions was the Liberian freighter Argo Merchant, which broke up after running aground on Nantucket Shoals in 1976. That disaster brought marine environmental protection to the attention of the nation.

ASCC is the second-largest unit in the Coast Guard with 400 employees and 1.9 million square feet of building space encompassing over 1400 acres of land. In addition, ASCC serves as the single largest housing authority within the Coast Guard and is responsible for the administration, maintenance, and well-being of 559 family housing units and over 2000 residents of the military housing community serving the Coast Guard, Army, Navy,

Air Force, Marines, National Oceanic and Atmospheric Administration (NOAA), Federal Aviation Administration (FAA), Massachusetts Environmental Police, and Massachusetts State Police. Of these housing units, 627 are located on the Massachusetts Military Reserve and 59 are dispersed throughout southeastern Massachusetts and Rhode Island.

ASCC's environmental program concentrates on four main areas of emphasis:

- Compliance/pollution prevention

- Recycling and affirmative procurement

- Natural resource protection

- Public/community involvement

The program took root in 1992. In 2001, ASCC became a charter member of EPA's National Environmental Performance Track. In 1999, ASCC compared its environmental management system to ISO 14001 and developed procedures in order to conform to that international standard. (Approximately 1600 federal facilities have implemented an environmental management system and almost all are using the ISO 14001 framework.)

According to ASCC's environmental protection specialist, the decision to conform to ISO 14001 reflected the belief that it was an excellent tool for communicating environmental information and transferring ownership from employees in the environmental department to the personnel responsible for various procedures and operations.

Relatively few federal facilities have opted for third-party registration and ASCC is no exception. It employs a self-declaration process (see Chapter 1). External audits are conducted on a three-year cycle by auditors certified by the National Registry of Environmental Professionals and ANSI–RAB.

Acknowledgments

This book would not have been possible without the assistance of some very special people.

U. S. Steel

John Armstrong, Manager, Public Affairs

Kenneth L. Mentzel, Manager, Environmental Control and Environmental Management Representative, Gary Works

and especially Jacqueline Gabel, Senior Environmental Engineer

Delaware North Companies

Dennis J. Szefel, President, Hospitality Group

Wendy A. Watkins, Vice President, Corporate Communications and Public Relations

and in particular John Huey, Director of Sustainability and Environmental Affairs, DNC Parks & Resorts

Federal Government

Edwin Piñero, Federal Environmental Executive, Office of the Federal Environmental Executive

Will Garvey, Chair, EO 13148 Interagency Environmental Leadership Workgroup

U.S. Coast Guard Air Station Cape Cod

Captain Thomas Ostebo, Commanding Officer

Commander Edward Gibbons, Executive Officer

Commander John Healy, Facility Engineer

and especially Bob Cannon, Environmental Health and
Safety Manager

Thank you, all. Thanks, too, to the countless men and women within each
of these organizations whose ongoing efforts to implement and enhance
their environmental management systems make our environment better.

1

Environmental Management

The concept of environmental management represents progression along a continuum that began on the first Earth Day in 1970. Command-and-control regulations of the 1970s, risk management efforts of the early 1980s, and attempts to fashion international environmental protocols in the late 1980s led organizations to recognize that preventing pollution is preferable to mitigation after the fact.

HISTORY OF ENVIRONMENTAL MANAGEMENT

During the 1960s, apprehension about environmental degradation began to emerge in the United States. Two unrelated events captured national attention and brought concerns about pollution to the forefront. One was publication of the book *Silent Spring* in which Rachel Carson denounced the use of pesticides. By itself, the book probably would not have created great alarm. Its publication, however, was followed by escalation of the U.S. presence in Viet Nam. Americans saw the damage caused by the use of defoliants, courtesy of the evening news. Images of jungles devastated by chemical agents reinforced Carson's contention, and the ecology movement was born.

In late 1969, the U.S. Congress approved the National Environmental Policy Act (NEPA). One of its primary purposes was to promote efforts that would prevent or eliminate damage to the environment. President Richard M. Nixon signed NEPA on January 1, 1970.

Several weeks later, President Nixon included remarks about the environment in his State of the Union address. In February, he announced an environmental action program to improve water and air quality. When more than 20 million Americans participated in Earth Day on April 22, it was clear that environmentalism was here to stay.

1

By July, President Nixon had come to believe that there was a need for an independent agency whose primary focus would be environmental protection. The blueprint for what would become the Environmental Protection Agency (EPA) was presented to Congress in a document titled *Reorganization Plan No. 3*. It pulled pollution-control functions and programs and pesticide research efforts from an array of government agencies and consolidated them. In December 1970, EPA came into being.

During the 1970s, environmentalism was characterized by command-and-control regulations. In an effort to control rampant pollution, a number of laws were enacted. Emphasis was placed on controlling industry practices and, by extension, the myriad of pollutants generated by previously uncontrolled practices.

The result was a piecemeal approach in which environmental problems—water pollution, air pollution, pesticides, hazardous waste, and so forth—and resulting regulations were segregated. This separation was reinforced by EPA's organizational structure of program offices with media-specific concerns. Thus, a regulation pertaining to air quality might require companies to use a particular chemical additive even though that chemical had adverse effects on drinking water.

Companies quickly realized that end-of-pipe fixes were costly and yielded only incremental improvements. Separately, EPA had reached the same conclusion and, in the 1980s, began the transition from command-and-control to risk management. *Risk* is the probability that life, health, property, and/or the environment will be harmed as a result of a given hazard. *Risk management* entails evaluating both regulatory and nonregulatory responses for dealing with such harm and putting into practice those responses that will reduce risk.

In 1987, EPA published the results of a landmark study, *Unfinished Business: A Comparative Assessment of Environmental Problems*. The report compared 31 environmental problems that contributed to human cancer risk, human non-cancer health risk, ecological risk, and welfare risk.

Unfinished Business and subsequent efforts, including the 1990 report *Reducing Risk: Setting Priorities and Strategies for Environmental Protection*, served as the foundation for a more integrated approach to addressing environmental issues. Pollution prevention became a guiding principle within EPA and multi-media strategies began to replace the single-medium focus that had been prevalent within program offices.

At the same time, attention was shifting to environmental issues that transcended local and national regulations. Widespread degradation, such as that caused by acid rain or depletion of the ozone layer, generated a number of international pacts and protocols to deal with local practices.

In 1985, representatives from 49 countries agreed on the need to protect the ozone layer but could not achieve consensus on how that would be accomplished. In 1987, the Montreal Protocol established a schedule for phasing out ozone-depleting substances.

In 1992, Rio de Janeiro, Brazil, was the site of the Earth Summit, a meeting of world leaders that occurred during the United Nations Conference on Environment and Development (UNCED). UNCED is inextricably linked to the *Framework Convention on Climate Change*. This treaty was open for signature at the conference. It required countries to address global warming by stabilizing greenhouse gases—primarily carbon dioxide (CO_2) and methane (CH_4)—in the atmosphere at levels that would prevent interference with the climate system.

Five years later, the *Framework Convention* was amended. The *Kyoto Protocol to the United Nations Framework Convention on Climate Change* (more commonly known as the Kyoto Protocol) required ratifying countries to either reduce emissions of CO_2 and other greenhouse gases based on 1990 emissions levels or participate in emissions trading if greenhouse gas emissions were maintained or increased.

The United States has not ratified the Kyoto Protocol because of concerns that the absence of binding targets and timetables for developing countries would be harmful to the U.S. economy. Despite an unwillingness to ratify the Kyoto Protocol, the U.S. has agreed to reduce emissions by seven percent of 1990 levels between 2008 and 2012.

An environmental ethic also was evolving in the global business community. In 1990, 50 business leaders from both developed and developing countries created the Business Council for Sustainable Development (BCSD). Unified by an interest in environmental and development issues, BCSD supported the somewhat controversial view that environmental protection and economic growth are compatible objectives.

That view was advanced when, in 1991, the International Chamber of Commerce (ICC) published the *Business Charter for Sustainable Development*. The *Business Charter* stops short of requiring specified performance levels of its signatories. Instead, it articulates 16 guiding principles that, if incorporated into business operations, contribute to improved environmental performance and sustainable development.

That same year, partly in response to the activities of the BCSD and ICC and partly in anticipation of the 1992 conference in Rio de Janeiro, the International Organization for Standardization (commonly referred to as ISO) established an *ad hoc* committee to determine whether there existed a need for an international standard on environmental management and, if so, whether developing such a standard was feasible. That committee—the

Strategic Advisory Group on the Environment (SAGE)—concluded that such a standard was warranted.

In 1993, ISO disbanded SAGE and established Technical Committee (TC) 207 to develop a standard on environmental management. The result, published in September, 1996, was *ISO 14001, Environmental management systems—Specification with guidance for use.* Other standards in the ISO 14000 series are listed in Table 1.1.

Although it can be argued that options such as design for the environment, lifecycle management, and pollution prevention are viable environmental management alternatives to ISO 14001, each is limited by a narrow focus that fails to place it within a larger, systemic context.

• *Design for the Environment(DfE).* DfE is a voluntary EPA program that provides information on specific industries so companies within an industry sector can incorporate environmental concerns into business decisions. It focuses on the design or redesign of products and processes that are clean, cost-effective, and safe for workers and the public. It is similar to the requirements imposed by ISO 14001:2004 for establishing environmental objectives and targets.

• *Lifecycle assessment (LCA).* LCA came about in response to energy shortages during the 1970s. As initially conceived, LCA focused on materials and energy associated with production systems. In the following 20 years, the focus of LCA shifted from production systems to products. It also moved beyond its original emphasis on the economics of energy and waste to assessing the environmental aspects and potential impacts of products.

In 1997, ISO published an informative standard on the principles and framework of LCA (ISO 14040) that defines LCA as a "compilation and evaluation of the inputs, outputs and the potential environmental impacts of a product system throughout its lifecycle." All of the ISO standards on LCA (see Table 1.1) are considered tools that can assist in the implementation of an environmental management system. Although LCA offers a specific technique for identifying environmental aspects and impacts, its use is not mandatory. ISO 14001:2004 states: "The identification of environmental aspects does not require a detailed lifecycle assessment." An organization is free to use any technique of its choosing.

• *Pollution prevention (P2).* P2 became the centerpiece of environmental activities in the United States with passage of the Pollution Prevention Act of 1990 (PPA). The PPA established pollution prevention as a national objective and shifted emphasis from end-of-pipe handling and disposal methods to preventing or reducing pollution at its source.

Table 1.1   Standards in the ISO 14000 series.

Number	Title	Date
14001	Environmental management systems—Requirements with guidance for use (second edition)	2004
14004	Environmental management systems—General guidelines on principles, systems and support techniques (second edition)	2004
14015	Environmental management—Environmental assessment of sites and organizations (EASO)	2001
14020	Environmental labels and declarations—General principles (second edition)	2000
14021	Environmental labels and declarations—Self-declared environmental claims (Type II environmental labeling)	1999
14024	Environmental labels and declarations—Type I environmental labeling—Principles and procedures	1999
TR 14025	Environmental labels and declarations—Type III environmental declarations	2000
14031	Environmental management—Environmental performance evaluation—Guidelines	1999
TR 14032	Environmental management—Examples of environmental performance evaluation (EPE)	1999
14040	Environmental management—Life cycle assessment—Principles and framework	1997
14041	Environmental management—Life cycle assessment—Goal and scope definition and inventory analysis	1998
14042	Environmental management—Life cycle assessment—Life cycle impact assessment	2000
14043	Environmental management—Life cycle assessment—Life cycle interpretation	2000
TR 14047	Environmental management—Life cycle assessment—Examples of application of ISO 14042	2003
TS 14048	Environmental management—Life cycle assessment—Data documentation format	2002
TR 14049	Environmental management—Life cycle assessment—Examples of application of ISO 14041 to goal and scope definition and inventory analysis	2000
14050	Environmental management—Vocabulary (second edition)	2002

Continued

Continued

Number	Title	Date
TR 14061	Information to assist forestry organizations in the use of environmental management system standards ISO 14001 and ISO 14004	1998
TR 14062	Environmental management—Integrating environmental aspects into product design and development	2002
FDIS 14063	Environmental management—Environmental communication—Guidelines and examples	2005
14064-1	Greenhouse gases—Part 1: Specification with guidance at the organization level for the quantification and reporting of greenhouse gas emissions and removals	2006
14064-2	Greenhouse gases—Part 2: Specification with guidance at the project level for the quantification, monitoring and reporting of greenhouse gas emission reductions and removal enhancements	2006
14064-3	Greenhouse gases—Part 3: Specification with guidance for the validation and verification of greenhouse gas assertions	2006
19011	Guidelines for quality and/or environmental management systems auditing (replaces ISO 14010, 14011, and 14012)	2002

Legend: FDIS = Final Draft International Standard; TR = Technical Report;
　　　　TS = Technical Specification

ISO 14001 uses a slightly different term—prevention of pollution—and definition from those imposed by the PPA to accommodate disparate environmental laws, regulations, enforcement priorities, and infrastructure in different parts of the world. The concept of eliminating or reducing adverse environmental impacts, however, is central to its purpose.

PURPOSE OF ENVIRONMENTAL MANAGEMENT

The fundamental goals of environmental management are prevention of pollution and environmental protection. If an organization's efforts to achieve those goals are to be effective, however, it must demonstrate:

- *Management commitment.* First and foremost, those in positions of authority must demonstrate their belief in and support for environmental values. Commitment at the top of the management hierarchy sends the message that an organization's environmental performance is viewed as an essential component of business activity. Without management commitment, it is unlikely that an organization would implement an environmental management system.

- *Employee involvement.* If management commitment sets the stage for effective environmental management, employee involvement ensures successful implementation. Workers throughout an organization are responsible for a myriad of activities that ultimately result in one of two outcomes—final product or waste. The manner in which activities are conducted, including handling and use of materials and disposition of waste, contributes directly to an organization's environmental performance.

- *Continual improvement.* Implementation of an environmental management system is not an end; it is the beginning of a dynamic process in which opportunities to change it for the better are actively sought and acted on.

- *Environmental ethic.* Finally, environmental management instills a sense of assurance that attention to environmental performance holds the same importance as product quality, customer satisfaction, efficiency, and profit.

The structure of ISO 14001:2004 ensures that these concepts are addressed. It emphasizes the importance of leadership by specifically requiring top management to define an organization's environmental policy, provide resources to implement and maintain the environmental management system, and regularly review all facets of the system to ensure its continuing viability.

It addresses the importance of employee involvement by requiring an understanding of the organization's environmental policy, an internal communication system, operating criteria for jobs that create adverse environmental effects, and demonstrated competence to perform such jobs.

A commitment to continual improvement must be articulated in the environmental policy and fulfilled, in part, by management review.

Mandates for awareness of and communication about the environmental management system throughout an organization foster an ethic that makes environmental concern part of every worker's job. The days of the environmental department working in isolation on regulatory compliance have been supplanted by multiple functions and departments working together to improve overall environmental performance.

ISO 14001 WORLDWIDE

Environmental management generally and ISO 14001 in particular have become an integral part of the business lexicon in more than 125 countries (See Table 1.2). The low number of ISO 14001 certificates awarded during the period from initial publication (September 1996) to December 1998 reflects the time lag between learning about ISO 14001:1996 and establishing an environmental management system ready for registration. By the end of 2000, however, the number of certificates conferred was triple the 1998 figure. And in 2004 there were four times as many certificates as in 2000.

The majority of certifications are found in Europe (44 percent) and East Asia (40 percent) (See Table 1.3). Although North America trails a distant third, at 7 percent, it is important to remember that only three countries are included (See Table 1.4), while the tally for Europe comprises 46 countries and the East Asia 19.

Examination of certificates awarded in individual countries instead of on a regional basis places the United States sixth in the world (See Table 1.5). Ten countries account for 71 percent of the world's total.

Table 1.2   ISO 14001 certifications worldwide, 1996–2004.

	Total certificates	Increase from previous year	Number of countries
Dec 2004	90,569	24,499 (37%)	127
Dec 2003	66,070	16,621 (34%)	113
Dec 2002	49,449	12,684 (35%)	117
Dec 2001	36,765	13,868 (61%)	112
Dec 2000	22,897	8,791 (62%)	98
Dec 1999	14,106	6,219 (79%)	84
Dec 1998	7,887	3,454 (78%)	72
Dec 1997	4,433	2,942 (197%)	55
Dec 1996	1,491		45

Sources: For 2001–2004, *The ISO Survey of Certifications 2004* (September 15, 2005); for 1996–2000, *The ISO Survey of ISO 9000 and ISO 14000 Certificates, Tenth Cycle* (2001).

Table 1.3   ISO 14001 certifications by region, 1996–2004.

	Africa and West Asia	Central and South America	North America	Europe	East Asia	Australia and New Zealand
Dec 2004	3,007	2,955	6,743	39,812	35,960	2,092
Dec 2003	1,997	1,691	5,233	31,997	23,747	1,405
Dec 2002	1,355	1,418	4,053	23,316	17,744	1,563
Dec 2001	923	681	2,700	18,243	12,796	1,422
Dec 2000	651	556	1,676	11,021	7,881	1,112
Dec 1999	337	309	975	7,365	4,350	770
Dec 1998	138	144	434	4,254	2,532	385
Dec 1997	73	98	117	2,626	1,356	163
Dec 1996	10	15	43	948	419	56

Sources: For 2001–2004, *The ISO Survey of Certifications 2004* (September 15, 2005); for 1996–2000, *The ISO Survey of ISO 9000 and ISO 14000 Certificates, Tenth Cycle* (2001).

Table 1.4   ISO 14001 certifications in North America, 1996–2004.

Year	United States	Canada	Mexico	Total
Dec 2004	4759	1492	492	6743
Dec 2003	3553	1274	406	5233
Dec 2002	2620	1064	369	4053
Dec 2001	1645	801	254	2700
Dec 2000	1042	475	159	1676
Dec 1999	636	276	63	975
Dec 1998	291	104	39	434
Dec 1997	79	27	11	117
Dec 1996	34	7	2	43

Sources: For 2001–2004, *The ISO Survey of Certifications 2004* (September 15, 2005); for 1996–2000, *The ISO Survey of ISO 9000 and ISO 14000 Certificates, Tenth Cycle* (2001).

Table 1.5 Top ten countries with ISO 14001 certifications, 2004.

Japan	19,584
China	8,862
Spain	6,473
United Kingdom	6,253
Italy	4,785
United States	4,759
Germany	4,320
Sweden	3,478
France	2,955
Republic of Korea	2,609
Total	64,078

Sources: For 2001–2004, *The ISO Survey of Certifications 2004* (September 15, 2005); for 1996–2000, *The ISO Survey of ISO 9000 and ISO 14000 Certificates, Tenth Cycle* (2001).

ENVIRONMENTAL MANAGEMENT IN THE PRIVATE SECTOR

Growing interest in environmental performance is apparent among the top 50 companies (based on annual revenues) in the world. Nearly two-thirds (32, or 64 percent) have an ISO 14001 environmental management system or other environmental programs in place.

In 2003, the industry sectors in which most certificates had been conferred were: electrical and optical equipment (seven percent); basic metal and fabricated metal (six percent); chemicals, chemical products, and fibers (six percent); construction (four percent); and machinery and equipment (four percent). For 2004, however, ISO 14001 certification worldwide is reported highest (at 31 percent) for service organizations.

ENVIRONMENTAL MANAGEMENT IN THE PUBLIC SECTOR

In the United States, federal government interest in environmental management predates ISO 14001. Executive Order 12856, signed by President Bill Clinton in August 1993, addressed the need for federal agencies to implement pollution prevention measures that would reduce use of toxic and hazardous chemicals and associated emissions.

The order also directed EPA to establish a code of environmental principles for pollution prevention, sustainable development, and state-of-the-art environmental management programs. In response, EPA developed the Code of Environmental Management Principles (CEMP), which was published in the Federal Register on October 16, 1996. This voluntary program articulated five principles:

- *Management commitment.* Senior agency officials create written policies that commit an agency to pollution prevention and improved environmental performance.

- *Compliance assurance and pollution prevention.* Potential compliance problems are identified and addressed before they worsen to the point of noncompliance; pollution prevention methods are employed to correct any identified noncompliance.

- *Enabling systems.* Measures are put into place to allow workers to perform their functions consistent with regulatory requirements and agency environmental policies.

- *Performance and accountability.* Tools are employed to assess employee environmental performance.

- *Measurement and improvement.* Progress toward meeting environmental goals is evaluated and results are used to improve environmental performance.

In April, 2000, 30 years after the first Earth Day, President Clinton signed Executive Order 13148, *Greening the Government Through Leadership in Environmental Management.* That order required every federal agency to implement an environmental management system at all *appropriate* facilities by December 2005. Based on the factors used to determine whether a facility is appropriate—size, complexity, and environmental aspects associated with operations—about half (1,140) of approximately 2,280 appropriate facilities have documented an environmental management system.

The majority of those agencies use the ISO 14001 framework. Some use CEMP, which is slightly less rigorous. The federal community uses self-declaration in lieu of registration. It remains to be seen whether this approach holds up over the long term.

Two months later, in June 2000, EPA launched its National Environmental Performance Track program. Voluntary in nature, this program encourages organizations to go beyond compliance and improve their environmental performance. Performance Track requires implementation of an environmental management system, compliance with regulatory requirements, compliance self-audits, and annual certification that all requirements are being met.

By 2003, EPA had developed guidance documents to help companies implement environmental management systems in the industry sectors of die casting, meat processing, and shipbuilding and repair. Other sector-specific guides address cement manufacturing, construction, forest products, iron and steel manufacturing, and specialty-batch chemical manufacturing.

REVISION OF ISO 14001:1996

ISO requires that its standards undergo a review every five years. The purpose of the review is to ascertain whether the standard of interest:

- Continues to be appropriate as initially written

- Is unnecessary and, therefore, should be rescinded

- Requires revision to improve its efficacy

To understand the review process employed for ISO 14001:1996, familiarity with the ISO 9001 standard is necessary. ISO 9001, originally published in 1987, had already been reviewed and revised once. The second edition, ISO 9001:1994, was reviewed in 1999 at which time it was determined that a technical revision was needed to make the standard "more compatible" with ISO 14001. The third edition of ISO 9001 was published in December 2000 as *ISO 9001, Quality management systems—Requirements.*

The ISO subcommittee tasked with review of ISO 14001:1996 concluded that this standard should be revised for clarification and for improved compatibility with ISO 9001:2000. It further concluded that the revision should not add any new requirements. The resulting second edition, *ISO 14001, Environmental management systems—Requirements with guidance for use*, was published in November 2004.

ORGANIZATION OF ISO 14001:2004

ISO 14001:2004 retains the same organization as its predecessor: a foreword and introduction are followed by four numbered sections—scope, normative references, terms and definitions, and environmental management system requirements—two annexes, and a bibliography.

Foreword

The foreword describes the International Organization for Standardization (ISO) and its work. It contains only two references to ISO 14001. The first identifies Technical Committee ISO/TC 207 as responsible for preparation of the standard. The second states that the 2004 edition cancels and replaces the 1996 edition.

Introduction

The purpose of ISO 14001:2004, as described in its introduction, is to support environmental protection and prevention of pollution by providing organizations with the elements of an effective environmental management system. It specifies a series of actions that enable an organization to develop an environmental policy and establish objectives, programs, and procedures to implement its policy and comply with environmental legal obligations.

ISO 14001:2004 is intended to apply to all types and sizes of organizations that operate under diverse geographical, cultural, and social conditions. Use of the standard by distinctly different organizations is fostered by the manner in which environmental management system elements are presented. ISO 14001:2004 articulates *what* an organization must do to achieve effective environmental management but does not specify *how* requirements are to be addressed. This enables any implementing organization to develop an environmental management system that reflects the realities of its own situation and operating conditions. As a result, two different organizations with different adverse effects on the environment (for example, a steel mill and a hospital) can each develop and implement an environmental management system that conforms to all ISO 14001:2004 requirements.

ISO 14001:2004 limits itself to *environmental* management. It does not address requirements for quality, health, safety, financial, or risk management. It does, however, recognize that environmental management efforts can be integrated with other management systems.

1 Scope

This section explains that ISO 14001:2004 delineates the requirements that must be met but does not state specific environmental performance criteria. In other words, the standard specifies *what* must be done without dictating *how* it must be done.

The scope also explains that an organization can demonstrate conformity to ISO 14001:2004 through self-determination and self-declaration (first-party audit), confirmation by parties with an interest in the organization, such as customers (second-party audit), or registration by an external organization (third-party audit).

The terms *registration* and *certification* are used synonymously. *Certification* is the preferred term in most countries. In the United States, certifications carry specific liability implications; therefore, the preferred term in that country is *registration*.

Once an organization initiates the process of designing and implementing an environmental management system, it must decide whether to self-declare its conformity to ISO 14001:2004 or seek third-party registration. Certainly, registration is not essential for an environmental management system to perform effectively. Internal auditors can be as valuable as third-party auditors in identifying the strengths and weaknesses of a system.

The decision to self-declare tends to be influenced by cost concerns. The costs of the initial application fee, registration audit, and periodic surveillance audits cause some organizations to forego formal registration. A belief that formal registration is less important to customers than actual environmental management and performance also causes some organizations to forego this step.

Three issues typically influence the decision to seek registration:

- *Requirement for doing business.* Some organizations pursue registration because a major customer has stipulated that its suppliers must have a certified environmental management system.

- *Public image.* Some organizations view registration as a mechanism for enhancing the way in which they are viewed by customers, the business community, regulatory agencies, and the general public.

- *Project milestone.* For some organizations, registration is a tangible result that validates the work of employees involved in system implementation.

2 Normative references

No normative references are cited. This clause is included as a placeholder in order to retain the clause numbers that correspond to those in ISO 14001:1996.

3 Terms and definitions

Seven terms have been added to the original list of 13. New terms are *auditor, corrective action, document, nonconformity, preventive action, procedure,* and *record. Internal audit* replaces *environmental management system audit.*

Definitions for the terms that are retained from the original edition have been revised for clarity.

4 Environmental management system requirements

This is the only section of ISO 14001:2004 with "normative" requirements—that is, they *must* be incorporated into an environmental management system subject to third-party registration/certification or self-declaration. All other sections and annexes of the standard are "informative"—they provide guidance intended to assist in the development and implementation of an environmental management system, but they do not contain any normative (auditable) requirements.

Clauses 4.1 and 4.2 address general requirements of an environmental management system and environmental policy respectively. The remaining clauses and subclauses (also referred to as elements) comprising section 4 are organized to reflect the Shewhart cycle, named for its creator, Walter A. Shewhart, a statistician at Bell Telephone Laboratories in New York. More commonly known as the PDCA cycle, for plan–do–check–act, it served as the foundation for W. Edwards Deming's management method.

The first step in the Shewhart cycle, *plan,* is to study a process in order to determine what changes might improve it. Conformity to ISO 14001:2004 requires that *planning* (clause 4.3) encompass three components—identification of environmental aspects, understanding of legal and other requirements, and establishment of objectives and targets—to ensure fulfillment of the environmental policy.

Implementation and operation (clause 4.4) corresponds to the second step in the Shewhart cycle, *do,* which involves carrying out actions that were identified during the planning stage. ISO 14001:2004 incorporates seven elements—resources, roles, responsibility, and authority; competence, training, and awareness; communication; documentation; control of documents; operational control; and emergency preparedness and response.

Clause 4.5 of ISO 14001:2004—*Checking*—corresponds to the *check* stage of the Shewhart cycle. The standard contains five elements that are intended to measure and evaluate the effects of actions taken during implementation and operation: monitoring and measurement, evaluation of compliance, nonconformity and associated corrective and preventive action, records, and internal audits of the environmental management system.

The final component of ISO 14001:2004, *Management review* (clause 4.6), parallels the final stage of the Shewhart cycle—*act*. The system is improved in response to what was learned during the *check* stage.

Annex A

This annex, *Guidance on the use of this International Standard*, is informative. It suggests things an organization might do in response to a stated requirement, but it does not add to nor detract from any of the requirements contained in clause 4.

Annex B

This annex, *Correspondence between ISO 14001:2004 and ISO 9001:2000*, contains two tables. The first lists in numerical order the numbered elements from ISO 14001 and shows which ISO 9001 clause contains a comparable or similar requirement. The second lists the ISO 9001 elements and identifies the corresponding clause from ISO 14001.

SUPPORTING GUIDELINES

Concurrent with development of ISO 14001:1996, a companion document— *ISO 14004, Environmental management systems—General guidelines on principles, systems and support techniques*—was created and published. Its purpose was to provide assistance to organizations that wanted to implement an environmental management system.

The effectiveness of ISO 14004:1996 was limited by unwillingness on the part of ISO/TC 207 to link it directly to the environmental management system requirements imposed by ISO 14001:1996. As a result, organizations seeking guidance often discovered that information related to a specific ISO 14001 requirement was lacking. This deficiency has been corrected in the second edition. ISO 14004:2004 is organized so that every numbered section in ISO 14001:2004, section 4, is addressed.

REFERENCES

Carson, R. *Silent Spring.* Boston: Houghton Mifflin, 1962.

Executive Order 13148. *Greening the Government Through Leadership in Environmental Management.* Federal Register 64, no. 81 (April 26, 2000): 24, 595–606.

Executive Order 12856. *Federal Compliance with Right-to-Know Laws and Pollution Prevention Requirements.* Federal Register 58, no. 150 (August 6, 1993): 41, 981–87.

ICC Business Charter for Sustainable Development. In Willums, J., and U. Golüke. *From Ideas to Action: Business and Sustainable Development. The ICC Report on the Greening of Enterprise 92.* Oslo: International Chamber of Commerce Publishing, 1992.

Lewis, J. "The Birth of EPA." *EPA Journal* (November 1985).

United Nations. *Kyoto Protocol to the United Nations Framework Convention on Climate Change.* 1997.

United Nations. *United Nations Framework Convention on Climate Change.* 1992.

United Nations Environment Programme. *The Montreal Protocol on Substances That Deplete the Ozone Layer.* Nairobi, Kenya: UNEP Ozone Secretariat, 2000.

U.S. Code. "Reorganization Plan No. 3 of 1970." *Congressional and Administrative News,* 91st Congress—2nd session, vol. 3. (1970).

U.S. Environmental Protection Agency. *Unfinished Business: A Comparative Assessment of Environmental Problems—Overview Report (EPA no. 400/02).* Washington, DC: EPA, 1987.

U.S. Environmental Protection Agency. Office of Enforcement and Compliance Assurance. *Implementation Guide for the Code of Environmental Management Principles for Federal Agencies (CEMP) (EPA no. 315-B-97-001).* Washington, DC: Government Printing Office, 1997.

U.S. Environmental Protection Agency. Science Advisory Board. *Reducing Risk: Setting Priorities and Strategies for Environmental Protection (EPA no. SAB-EC 90-021).* Washington, DC: EPA, 1990.

2

General Requirements

An environmental management system helps organizations manage their various processes and activities in a way that lessens adverse effects on the environment.

ISO 14001:2004 Text	ISO 14001:1996 Text
4.1 General requirements The organization shall establish, document, implement, maintain and continually improve an environmental management system, in accordance with the requirements of this International Standard and determine how it will fulfill these requirements. The organization shall define and document the scope of its environmental management system.	*4.1 General requirements* The organization shall establish and maintain an environmental management system, the requirements of which are described in the whole of clause 4.

SIGNIFICANT CHANGES

The original language required an organization to *establish* and *maintain* an environmental management system. As revised, ISO 14001:2004 now requires that an organization also document, implement, and continually improve the environmental management system.

ISO 14001:2004 clarifies that it is up to an organization to decide how it will meet stated requirements.

A new second paragraph specifies that the scope of the environmental management system must be defined and documented. ISO 14001:1996 made no reference to the scope of the system.

INTENT OF ISO 14001:2004

This clause introduces a number of terms that appear throughout ISO 14001:2004. When a term is intended to convey a specific meaning, the definition is presented in section 3 of the standard. Absent such a definition, the meaning of a term can be found in a standard dictionary.

Organization is defined in section 3.16 as "company, corporation, firm, enterprise, authority or institution, or part or combination thereof, whether incorporated or not, public or private, that has its own functions and administration." An accompanying note states: "For organizations with more than one operating unit, a single operating unit may be defined as an organization."

Examples of private-sector organizations range from large corporate entities that own a large number of companies, to individual companies (that may or may not be owned by a corporation), to subsets within an individual company, such as a department or facility. Public-sector organizations, situated at federal, state, county, and local levels, include agencies, individual offices within agencies, and programs within offices.

For purposes of implementing ISO 14001:2004, an organization can be any size as long as it meets two criteria. First, it must have a defined function. Second, it must have an autonomous management structure with the authority to make decisions about and provide resources to an environmental management system.

The verb *shall*, as used in any ISO normative standard, means that the activity in question must be undertaken. Each "shall" statement contains one or more requirements that must be met if an organization wishes to conform to ISO 14001:2004.

When instructed to *establish* something, an organization must create the item of interest. A requirement to establish a procedure, for example, means that an organization must take whatever course of action is appropriate to bring that procedure into existence.

Document is defined (as a noun) in section 3.4 as "information and its supporting medium." Supporting media can be paper, magnetic, electronic or optical computer disc, photographic, master sample, or a combination thereof.

Although not defined as a verb, a requirement to document a procedure, decision, or other activity means that an organization must create a tangible manifestation of the procedure, decision, or activity in an acceptable medium. With only one exception (clause 4.4.6a), organizations are instructed to establish procedures instead of *documented* procedures. It is up to an individual organization to decide whether there is value in documenting its procedures. If an organization decides not to document required procedures, it still must be able to demonstrate that it has established such procedures.

In practice, almost all organizations document their procedures despite the flexibility offered by ISO 14001:2004. Because the purpose of a procedure is to ensure that all workers perform the activity of interest in a specified manner, the risk of nonconformity is lessened when written guidance is available.

Implement means that an organization must carry out or accomplish by concrete measures a specified activity. When instructed to implement a procedure, it is expected that an organization will employ the procedure and follow all steps therein.

An organization that *maintains* a system or procedures keeps them in their intended state by taking steps to prevent failure or decline.

Continual improvement is defined in section 3.2 as a "recurring process of enhancing the environmental management system in order to achieve improvements in overall environmental performance consistent with the organization's environmental policy." Continual improvement does not have to take place in all areas of activity simultaneously (see Chapters 3 and 19).

As defined in section 3.8, an *environmental management system* is "part of an organization's management system used to develop and implement its environmental policy and manage its environmental aspects." ISO 14001:2004 goes on to explain that a management system comprises organizational structure, planning activities, responsibilities, practices, procedures, processes, and resources.

When instructed to *define* some component of the environmental management system, it is expected that an organization will provide a distinct, clear explanation of its characteristics and demarcation of its limits. Thus, the mandate to define the scope of an environmental management system requires an organization to specify the physical and functional boundaries of the system.

Physical boundaries are those locations at an organization's site that are included within an environmental management system. A coal mine, for example, might define physical boundaries to include all surface operations and exclude all below-surface activities.

Functional boundaries are those operations, processes, and activities encompassed by an environmental management system. An organization might define the scope of a system to include all manufacturing and administrative operations with the exception of sales.

Once the scope of an environmental management system is described, all processes, activities, products, and services that fall within the scope must be included.

Interestingly, ISO 14001:2004 does not directly address management commitment, although three clauses delineate requirements that are explicitly identified as top management obligations. These are:

- *4.2 Environmental policy.* Top management must define the policy and ensure that it fulfills all requirements specified in paragraphs (a) through (g).

- *4.4.1 Resources, roles, responsibility and authority.* Management must ensure that appropriate resources are available to establish, support, and improve the environmental management system; top management must appoint a specific representative who, among other responsibilities, reports to top management on all facets of the environmental management system.

- *4.6 Management review.* Top management must review the environmental management system on a regular basis to ensure its continuing suitability, adequacy, and effectiveness.

These requirements suggest that the single most important factor for successful implementation of an environmental management system is management commitment to improved environmental performance. Top managers demonstrate their commitment by articulating the environmental values by which their organization will be guided and providing necessary equipment, manpower, and funding to assimilate those values into day-to-day activities.

3

Environmental Policy

ISO 14001:2004 requires an environmental policy statement that serves as a guiding document for specific activities of an organization.* It defines the environmental policy as a statement of an organization's intentions and direction in relation to its environmental performance.

Many companies had some sort of environmental policy prior to publication of ISO 14001:1996. Typically, such policy statements asserted that the company would comply with all applicable laws and regulations, protect the health and safety of employees, and safeguard the environment.

Neither ISO 14001:1996 nor ISO 14001:2004 consider such general statements acceptable. The environmental policy must be appropriate to the organization for which it is written. The type of business and the environmental impacts associated with its operations must be addressed. The policy statement for a company that *manufactures* nondurable consumer goods likely would differ from the policy statement for an organization that *assembles* nondurable consumer goods or one that *transports* them.

ISO 14001:2004 Text	ISO 14001:1996 Text
4.2 Environmental policy	*4.2 Environmental policy*
Top management shall define the organization's environmental policy and ensure that, within the defined scope of its environmental management system, it a) is appropriate to the nature, scale and environmental	Top management shall define the organization's environmental policy and ensure that it a) is appropriate to the nature, scale and environmental impacts of its activities, products and services;

Continued

Continued

ISO 14001:2004 Text	ISO 14001:1996 Text
impacts of its activities, products and services, b) includes a commitment to continual improvement and prevention of pollution, c) includes a commitment to comply with applicable environmental legal requirements and with other environmental requirements to which the organization subscribes which relate to its environmental aspects, d) provides the framework for setting and reviewing environmental objectives and targets, e) is documented, implemented and maintained, f) is communicated to all persons working for or on behalf of the organization, and g) is available to the public.	b) includes a commitment to continual improvement and prevention of pollution; c) includes a commitment to comply with relevant environmental legislation and regulations, and with other requirements to which the organization subscribes; d) provides the framework for setting and reviewing environmental objectives and targets; e) is documented, implemented and maintained and communicated to all employees; f) is available to the public.

SIGNIFICANT CHANGES

The requirements associated with articulating an environmental policy are unchanged. Revisions to this clause were made for the purpose of clarification.

The first sentence now includes a reference to the scope of the system. Wording contained in the original standard implied that the environmental policy must be applicable across the entire organization. In other words, the policy would be appropriate for *all* organizational activities, products, and services. ISO 14001:2004 makes clear that the policy is intended to pertain only to those organizational entities that fall within the defined scope of the system.

Paragraph (c) now refers to applicable (instead of relevant) environmental legal requirements. It also links legal requirements and other requirements with environmental aspects in an effort to be more specific about what is considered applicable.

Communication of the policy is more prominent in ISO 14001:2004. Formerly mentioned in paragraph (e), it has been moved to a separate paragraph. Unlike the original language that required communication to all employees, the revised standard requires communication to all persons working for or on behalf of the organization.

INTENT OF
ISO 14001:2004

ISO 14001:2004 requires that the environmental policy commit the organization to four specific efforts. These are:

• *Continual improvement.* As defined in ISO 14001:2004, continual improvement is a recurring process of enhancing the environmental management system in order to achieve improvements in overall environmental performance. Many of the requirements embedded in other clauses of the standard contribute to improved environmental performance. Clause 4.6, however, focuses on activities intended to improve the environmental management system (see Chapter 19).

• *Prevention of pollution.* It is important to understand the distinction between the terms *prevention of pollution* and *pollution prevention.* ISO 14001:2004 defines prevention of pollution as the use of processes, practices, techniques, materials, products, services, or energy to avoid, reduce, or control the creation, emission, or discharge of any type of pollutant or waste, in order to reduce adverse environmental impacts.

In the United States, this differs from pollution prevention, which EPA defines as the use of materials, processes, or practices that reduce or eliminate the creation of pollutants or wastes at the source.

The two definitions differ in one important regard. The ISO 14001:2004 definition incorporates the concept of end-of-pipe control; the EPA definition does not. The terms, therefore, should not be used interchangeably. An organization should choose the definition that will guide its activities and insert the appropriate terminology into the environmental policy.

• *Compliance with applicable legal requirements.* This commitment is the first of three references to regulatory compliance in the standard. By endorsing this commitment, an organization agrees to make every effort to comply with its legal obligations, to promptly correct noncompliance, and to take steps that will prevent recurrence of noncompliance.

It is important to understand that conformity to two other clauses in ISO 14001:2004 enables an organization to fulfill this commitment. Clause 4.3.2 requires identification of the legal requirements with which an organization must comply (see Chapter 5). Clause 4.5.2 mandates periodic evaluation to see whether an organization is in compliance with all identified legal requirements (see Chapter 15).

• *Compliance with other requirements to which the organization subscribes.* Some organizations voluntarily agree to abide by codes of practice that are not legally binding (see Chapter 5). Any voluntary commitments associated with an organization's environmental aspects must be articulated in the environmental policy.

ISO 14001:2004 treats these nonlegal requirements in the same manner as legal requirements. An organization must adhere to all governing requirements contained in the applicable code of practice, correct any failures to comply, and prevent recurrence.

Despite the necessity of including these commitments, environmental policies differ from one organization to the next as illustrated by the examples at the end of this chapter. This is because ISO 14001:2004 requires a policy that reflects the type and size of an organization's operations and the environmental impacts that result from its operations.

In crafting its policy, an organization must decide whether it is preferable to:

• *Employ an existing environmental policy.* Organizations that reside within larger entities, such as a single facility within a company or a single company within a corporation, may be obligated to use an existing environmental policy. If the existing policy conforms to the requirements imposed by ISO 14001:2004, it can be used without revision.

• *Modify an existing environmental policy.* If an existing environmental policy does not conform to ISO 14001:2004 but must be used, an organization can revise it so that all requirements are incorporated.

• *Connect an existing environmental policy and an additional policy.* Sometimes an existing policy can not be revised because it applies to entities that fall outside the scope of an environmental management system. In such a situation, where the existing policy must be used, the organization for which an environmental management system is implemented can create an additional policy that is linked to the original.

• *Create a new environmental policy.* If an existing environmental policy does not conform to ISO 14001:2004 requirements, or if no environmental policy exists, an organization can create a new policy.

The environmental policy is a statement of intention. As such, it is merely a document that contains some promises. The degree to which its intentions are achieved results from an organization's efforts to effectively fulfill the requirements found throughout the remainder of the standard.

Thus, a nonconformity associated with the environmental policy does not necessarily mean that an organization has failed to implement an effective system. For example, an organization might fail to commit to continual improvement in the policy, yet provide ample evidence of continual improvement activities despite that omission.

In addition to the commitments delineated in paragraphs (b) and (c), ISO 14001:2004 requires that the environmental policy provide a framework for establishing and reviewing environmental objectives and targets (see Chapter 4). The environmental policy also must be:

• *Documented, implemented, and maintained.* These terms are discussed in Chapter 2.

• *Communicated.* Originally, ISO 14001:1994 required that the policy be communicated only to employees. ISO 14001:2004 expands the audience beyond employees to include all persons working on behalf of the organization. Communication efforts, therefore, must address applicable suppliers, contractors, and temporary workers in addition to full-time and part-time employees.

Management must convey the meaning of the policy to all persons working for or on behalf of the organization. This can be done through a variety of mechanisms such as new-employee orientation, contractor training, videotapes, audiotapes, and written statements.

There is a distinct difference between *distribution* of information and *communication* of information. It is critical, therefore, to determine whether employees and other workers understand the environmental policy. This is best assessed by going directly to these individuals and asking whether they are familiar with the organization's environmental policy. Understanding has been achieved when an individual can describe the principles articulated in the policy and explain how those principles affect that individual's job.

• *Available to the public.* The environmental policy must be accessible to or obtainable by any individual who requests it. At the very least, this requires some mechanism to respond to such information requests.

Thus, posting the policy in the organization's reception area or printing it on objects distributed to workers (for example, badges or computer mouse pads) are inadequate. Wider access can be obtained by publishing the policy in company reports or posting it on the organization's Web site. However, availability is ensured when the policy is mailed to anyone who requests it.

EXAMPLES

The three examples that follow all conform to ISO 14001 requirements. Each reflects the environmental impacts of its operations. U. S. Steel Gary Works mentions air emissions; Delaware North Companies Parks & Resorts addresses stewardship of resources; U.S. Coast Guard Air Station Cape Cod focuses on marine biodiversity and the prevention of marine ecosystem degradation.

Although ISO 14001:2004 does not require a procedure, Gary Works created a procedure that contains the environmental policy as well as describing how it will be implemented and maintained. The environmental policies of the other organizations are not linked to formal procedures.

U. S. Steel Gary Works
EMS Procedure 4.2—Environmental Policy
(Effective October 4, 2005)

1.0 Purpose

    1.1 The purpose of this procedure is to describe the process of documenting, implementing, maintaining, and communicating the Gary Complex Environmental Policy.

2.0 Scope

    2.1 This procedure applies to all employees.

3.0 References

    3.1 ISO 14001:2004 Standard

    3.2 EMS Procedure 4.4.2—Competence, Training, and Awareness

    3.3 EMS Procedure 4.5.5—Internal Audit

    3.4 USS Web site:
        http://www.ussteel.com/corp/facilities/gary_env.htm

4.0   Definitions

For the purpose of this procedure, the following definitions
shall apply.

4.1   The Environmental Policy provides the Gary Complex
commitment to:

- Comply with all regulations, improve performance, prevent
  pollution, train employees, and evaluate results.

4.2   Gary Complex Environmental Policy

*The U. S. Steel Gary Complex, an integrated steelmaking
operation, is committed to prevention of pollution to achieve
minimal adverse impact on the air, water, and land, through
programs that incorporate responsible environmental
management practices.*

Continuous Improvement to Environment

*Continuous compliance with applicable environmental laws,
regulations, and other requirements is our commitment.
If an environmental noncompliance occurs, it will be
documented and the implemented corrective measures
verified for effectiveness. Preventive measures to improve
environmental compliance are reviewed for relevance, and
if applicable, implemented and evaluated for effectiveness.
U. S. Steel Gary Complex personnel participate, where
appropriate, in the development of public policy and
governmental and intergovernmental programs.*

*Improvement in our environmental performance occurs
through the continuous improvement process and through
annual management reviews of our environmental
management system, including periodic review of our
environmental objectives and targets. Our main objectives
are to:*

- *Improve air emissions*

- *Investigate waste minimization opportunities*

*The Environmental Policy along with appropriate information
regarding environmental performance is periodically provided
to executive management and employees and is also made
available to the public.*

To train and educate employees to conduct their activities in an environmentally responsible manner is an ongoing process. Protecting our environment is everyone's responsibility.

Environmental impact evaluations of proposed actions, including process and practice changes, are conducted to minimize adverse consequences.

5.0   Responsibilities

5.1   The following job positions have responsibilities in this EMS procedure:

- Gary Complex Environmental Management System Steering Team

- Environmental Management Representative (EMR)

- All employees

6.0   Procedure

6.1   The Gary Complex Environmental Policy has been written and approved by the Gary Complex EMS Steering Team to provide direction, to promote understanding, and to demonstrate commitment to the Gary Complex Environmental Management System.

6.2   The Gary Complex Environmental Policy is communicated to all employees.

6.2.1   The Manager, Environmental Control or designee ensures that the Gary Complex Environmental Policy and Environmental Policy Focus are communicated to *all* employees as part of ISO 14001 Awareness Training. (See EMS Procedure 4.4.2).

6.2.2   Copies of the Gary Complex Environmental Policy and Environmental Policy Focus are posted throughout the Gary Complex.

6.2.3   Periodic audits are conducted to ensure that the policy is communicated. (See EMS Procedure 4.5.5.)

6.2.4   The Environmental Policy is made available to employees on the Environmental Control intranet

Web site. The policy is also made available to employees and the public on the USS Web site at location: http://www.ussteel.com/corp/facilities/gary_env.htm.

7.0   Approval

7.1   Approval of this procedure by the Gary Complex Environmental Management System Steering Team is effected by the signature (on the Document Validation Form) of the Manager, Environmental Control that has been designated as the Environmental Management Representative.

7.2   Approved for use:

Manager, Environmental Control and Environmental Management Representative

[The environmental policy in section 4.1.2 of the procedure was issued on March 10, 2000. It was approved by the EMS Steering Team. The policy was reviewed and reaffirmed by the EMS Steering Team in September 2004.]

Delaware North Companies
Parks & Resorts

Delaware North Companies Parks & Resorts (DNCP&R) is fortunate to do business in very special and scenic locations, some designated as national treasures. DNCP&R is committed to responsible stewardship of the resources in all these locales, and has developed GreenPath, an environmental management system, to guide us in achieving our commitment to environmental excellence.

Delaware North Companies Parks & Resorts acknowledges that it is essential to the environment that all operations and activities of the company be conducted in strict accordance with sound environmental, health, and safety practices. Therefore, all DNCP&R operations will be managed in compliance with all laws, regulations, and requirements related to environmental quality and human health and safety applicable to our business activities. DNCP&R is committed to build from a foundation of compliance with the aim of preventing pollution in the areas where we do business and to continually improving our environmental performance. To achieve these goals, DNCP&R will adopt the best available practices in environmental matters. Specifically, DNCP&R shall:

- Incorporate environmental considerations into business decisions, including planning and design activities

- Set measurable objectives and targets to improve environmental performance

- Reduce, where practicable, pollution and the generation, discharge, and emission of waste to all environmental media—air, land, surface water, and groundwater

- Anticipate emerging environmental issues and develop programs to respond to future requirements

- Allocate and maintain resources for the effective implementation of environmental management and compliance programs

- Encourage communication among employees, visitors, neighbors, surrounding communities, business associates, customers, regulatory agencies, and the general public regarding DNCP&R's environmental issues

- Strive to make a positive environmental contribution to the communities where we operate

Every DNCP&R employee, vendor, and contractor has an obligation to comply with all applicable environmental laws and regulations and other DNCP&R requirements. Employee training will include a review of this policy and all applicable elements of GreenPath, our environmental management system.

[This environmental policy, issued on May 27, 2005, is signed by the President, Hospitality Group. It supersedes a previous policy dated January 15, 2004.]

Coast Guard Air Station Cape Cod

As the world's premier maritime service and steward of our nation's marine environment, our goal is to manage the land, sea, and air resources under our cognizance in an environmentally responsible manner. The preservation of marine biodiversity and the prevention of marine ecosystem degradation from land-based activities, including our own, is central to our environmental efforts.

We will comply with all applicable environmental regulations. Operations shall be planned and executed to reduce or eliminate the potential for pollution and waste of the earth's limited resources. We will work aggressively, in partnership with federal, state, and local agencies, environmental interest groups, and private industry, to provide for long-term environmental quality and improvement. Our environmental program will focus on marine emergency preparedness, marine transportation management, environmental law, environmental justice, pollution response, and internal programs of compliance and restoration.

Our goal is to be the world's leader in maritime environmental stewardship. Protecting the environment is inherent in every mission and operation at Air Station Cape Cod. The leadership of all personnel at Air Station Cape Cod is expected to execute this policy.

[This policy was initially issued on February 1, 2001. It was most recently revised on September 15, 2005, and is signed by the Commanding Officer.]

4

Environmental Aspects

Effective environmental management requires a comprehensive understanding of an organization's effect on the environment. Because most organizations affect the environment in numerous ways, ISO 14001:2004 requires a comprehensive analysis of all components integral to daily operations.

ISO 14001:2004 Text	ISO 14001:1996 Text
4.3.1 Environmental aspects The organization shall establish, implement and maintain a procedure(s) a) to identify the environmental aspects of its activities, products and services within the defined scope of the environmental management system that it can control and those that it can influence taking into account planned or new developments, or new or modified activities, products and services, and b) to determine those aspects that have or can have significant impact(s) on the environment (i.e. significant environmental aspects).	*4.3.1 Environmental aspects* The organization shall establish and maintain (a) procedure(s) to identify the environmental aspects of its activities, products or services that it can control and over which it can be expected to have an influence, in order to determine those which have or can have significant impacts on the environment. The organization shall ensure that the aspects related to these significant impacts are considered in setting the environmental objectives. The organization shall keep this information up to date.

Continued

Continued

ISO 14001:2004 Text	ISO 14001:1996 Text
The organization shall document this information and keep it up to date. The organization shall ensure that the significant environmental aspects are taken into account in establishing, implementing and maintaining its environmental management system.	

SIGNIFICANT CHANGES

Additional language in ISO 14001:2004 specifies that information about environmental aspects and impacts must be documented. All other changes are intended to clarify the original wording:

• The phrase "activities, products *and* services" replaces "activities, products *or* services." An organization cannot selectively identify environmental aspects. All facets of an enterprise must be evaluated.

• ISO 14001:2004 requires an organization to define the scope of its environmental management system (see Chapter 2). Environmental aspects must be identified only for those activities, products, and services that fall within the defined scope.

• The original standard mandated identification of environmental aspects over which an organization could be *expected* to have an influence. Because the concept of "expectation" was ambiguous, ISO 14001:2004 explicitly restates this requirement as identifying environmental aspects that the organization *can* influence. Although an organization can not control consumer behavior, decisions about product characteristics and packaging can influence use and disposal behaviors of consumers. Similarly, an organization might be in a position to influence some suppliers of purchased products and services.

• Reference to "planned or new developments" and "new or modified activities, products and services" is new to this clause, but not new to the standard. Originally, that language appeared in conjunction with requirements to achieve stated objectives and targets (clause 4.3.4). This direct reference to change emphasizes the requirement for an organization to be familiar with the environmental aspects and impacts associated with all current endeavors.

• ISO 14001:1996 required that significant environmental aspects be considered in setting environmental objectives and targets. ISO 14001:2004 broadens this requirement so that significant environmental aspects are taken into account in establishing, implementing, and maintaining the entire environmental management system.

INTENT OF ISO 14001:2004

This requirement constitutes one of the most misunderstood sections of ISO 14001:2004. As defined in section 3.6 of the standard, an environmental aspect is any element of an organization's activities or products or services that can interact with the environment (for example, the use of lead in the manufacture of steel). An environmental impact (defined in section 3.7) is any change to the environment, whether adverse or beneficial, wholly or partially resulting from an aspect (for example, lead dust in the air). Table 4.1 illustrates the distinction between environmental aspects and impacts for a manufacturing process, a product, and a service.

ISO 14001:2004 requires that an organization have a procedure to identify its environmental aspects and their associated impacts. The most typical approach to identification of environmental aspects involves examination of individual processes. Because every process is bounded by the

Table 4.1 Examples of environmental aspects and impacts.

	Process	**Product**	**Service**
Example	Manufacture of acrylonitrile monomer	Styrofoam coffee cup	Lawn maintenance
Aspect	Ammonium sulfate	Not degradable or recyclable	Application of herbicides and pesticides
Method of transfer	Injection of ammonium sulfate into deep wells	Disposal of solid waste	Rain causes runoff into storm drains
Impact	Soil, water contamination	Depletion of landfill space	Nonpoint source pollution

discrete parameters of inputs (such as materials, energy), a value-added transformation, and outputs (such as finished product, reusable materials, wastes), a procedure for identification of environmental aspects is rendered straightforward and manageable.

Depending on the nature of the specific operation under review, consideration usually is given to the following categories of aspects:

- Raw materials
- Processed materials
- Recycled materials
- Reused materials
- Chemicals
- Natural resources
- Energy
- Packaging

The standard is not intended, and should not be interpreted, to require a detailed lifecycle assessment. Nor do organizations need to evaluate each product, component, or raw material input. An organization may select categories of activities, products, and services to identify its aspects.

Less common, but no less important, is identification of the environmental aspects associated with activities that are not directly related to an organization's processes. Examples include janitorial services, pest control, food service (such as a cafeteria), and building construction.

Once an organization has identified its environmental aspects, it must determine their impact on the environment. Environmental impacts can be acute or chronic. Acute impacts are associated with episodic or short-term events, such as an accidental oil spill. Chronic impacts result from long-term events, such as improper disposal of used oil by car owners. Typically, environmental impact is assessed by estimating factors such as:

- *Severity.* The degree to which an organization's surroundings are affected.
- *Likelihood.* The probability of occurrence.
- *Frequency.* How often it will occur.
- *Duration.* The length of time it will be felt.
- *Boundaries.* Physical area in which it occurs.

To the extent allowed by science and technology, the impact of each environmental aspect should be quantified. Resulting values provide a basis for determining whether a specific impact is *significant*. A significant environmental aspect is one that has or can have a significant environmental impact.

ISO 14001:2004 does not define significance. Rather, it is left to an organization to determine what it deems significant based on the nature of its business. What is considered significant in one setting is not necessarily significant in another. For example, used toner cartridges might be identified as the most significant environmental aspect in a training organization and the lowest-ranking aspect in a coal mining operation.

Although some organizations have argued that they have no significant environmental aspects, such a position demonstrates a limited understanding of the intent of ISO 14001:2004. First, there is no absolute value of significance assigned to a specific aspect; significance is always relative to other identified aspects. It follows, then, that the aspect with the worst environmental impact is significant even if that impact is not particularly bad.

Second, ISO 14001:2004 relies on identified significant environmental aspects as the basis for activities associated with other requirements. An organization that purports to have no significant aspects would be unable to fulfill those requirements and would, therefore, be unable to provide evidence of conformity.

Environmental aspects or impacts are the focus of two clauses in ISO 14001:2004; *significant* environmental aspects or impacts are the focus of five clauses:

- *4.2a Environmental policy.* Requires that the policy is appropriate to the environmental impacts of its activities, products, and services.

- *4.3.2 Legal requirements.* Requires identification of and access to applicable legal requirements and other requirements related to environmental aspects.

- *4.3.3 Objectives, targets and programs.* Requires that significant environmental aspects are taken into account.

- *4.4.2 Competence, training and awareness.* Requires that workers performing tasks with the potential to cause a significant environmental impact must be competent, training needs associated with environmental aspects must be identified, and awareness training related to significant environmental aspects and related actual or potential impacts must be provided.

- *4.4.3 Communication.* Requires a decision concerning external communication about significant environmental aspects.

- *4.4.6 Operational control.* Requires identification and planning of operations associated with significant environmental aspects; requires procedures related to significant environmental aspects of goods and services provided by suppliers and contractors.

- *4.5.1 Monitoring and measurement.* Requires regular monitoring and measurement of operations that can have significant environmental impacts.

Identification of significant environmental aspects and impacts constitutes the single most important activity required by ISO 14001:2004. If an organization's environmental management system is to be effective, it must reduce or eliminate adverse environmental effects that result from its operations.

EXAMPLES

U. S. Steel Gary Complex
EMS Procedure 4.3.1—Environmental Aspects
(Effective September 19, 2005)

1.0 Purpose

    1.1 This procedure describes the identification, prioritization, and periodic review of new and/or modified environmental aspects associated with operations at the Gary Complex.

2.0 Scope

    2.1 Personnel involved with the identification, prioritization, and periodic review of new and/or modified environmental aspects use this procedure.

3.0 References

    3.1 ISO 14001:2004 Standard

    3.2 Gary Complex process flow diagrams (PFDs)

    3.3 Environmental Aspect Inventory and Evaluation Worksheet 70100060FRM—Exhibit I (see page 46)

3.4   Significant Aspect Web page—Exhibit II

3.5   Environmental Incident Reporting System

3.6   Environmental Preventive/Corrective Action Requests (EPCAR)

4.0   Definitions

4.1   An environmental aspect is an element of the Gary Complex activities, products, and services that can interact with the environment.

4.2   An environmental impact is any change to the environment, whether adverse or beneficial, wholly or partially resulting from the Gary Complex activities, products, or services.

4.3   A significant environmental aspect is an environmental aspect that has or can have a significant environmental impact.

4.4   An abnormal condition is a departure from normal operations that may result in a significant environmental impact.

5.0   Responsibilities

5.1   The following job positions/functions have responsibilities in this EMS procedure:

- Business Unit Cross-Functional Teams (CFT)

- Environmental Control ISO 14001 Steering Team

- Gary Complex Environmental Management System Steering Team

6.0   Procedure

6.1   Process Flow Diagrams (PFDs) and Other Information Resources

6.1.1   The ISO 14001 Coordinator maintains process flow diagrams that illustrate Gary Complex operational activities. The diagrams include inputs and outputs of each process.

6.1.2   Reviews of process flow diagrams and other information resources are conducted to identify any process changes and associated environmental aspects. This review is conducted at least annually.

6.1.3   The ISO 14001 Coordinator ensures the revision of the process flow diagrams to include process changes identified by the CFT.

6.2   Environmental Aspects and Environmental Impacts

6.2.1   A baseline evaluation of environmental aspects at the Gary Complex has been conducted. The results of this evaluation are recorded on Aspect Inventory and Evaluation Worksheets for each business unit.

6.2.2   The ISO 14001 Coordinator ensures the revision of the Environmental Aspect Inventory and Evaluation Worksheet to include environmental aspects associated with process changes identified by the CFT. This revision, depending on the nature of the process change, may include the addition of new environmental aspects or the modification or deletion of existing environmental aspects.

6.2.3   An evaluation of new or modified environmental aspects is conducted annually. This evaluation is conducted by appraising mutually exclusive elements associated with the aspect using four evaluation criteria and a numerical rating scale for each criterion. A record of this evaluation is maintained on the Environmental Aspect Inventory and Evaluation Worksheet. The evaluation criteria and their associated rating scales are as follows:

6.2.3.1   Severity of environmental impact:

5 = Severe—very harmful, great effort to correct and recover

4 = Serious—harmful, difficult to correct but recoverable

3 = Moderate—somewhat harmful, correctable

2 = Mild—little potential for harm, easily correctable

1 = Harmless—no potential for harm, potentially beneficial

6.2.3.2 Likelihood that an abnormal condition will occur:

5 = Very likely—high probability that an abnormal condition will occur (53 or more events/year)

4 = Likely—strong probability that an abnormal condition will occur (25 to 52 events/year)

3 = Moderate—reasonable probability that an abnormal condition will occur (seven to 24 events/year)

2 = Low—low probability that an abnormal condition will occur (four to six events/year)

1 = Remote—very unlikely that an abnormal condition will occur (zero to three events/year)

6.2.3.3 Detectability of an abnormal condition:

5 = Low detectability—abnormal condition apparent after 24 hours

4 = Poor detectability—abnormal condition apparent within 16 to 24 hours

3 = Moderate detectability—abnormal condition apparent within eight to 16 hours

2 = Good detectability—abnormal condition apparent within eight hours

1 = High detectability—abnormal condition immediately apparent

6.2.3.4 Controllability of environmental aspect:

5 = Uncontrolled—no apparent control capability

4 = Poor control—not regularly monitored, manual control capability

3 = Moderate control—monitored at established intervals, manual control capability

2 = Controlled—continuous monitoring, manual control capability

1 = Immediate control—continuous monitoring, automatic control capability

6.2.4 The evaluation total for each environmental aspect is determined by multiplying each of the evaluation results for each criterion in sequence. The range of aspect evaluation totals is from 1 to 625.

6.2.5 The results of aspect evaluations for each applicable business unit/staff organization are arranged by the CFT according to aspect evaluation total. The CFT reviews the sorted list of environmental aspects for each business unit/staff organization and determines the significant aspect definition level for that business unit. Environmental aspects with an aspect evaluation total equal to or greater than the significant aspect definition level are designated as significant environmental aspects. Environmental aspects with aspect evaluation totals below the significant aspect definition level remain environmental aspects.

6.2.6 The Environmental Control ISO 14001 Steering Team reviews, revises, and approves the designated significant environmental aspects. This review is conducted at least annually but may be conducted more frequently. The review shall be conducted by the end of the third quarter of the current calendar year for development of significant aspect objectives and targets, which are considered during development of business unit annual business plans. Changes in significant aspects are effective upon the implementation of the annual business plans.

6.2.6.1 The Environmental Control ISO 14001 Steering Team will review and revise the active status of significant environmental aspects any time operations within a business unit are suspended or terminated. Significant aspects associated with those operations will assume a status equivalent to those operations (suspended or terminated). Significant aspects will be reinstated to active status within 30 days after operations resume.

6.2.7 Environmental Control conducts an annual review of a list of contractors/suppliers to determine relevance to Gary Complex environmental aspects. A CFT, comprising Environmental Control and affected business units, reviews a list of relevant contractors/suppliers to determine association with Gary Complex significant environmental aspects. This review will utilize the following EMS components:

- Significant Environmental Aspects

- Environmental Incident Reporting System (EIRS)

- Environmental Preventive and Corrective Action Request (EPCAR) System

Identified relevant contractors/suppliers associated with significant environmental aspects are included on the Significant Aspect Web page.

6.2.8 Approved significant environmental aspects are presented to the Gary Complex Environmental Management System Steering Team at the next scheduled management review meeting. The Gary Complex EMS Steering Team reviews approved significant environmental aspects to ensure that they are consistent with the Gary Complex Environmental Policy and goals.

7.0 Approval

7.1 Approval of this procedure by the Gary Complex Environmental Management System Steering Team is effected by the signature (on the Document Validation Form) of the Manager, Environmental Control that has been designated as the EMR.

7.2 Approved for use:

Manager, Environmental Control and Environmental Management Representative

Aspect ref. code	Aspect location	Aspect type	Activity/upset condition	Aspect description	Environmental impact	Severity	Likelihood	Detectability	Controllability	Significance total

Continued

Exhibit I EMS Procedure 4.3.1—Environmental Aspect Inventory and Evaluation Worksheet.

Continued

Rating scale	Severity	Likelihood	Detectability	Controllability
5	Severe	Very likely	Low detectability	Uncontrolled
4	Serious	Likely	Poor detectability	Poor control
3	Moderate	Moderate	Moderate detectability	Moderate control
2	Mild	Low	Good detectability	Controlled
1	Harmless	Remote	High detectability	Immediate control

Severity

Very harmful—great effort to correct and recover

Serious—harmful, difficult to correct but recoverable

Moderate—somewhat harmful, correctable

Mild—little potential for harm, easily correctable

Harmless—no potential for harm, potentially beneficial

Likelihood

Very likely—high probability that an abnormal condition will occur at 53 or more events/year

Likely—strong probability that an abnormal condition will occur at 25 to 52 events/year

Moderate—reasonable probability that an abnormal condition will occur at seven to 24 events/year

Low—low probability that an abnormal condition will occur at four to six events/year

Remote—very unlikely that an abnormal condition will occur at zero to three events/year

Detectability

Low detectability—abnormal condition apparent greater than 24 hours

Poor detectability—abnormal condition apparent within 24 hours

Moderate detectability—abnormal condition apparent within eight to 16 hours

Good detectability—abnormal condition apparent within eight hours

High detectability—abnormal condition immediately apparent

Controllability

Uncontrolled—no apparent control capability

Poor control—not regularly monitored, manual control capability

Moderate control—monitored at established intervals, manual control capability

Controlled—continuous monitoring, manual control capability

Immediate control—continuous monitoring, automatic control capability

Exhibit I EMS Procedure 4.3.1—Environmental Aspect Inventory and Evaluation Worksheet.

Delaware North Companies Parks & Resorts
P1400.02—GreenPath Environmental Aspects
(Effective August 5, 2005)

Policy

Delaware North Companies (DNC) GreenPath locations will identify and evaluate the environmental aspects that they can control and those that they can influence that are associated with the services, activities, and products at their location. The significant environmental aspects will then be managed in a manner that endeavors to reduce or eliminate the environmental impacts associated with them.

Purpose

To identify and evaluate the environmental aspects associated with DNC GreenPath locations, with the goal of establishing and prioritizing environmental objectives, targets, and programs to achieve overall continual improvement in environmental performance.

Procedure

Responsibility:

The Environmental Manager at each GreenPath location, with input, as appropriate, from local staff, the Director of Environmental Affairs, company personnel, and others, is responsible for conducting the initial environmental aspects evaluation and for annually reviewing the aspects for continued relevance. The top manager at the GreenPath location will approve the significant environmental aspects. The Director of Environmental Affairs will annually review the environmental aspects.

Definitions:

Environment—Surroundings in which an organization operates, including air, water, land, natural resources, flora, fauna, humans, and their interrelation.

Environmental aspect—Element of an organization's activities or products or services that can interact with the environment.

Significant environmental aspect—An environmental aspect that has or can have a significant environmental impact.

Environmental impact—Any change to the environment, whether adverse or beneficial, wholly or partially resulting from an organization's environmental aspects.

Environmental objective—Overall environmental goal, consistent with the environmental policy, that an organization sets itself to achieve.

Environmental target—Detailed performance requirement, applicable to the organization or parts thereof, that arises from the environmental objectives, and that needs to be set and met in order to achieve those objectives.

Process:

1. The Environmental Manager at each GreenPath location will review the environmental aspects at the facility during the first quarter of every calendar year, or when warranted by physical or operational changes to facility operations. The Environmental Manager:

   • May solicit input from operations personnel, the Director of Environmental Affairs, and other personnel in order to accomplish this process

   • Will consult the file of External Communication Record forms to incorporate appropriate outside communications

2. Will evaluate services, activities, and products associated with the operating location to determine how they impact the following environmental issues:

   • Air emissions

   • Water emissions

   • Water use

   • Waste disposal (solid, hazardous, and so on)

   • Energy use

   • Animals and plants

   • Material use

3. The Environmental Manager will use this evaluation to identify environmental aspects. Each environmental aspect will be evaluated under normal and abnormal conditions, as deemed necessary.

4. The environmental aspects will be listed on the Environmental Aspect Matrix form, or a similar form.

5. The Environmental Manager will evaluate the identified impacts with appropriate location staff to determine if the impacts are significant or potentially significant.

   • Significance will be determined by consensus with the individuals involved in the evaluation.

   • The general screening criteria might include an evaluation of the views of interested parties (including the client, the public, employees, and others as determined appropriate) and the estimated environmental impact (that is, severity of impact, the frequency of impact, and the business impact to the company).

   • The Environmental Manager will document the significant environmental aspects, along with an explanation as to how they were determined to be significant.

   • Agreement with the unit's top executive is required in order to complete the process of identifying the significant environmental aspects.

   • Significant environmental aspects will be made available to the public upon request.

6. For each significant environmental aspect, the Environmental Manager will consider developing appropriate objectives, targets, environmental management plans, and programs with the goal of reducing the overall impact of that aspect.

   • Environmental management plans will be documented on the Environmental Management Plan form, F1400.02. Plans will include specific tasks that will be required to accomplish the target, the name of the person or group who is assigned to complete each task, and a projected date of completion for each task.

   • The Environmental Management Plan Activity Log will be used to document action on the tasks listed on the Environmental Management Plan. Information logged should be identified by a number corresponding with the numbered task/action item.

Required Documentation:

• Environmental Aspects Matrix

• Documentation concerning the results of each annual review of the environmental aspects

- Environmental Management Plan form, F1400.02

- Environmental Management Plan Activity Log, F1400.02.01

This documentation will be kept in the environmental files.

Coast Guard Air Station Cape Cod
Procedure 01—Environmental Aspects Review Procedure
(Effective January 17, 2003)

1.0 Purpose:

Identify the significant environmental aspects of the U.S. Coast Guard Air Station Cape Cod's (USCG–ASCC) activities, products, and services.

2.0 Scope:

2.1 This procedure will include the review of all areas of Air Station Cape Cod that are under the ownership or operation of the USCG, including areas that are within the USCG's control and/or influence.

2.2 This procedure will include both USCG and civilian operations within these areas as well as all contracted services.

3.0 Procedure:

3.1 The Environmental Health and Safety Manager will assemble a team to conduct a baseline environmental aspects review. Team members should include, at a minimum, the USCG–ASCC environmental staff.

3.2 The team will conduct an inventory of ASCC activities, products, and services within the above-stated scope. A list of the facility's functional areas will be created/reviewed to ensure a comprehensive review. A list of the functional areas is attached to this procedure in Appendix A (page 54).

3.3 For each functional area, the team will identify the environmental aspects of the area's activities, products, and services.

3.4 Using the worksheet provided in Appendix B (page 55), the team will identify the potential environmental impacts for the activities, products, and services within each functional area, taking into consideration normal and abnormal operations. For guidance, a list of possible environmental impacts that should be considered is provided in Appendix C (page 56).

3.5   Using the Environmental Aspects Worksheet, the team will rank the significance of the identified environmental impacts, using a scale of 1 (lowest significance) to 5 (highest significance).

3.6   The determination of significance is an educated judgment made by the team based on the following criteria:

- Frequency or likelihood of occurrence

- Severity of environmental impact

- Scale of use or environmental impact

- Legal or regulatory concern

- Ability of the organization to control or influence

- Public relations/stakeholder issue

The significance of each environmental aspect/impact will be assessed using the above criteria, following the guidance provided in Appendix D (page 58). Each aspect must be considered under both normal operations as well as abnormal situations (for example, in the event of a spill, malfunction, or emergency situation). The significance of each aspect will then be ranked on a scale of 1 to 5.

3.7   The Environmental Aspects Worksheet information will be evaluated, and a cutoff significance ranking score will be selected. Environmental aspects that have rankings equal to or greater than 18 will be designated as "significant." Where it makes sense, environmental aspects may be considered either individually or in groups. For example, there may be multiple items related to air emissions, spills, or hazardous waste generation.

3.8   After evaluating categories and trends among those environmental aspects determined to be significant, a final list of the USCG–ASCC's "significant environmental aspects" will be generated. Aspects ranked high in significance will be targeted for attention and improvement through the selection of objectives and targets and will be the focus for operational controls and/or monitoring and measurement. The list of significant environmental aspects is included as Appendix E (page 59).

3.9 The list of environmental aspects will be periodically reviewed and kept up to date. The team will meet at a minimum on an annual basis to update the baseline inventory of environmental aspects, which will be modified as necessary due to facility changes or other information. Aspects that are initially ranked as high in significance may be re-designated with a lower ranking upon the application of physical controls (for example, containment system or emissions control device), operational controls (for example, documented standard operating procedure) and/or the lessening of environmental impacts via the achievement of environmental improvement objectives. The "notes" section of the Environmental Aspects Worksheet should be used to provide explanations for changes in significance rankings. Environmental aspect review sessions will be documented using the form provided as Appendix F (page 60).

3.10 Environmental aspects associated with facility changes will be identified in accordance with the National Environmental Policy Act (NEPA) process and Procedure 05—New Chemical Review and Pharmacy. Each of these procedures makes provision for the review of environmental aspects associated with facility changes, and for update of the environmental aspects inventory as necessary.

3.11 Each update of the list of environmental aspects will be assigned a revision number and date and maintained as Appendix E to this procedure. Upon the completion of each environmental aspects update session, the previous list of aspects will be retained as a record, in accordance with Procedure 03—Recordkeeping and Record Retention.

4.0 Responsibilities:

The USCG–ASCC EHS Manager is responsible for the implementation of this procedure. This includes the selection of the aspects review team and oversight of the team's activities.

5.0 Appendixes

A. USCG–ASCC functional areas and locations

B. Environmental Aspects Worksheet

C. Environmental aspects and impacts guidance list

D. Significance ranking criteria

E. USCG–ASCC list of significant environmental aspects

F. Environmental Aspects Review Documentation form

6.0 Related Documentation:

Procedure 06—Environmental Aspects Procedure

Procedure 07—Document Control System

Procedure 03—Recordkeeping and Record Retention

7.0 Records:

Records generated by this procedure include:

- Environmental Aspects Review Worksheets

- Environmental Aspects Review Documentation forms

- USCG–ASCC list of significant environmental aspects (obsolete lists retained as records).

APPENDIXES TO COAST GUARD AIR STATION CAPE COD PROCEDURE 01

3-in-1 Variety Store	Medical Clinic
Roadways	Housing
Activities Center	Vehicles
Golf Course	Emergency Generators
Aircraft Air Operations	Purchasing
Aircraft Ground Operations	Demolition and Construction
Administrative Offices	Hazardous Waste Accumulation Areas
GSE Shops	
Roads and Grounds/FED Shops	Chapel and Chapel Support

Appendix A USCG–ASCC functional areas and locations.

Environmental impacts	Present	Frequency likelihood	Severity	Scale	Legal/regulatory	Control/influence	Stakeholder concern	Ranking score	Notes
Date:									
Functional area:									
Normal activity/environmental aspect									
Inputs									
Electricity use									
Water use									
Fuel use									
Chemical or toxic substances use									
Land use									
Raw materials									
Outputs									
Air emissions									
Wastewater									
Storm water									
Solid waste									
Hazardous waste									
Abnormal operations									

Appendix B   Environmental Aspects Worksheet.

Air emissions:	
Organics or solvent fumes	Dust or particulate
Odors	CFCs or refrigerants
Ozone-depleting substances	Combustion emissions
Hoods and vents	Vehicle emissions
Fugitive emissions	Tank vent emissions
Greenhouse gases	Painting
Sandblasting	Welding
Oil mists	Radiation

Water:	
Sanitary wastewater	Industrial wastewater
Stormwater runoff	Water usage
Cooling water	Blowdown or condensate
Water treatment chemicals	Floor drain discharges

Solid and hazardous waste:	
General trash	Food waste
Yard waste	Office waste
Nonrecyclable waste	Spent chemicals
Used oil	Packaging waste
Electronic equipment waste	Asbestos
Hazardous waste	Construction debris
Medical or biohazard waste	Spent pesticides
Spill clean-up debris	PCBs
Lead-based paint	Batteries
Mercury-containing waste	Fluorescent light tubes and ballasts

Land use:	
Erosion and sedimentation	Visual impact
Natural resources	Endangered species
Open spaces	Tree growth
Wildlife habitat	Zoning
Pesticide use	Agricultural/forestry issues
Illegal dumping	Historic preservation

Appendix C Environmental aspects and impacts guidance list. *Continued*

Continued

Raw materials:	
Chemical usage	Toxicity
Natural resource depletion	Packaging
Waste impacts	Warehousing
Transportation	Supplier environmental issues
Toxics use (reporting requirements)	Toxics release
Janitorial supplies	

Bulk material storage:	
Underground tank leaks	Piping leaks
Transfer activities	Drips and spills
Vent emissions	

Utilities:	
Electricity consumption	Water use
Electricity supplier source issues	Fuel consumption

Vehicles and transportation:	
Air emissions	Fuel consumption
Traffic congestion	Fuel leaks
Waste oil	Security

Abnormal operations:	
Spills	Accidental discharge
Leaks	Abnormal raw material usage
Fire	

Appendix C   Environmental aspects and impacts guidance list.

Frequency or likelihood of occurrence	
1	Once in a lifetime
2	Rarely—for example, once every few years
3	Occurs on a regular basis—for example, several times a month
4	High frequency—for example, daily
5	Continuous

Severity of impact	
1	No adverse environmental impact
2	Low environmental impact
3	Moderate environmental impact, does not cause irreversible damage, can be controlled
4	Significant environmental impact, difficult to control
5	High adverse impact—results in contamination, irreversible damage, or other serious environmental issue

Scale of use or impact	
1	Inconsequential use or discharge
2	Minor use or minor volume discharge
3	Moderate use or moderate volume discharge
4	Significant use or significant volume discharge
5	High-scale use or high volume discharge

Legal or regulatory concern	
1	Not regulated
2	Regulated area but no restrictions
3	Subject to moderate regulatory requirements—for example, recordkeeping, reporting
4	Highly regulated—for example, subject to permit conditions, emission limits, operating restrictions, usage limitations
5	Violates regulatory requirements or permit conditions

Appendix D   Significance ranking criteria.   *Continued*

Continued

Degree of control or influence	
1	Little or no ability to influence
2	Able to influence somewhat—for example, via selection of contractors, vendors
3	Somewhat within the site's control
4	Generally within the site's control
5	Completely within the site's control

Stakeholder concern	
1	No site personnel, public, regulatory agency, or interest group concern
2	Minor concern
3	Moderate concern
4	Significant concern, could cause adverse publicity
5	Serious concern, reputation at stake

Appendix D Significance ranking criteria.

Golf Course—Water use

Golf Course—Pesticide application

Golf Course, GSE Shops, Roads and Grounds/FED Shops—Fuel spill or release

Aircraft Ground Operations—Tanker truck release

3-in-1 Variety Store—Fuel spill or release

Roads and Grounds/FED Shops—Ozone-depleting substance release

Roads and Grounds/FED Shops—Improper hazardous waste disposal

Purchasing—Raw material procurement

Demolition and Construction—Construction in environmentally sensitive area

Demolition and Construction—Demolition without abatement

Medical Clinic—Failure of silver recovery unit

Hazardous Waste Accumulation Areas—Hazardous waste management

Sitewide—Air emissions permit compliance

Solid Waste

Recycling

Appendix E USCG–ASCC list of significant environmental aspects.

| Meeting date: |
| Participants: |
| Agenda: |
| Action items: |

Appendix F   Environmental aspects review documentation form.

5

Legal and Other Requirements

Implementation of an environmental management system does not absolve an organization of its legal obligations. ISO 14001:2004 is not a substitute for regulatory requirements. It is intended to improve an organization's environmental performance beyond the level imposed by governmental authority.

ISO 14001:2004 Text	ISO 14001:1996 Text
4.3.2 Legal and other requirements The organization shall establish, implement and maintain a procedure(s) a) to identify and have access to the applicable legal requirements and other requirements to which the organization subscribes related to its environmental aspects, and b) to determine how these requirements apply to its environmental aspects.	*4.3.2 Legal and other requirements* The organization shall establish and maintain a procedure to identify and have access to legal and other requirements to which the organization subscribes, that are applicable to the environmental aspects of its activities, products or services.

Continued

Continued

ISO 14001:2004 Text	ISO 14001:1996 Text
The organization shall ensure that these applicable legal requirements and other requirements to which the organization subscribes are taken into account in establishing, implementing and maintaining its environmental management system.	

SIGNIFICANT CHANGES

The language employed in the revised text is intended to clarify the original language. In 1996, ISO 14001 instructed organizations to focus on legal and other requirements that were "applicable" to their environmental aspects.

The 2004 revision is less ambiguous. Paragraph (b) explicitly requires an organization to ascertain *how* its legal and other requirements apply to its environmental aspects. The last paragraph further instructs an organization to explicitly consider those requirements in the creation and execution of its environmental management system.

INTENT OF ISO 14001:2004

ISO 14001:2004 differentiates between legal requirements and "other" requirements. Legal requirements encompass laws and regulations imposed by federal (or national), provincial, state, county, city, and local agencies.

"Other" requirements are voluntary initiatives that an organization imposes upon itself such as:

- *Industry codes of practice.* Guidelines that have been established for companies within a specific business sector, such as Responsible Care (American Chemistry Council) and STEP—Strategy for Environmental Protection (American Petroleum Institute).

- *Environmental guiding principles.* General guidelines that have been established for companies across a diverse array of business sectors, such as the Business Charter for Sustainable Development (International Chamber of Commerce).

- *Agreements with public authorities.* Activities not mandated by laws or regulations, such as the National Environmental Performance Track (EPA).

Although ISO 14001:2004 says that an organization must identify its applicable legal requirements, it is acceptable for an outside individual or entity to provide this information. In large organizations, such information tends to reside with corporate counsel or corporate environmental, health, and safety (EHS) staff. Designated individuals within these functions are likely to be aware of every legal obligation with which their organization must comply and, therefore, responsible for sharing such information with relevant business units.

In organizations that have neither expertise in this area nor a centralized administrative structure with the capability to assemble such information, it is acceptable to rely on consultants or research firms with specialized knowledge about environmental laws and regulations. As long as an organization's legal requirements are identified, it does not matter whether the information is obtained by an employee of the organization or an outside expert.

A thorough assessment will extend beyond identifying which legal requirements affect specific operations and activities. As required elsewhere in ISO 14001:2004 (see Chapter 8), it will also ascertain whether appropriate personnel affiliated with those operations and activities are familiar with the associated legal requirements. Workers must perform their tasks in a manner that complies with the constraints imposed by such legal requirements.

An organization also must have access to its environmental legal requirements. This means that it has the ability to obtain relevant information in a timely manner. Although many organizations rely on electronic databases to provide access to legal requirements, workers throughout an organization rarely are expected to use such databases on a daily basis. Typically, information from such databases is incorporated into operating procedures and work instructions associated with specific activities and tasks.

Similarly, all other environmental requirements to which the organization voluntarily subscribes also must be identified. Frequently, a company's senior management signs on to such initiatives without communicating to employees how they will be affected. The voluntary nature of such initiatives may lull decision makers into a sense of complacency. However, ISO 14001:2004 requires that such obligations be treated with the same commitment as legal requirements.

Remember that the environmental policy statement contains language that commits to compliance with legal and other requirements. That commitment is supported by clause 4.3.2, which is intended to ensure that the organization knows what requirements it is to comply with. (Clause 4.5.2, discussed in Chapter 15, focuses on evaluating compliance.)

EXAMPLES

U. S. Steel Gary Works
EMS Procedure 4.3.2—Legal and Other Requirements
(Effective September 19, 2005)

1.0 Purpose

    1.1 This procedure describes the identification and communication of legal and other environmental requirements that are associated with operations at the Gary Complex.

2.0 Scope

    2.1 Personnel who are responsible for the identification and communication of legal and other environmental requirements use this procedure.

3.0 References

    3.1 ISO 14001:2004 Standard

    3.2 Environmental Requirement Notice 70100062FRM—Exhibit I (page 67) (Guidance for Completion)

    3.3 Table of Legal and Other Requirements—Exhibit II (page 69)

4.0 Definitions

    4.1 A *legal requirement* is a permit condition, ordinance, settlement agreement, or rule that specifies environmental performance standards for the Gary Complex.

    4.2 *Other requirements* are voluntary agreements made between the Gary Complex and interested parties. Other requirements may also include participation in voluntary environmental programs and agreements with governmental agencies.

5.0 Responsibilities

    5.1 The following job positions have responsibilities in this procedure:

- Area Manager, Environmental Technical Services

- Environmental Technical Services Managers

- ISO 14001 Coordinator

6.0   Procedure

   6.1   Identification of Legal and Other Requirements

      6.1.1   The Area Manager, Environmental Technical Services receives information regarding new/revised regulations, voluntary environmental programs, and environmental agreements that are applicable to environmental aspects at the Gary Complex. This information is derived from both organizational and published resources. Organizational resources include the following:

        - U. S. Steel Environmental Affairs Department

        - U. S. Steel Law Department

      Published resources may include, but are not limited to, the following:

        - Corporate publications

        - Industry newsletters and bulletins

        - Subscription environmental compliance services

        - Government publications

      6.1.2   The Area Manager, Environmental Technical Services evaluates information from these resources to determine if a detailed review of information regarding new/revised regulations, voluntary environmental programs, and environmental agreements is required. The Area Manager determines the appropriate Environmental Technical Services Manager to conduct a detailed review of received information.

      6.1.3   Environmental Technical Services Managers are charged with the responsibility of evaluating new/revised regulations, voluntary environmental programs, and environmental agreements that are applicable to environmental aspects at the Gary Complex. These responsibilities are assigned according to the manager's area of responsibility.

6.2 Communication of Legal and Other Requirements

6.2.1 Identified new or revised regulations, voluntary environmental programs, and environmental agreements are communicated to plant personnel through Environmental Requirement Notices. The Environmental Technical Services Managers determine the need for communication following a detailed review of the requirement. Environmental Requirement Notices serve as the notification of new/revised legal and other requirements. This notice identifies the status of the requirement, summarizes compliance issues, and provides an evaluation of impacts on operations. Additional actions to ensure compliance with the requirement are also identified in the notice.

6.3 Table of Legal and Other Requirements

6.3.1 At least annually, Environmental Technical Services Managers review the Table of Legal and Other Requirements to ensure that they are accurate and current. New or revised requirements are highlighted and forwarded to the ISO 14001 Coordinator.

6.3.2 The ISO 14001 Coordinator maintains a Table of Legal and Other Requirements for the plant and each business unit or staff group on the Gary Works ISO 14001 intranet Web site. The ISO 14001 Coordinator receives copies of issued notices to update the table as appropriate.

6.4 Conformance with Legal and Other Requirements

6.4.1 Conformance with Gary Complex legal and other requirements is evaluated through means identified in EMS Procedure 4.5.2—Evaluation of Compliance. Additionally, Gary Complex legal and other requirements are the subject of EMS audits described in EMS Procedure 4.5.5—Environmental Management System Audit.

7.0 Approval

7.1 Approval of this procedure by the Gary Complex Environmental Management System Steering Team is effected by the signature (on the Document Validation Form) of the Manager,

Environmental Control that has been designated
as the Environmental Management Representative.

7.2   Approved for use:

Manager, Environmental Control and Environmental
Management Representative

EMS PROCEDURE 4.3.2— ENVIRONMENTAL REQUIREMENT NOTICE

1.0   Purpose

State purpose for notification: "This provides notification of a
(regulatory or other) requirement that may impact operations at
facilities that . . ."

2.0   Background

Provide background of requirement:

- Provide the status of requirement, proposed rule, final rule, consent
  decree item, agreed order item, voluntary agreement, and so on

- Provide a summary of the requirement

- Provide critical compliance dates

3.0   Impact on Operations

Preliminary evaluation of significance of requirement:

- List potentially affected operations

- Summarize potential impacts to operations

- Evaluate current compliance status with requirement

4.0   Compliance Performance

Provide an evaluation of current compliance performance of the
affected operations/process equipment using the requirements
(above) as the compliance standard: "The (affected operations/
process equipment) is currently in (compliance or noncompliance)
with the regulatory requirement."

5.0   Recommendations

Provide recommendations (action items) to ensure compliance
with requirement:

- No action required, current compliance status is satisfactory

- Develop Compliance Action Plan

- Modifications to equipment and/or work practices

- Conduct evaluations to determine compliance approach

Exhibit I   EMS Procedure 4.3.2.   *Continued*

Continued

Action Items	Responsibility	Target completion date(s)
1)		
2)		
3)		
4)		

6.0 Responsibility for Compliance

Identify the position titles that are responsible for ensuring compliance with the requirement.

7.0 Contact

Identify environmental control manager(s) assigned the responsibility for compliance with the requirement.

8.0 Approval

Approved for distribution and use.

_____

Area Manager
Environmental and Program Services

9.0 Notice Distribution

Environmental
Compliance Manager: _____ Date: _____

Business Unit Manager: _____ Date: _____

10.0 Returned To

Area Manager
Environmental and
Program Services: _____ Date: _____

11.0 Action Item Completion

Action item number	Completion date
1	
2	
3	
4	

Exhibit I EMS Procedure 4.3.2.

Regulatory requirement			EMS implementation
Citation	Media	Description	Documentation vehicles
40 CFR Part 61, Subpart L	Air	Benzene NESHAP—Coke by-product recovery plants	GCO: ER&S, CMP

Voluntary programs			EMS implementation
Citation	Media	Description	Documentation vehicles
Wildlife Habitat Council (WHC)	Air, land, water	Wildlife habitat restoration and educational activity	WHC activity calendar

Exhibit II   EMS Procedure 4.3.2—Table of Legal and Other Requirements.*

* Table contains 15 pages; these two entries provided for illustration.

Delaware North Companies Parks & Resorts
P1400.03—GreenPath Legal and Other Requirements
(Effective August 5, 2005)

Policy

Delaware North Companies (DNC) shall endeavor to comply with all applicable federal, state, and local environmental laws and regulations, and other requirements to which DNC subscribes that are related to environmental aspects.

Purpose

To ensure that all legal and other requirements applicable to Delaware North Companies' Environmental Management System (EMS) have been identified, documented, complied with, and are kept up to date.

Procedure

Responsibility:

The Environmental Manager at each GreenPath location, with input from the operations and DNC staff, is responsible for identifying and documenting the legal and other requirements that apply to the unit's environmental aspects and operations.

Policy:

Management will identify and evaluate legal and other requirements that are applicable to the unit's environmental aspects and operations, and ensure that such information is documented and kept up to date.

Process:

1. The Environmental Manager at each GreenPath location identifies the legal and other requirements that apply to the unit's environmental aspects by:

   - Subscribing to publications that summarize current and proposed regulations, and/or

   - Attending conferences and seminars that address regulatory issues, and/or

   - Getting periodic input on regulatory issues from experienced regulatory consultants, government agencies, company personnel, and/or

   - Searching for relevant information on the Internet, and/or

   - Reviewing federal and state regulations on the Internet, and/or

   - Reviewing contracts between DNC and other entities

2. The Environmental Manager at each GreenPath location will create a list of legal and other requirements pertaining to the unit's environmental aspects. Environmental managers will review the current list at least once per year to ensure that it is up to date and reflects current local conditions. The Environmental Managers will make appropriate changes to the list, and inform personnel of any change that affects the work activities at the operating location.

3. The legal and other requirements that may be applicable to a unit's environmental aspects may include:

   - National and international legal requirements

   - State/provincial/departmental legal requirements

   - Local governmental legal requirements

   - ISO 14001:2004

   - Agreements with public authorities

- Agreements with customers

- Contracts with government agencies/organizations

- Nonregulatory guidelines

- Voluntary principles or codes of practice

- Voluntary environmental labeling or product stewardship commitments

- Requirements of trade associations

- Agreements with community groups or nongovernmental organizations

- Public commitments of the organization or its parent organization

- Corporate/company requirements

- Unit environmental objectives, targets, environmental management plans, and operation controls

- Calibration of environmental equipment

4. Using GreenPath form F1400.03, or a similar form, the unit's Environmental Manager shall attempt to identify and document the legal and other requirements that apply to the unit's environmental aspects.

Required Documentation:

- Current list of legal and other requirements, GreenPath form F1400.03, or similar documentation.

- Current permits will be kept in the environmental files, or other appropriate place, at each operating location.

Coast Guard Air Station Cape Cod
Procedure 02—Legal Requirements
(Effective February 1, 2001)

1.0 Purpose:

To identify state and federal environmental rules and regulations to ensure USCG–ASCC's operational compliance.

2.0 Scope:

    2.1 This procedure affects ASCC's operations and is the baseline for its EMS.

3.0 Procedure:

    3.1 In order to ensure environmental compliance with state and federal rules and regulations, a complete list of environmental regulations that are relevant for each division is to be generated. By compiling this list the command and department heads are aware of what they must comply with. [The list appears at the end of this procedure.]

    3.2 This list may be maintained in the EMS.

    3.3 At a minimum, the list will be reviewed annually. The review may be conducted with an internal/external audit, during an environmental aspects review, or when new regulation is introduced.

    3.4 The review may be evidenced by updates/revisions to the EMS or, where there have been no changes made to the EMS, a log entry made in the appropriate review documentation form or audit report.

4.0 Responsibilities:

    4.1 The Commanding Officer, command staff, EH&S Department Head, and EH&S department personnel are responsible for keeping current with regulatory issues and evolutions.

    4.2 The EH&S department shall ensure the accuracy of and maintain and update the regulatory list.

    4.3 All USCG–ASCC military and civilian personnel shall comply with the regulatory requirements.

ASCC environmental regulations

Category	Regulatory reference	Description (of regulations/requirements)	Program (How ASCC complies)	Due date
Air				
Clean Air Act	40 CFR 70	Estimate of state air quality permitting in accord with Title V of CAA; source shall have permit assuring compliance with requirements; emissions monitoring	Emissions monitoring permit	
	310 CMR 7.02	State restricted emissions status		
	310 CMR 7.12	Source registration	Verify state registration statement and resubmit; Procedure 21, *Monitoring Sitewide Air Emissions Permit Compliance*	Annually (around February)
	310 CMR 7.24(6)	Dispensing of motor vehicle fuel (Stage II vapor recovery)	Under the EMS umbrella, Vapor Recovery Program inspections and checklist	Annual testing— Report due to state in June; monthly PMS; weekly inspections
	40 CFR 82.150	Recycling emissions reductions (ODS)	Registering ODS reclamation unit; certifying technicians; Procedure 16	Annual review of program in January

Continued

Continued

ASCC environmental regulations

Category	Regulatory reference	Description (of regulations/requirements)	Program (How ASCC complies)	Due date
	310 CMR 7.25	VOC industrial maintenance coatings	NEPA review and tracking POs for quantities	Ongoing
	310 CMR 7.07 part (3) (a) exemption	Open burning regulations, requirements, and exemptions	Fire Department training on CG facility, Permit (application no. 4F98009) to conduct fire training and sprinkler system test at MMR	Case-by-case basis
	310 CMR 7.00	Air pollution control for street sweeper	Operate all mechanical street sweeping equipment in 'wet mode'	Ongoing ops
Noise Control Act (of 1972)	Air Force Instruction 32-7063	Air Installation Compatible Use Zone (Air Force Instruction) (Noise)	Monitor different zones for noise from airfield	Ongoing coordination
	30 CMR 7.15 Asbestos standards for demolition/ renovation for air pollutants	Requirements for demolition/ renovation/installation of material that contains asbestos		

ASCC environmental regulations

Continued

Category	Regulatory reference	Description (of regulations/requirements)	Program (How ASCC complies)	Due date
WATER				
Clean Water Act	40 CFR Part 110 Discharge of Oil Prohibited; Part 112 Oil Pollution Prevention	Establish procedures, methods, and equipment to prevent the discharge of oil from non–transportation related onshore/offshore facilities into or upon the navigable waters of U.S. or adjoining shoreline	Spill Prevention Control and Countermeasure Plan; spill response training and annual refresher training; COMDTINST M5090.9 Storage Tank Management Manual; and COMDTINST M16478 Hazardous Waste Management Manual	PE certification every three years (beginning with 1999); annual internal review around June
	310 CMR 40	Provide for protection of health, safety, public welfare, and the environment; procedures for prevention and control of activities that may cause or contribute to a release or threat of release of oil and/or hazardous material		
Safe Drinking Water Act	40 CFR 141 310 CMR 22	Safe Drinking Water requirements	Lead and copper analysis; draw samples and 102nd tests and reports	
	310 CMR 22	The permitting, renewal, and reporting process associated with water withdrawals from a river basin or aquifer	B-Well Annually Registered and Permitted Withdrawal Report form must be completed and submitted to the DEP	Annual report in February; calibration of well annually in June

ASCC environmental regulations

Category	Regulatory reference	Description (of regulations/requirements)	Program (How ASCC complies)	Due date
	314 CMR 7 310 CMR 22.22	Sewer Connections/Cross Connections	Tie into POTW (SOP under development by 102nd)	Annual inspection of devices
	314 CMR 7 310 CMR 27.00	Establishes water quality (to sustain designated uses) and prohibition of discharges; Underground Injection Control Regulations	Floor drains tied to sanitary sewer; verified with "as built" and dye testing—1X original testing; for new buildings—NEPA; underground injection well program	Initial 1X survey, NEPA review as needed for new construction
	310 CMR 22	Safe Drinking Water requirements	Interface with Water Dept./102 Division	
	40 CFR 122.26	Storm Water Discharge NPDES Phase II, Storm Water Program	Obtain permit; develop and implement storm water pollution prevention plan	Initial Notice of Intent due 3/10/03 and annually thereafter (due May 1)
	310 CMR 36.25	Water Conservation Program and Permit Application (reasonable conservation practices and measures)	Air National Guard Water Management Plan (drought watch; drought warning; drought emergency); voluntary and mandatory restrictions within those levels	As 102nd dictates

Continued

ASCC environmental regulations

Continued

Category	Regulatory reference	Description (of regulations/requirements)	Program (How ASCC complies)	Due date
	333 CMR 1-12	Pesticide use	EMS Procedure 5; NEPA categorical exclusion assessment	Annual NEPA categorical exclusion assessment; ongoing ops
	310 CMR 10	Wetlands	Protect activities around wetlands via NEPA process	As needed
	Voluntary	Testing ponds	Establish baseline of water quality; annual testing and review of health of the pond	Annual analyses in November
Solid and hazardous waste				
Comprehensive Environmental Response, Compensation and Liability Act	40 CFR 300	Identify contaminated sites as a result of past activities on Coast Guard property	Sites identified, processed, and closed via CECLA requirements	Ongoing

ASCC environmental regulations

Category	Regulatory reference	Description (of regulations/requirements)	Program (How ASCC complies)	Due date
Resource Conservation and Recovery Act	40 CFR Parts 260, 265 310 CMR 30—Hazwaste management, recycling permits, and so on	Comprehensive regulations regarding generation, storage, collection, transportation, treatment, disposal, use, reuse, and recycling of hazwaste	• EPA generator ID • 180 storage limitation • Satellite Point Managers Hazwaste/Hazwoper training and refresher training • HHW collections • Hazwaste Management Contingency Plan • COMDTINST M16478 Hazwaste Management Manual • Airstainst 11000.1 Environmental Compliance and Hazwaste Management	Ongoing
	310 CMR 22.22	Cross Connections Distribution System Protection	Cross Connection Control Program	
	453 CMR 6.00	Removal, Containment, or Encapsulation of Asbestos	COMDTINST M6260.16A Asbestos Exposure Control Manual	
	310 CMR 19.060	Disposal of street sweepings; allows for alternate beneficial use of street sweepings	Procedure 26, Street Sweepings	Ongoing

Continued

ASCC environmental regulations

Continued

Category	Regulatory reference	Description (of regulations/requirements)	Program (How ASCC complies)	Due date
Miscellaneous				
Occupational Safety and Health Act	29 CFR Part 1910.120; Part 1910.120 (b)–o); Part 1910.132	Hazwaste Ops and Emergency Response; 40 Hour Hazwaste site worker; PPE	Approved Hazardous Waste Management and Contingency Plan	Annual review of the plan; initial 40-hour training with eight-hour annual refresher training; ongoing as needed for PPE
The Federal Insecticide, Fungicide and Rodenticide Act	333 CMR Parts 8, 10, 12	Registration of Pesticide Products—Part 10, Licensing of Pesticide Products; Part 12 Protection of Groundwater Sources of Public Drinking Water Supplies from Nonpoint Source Pesticide Contamination	Procedure 5	Annual review of the contract and a NEPA Categorical Exclusion Assessment
Medical Wastes Tracking Act of 1988	105 CMR 480	Medical Waste	Procedure 22	As needed

Continued

ASCC environmental regulations

Category	Regulatory reference	Description (of regulations/requirements)	Program (How ASCC complies)	Due date
The Toxic Substance Control Act—Title III—Indoor Radon Abatement Act; Title IV—Lead-Based Paint Exposure Reduction Act.	24 CFR 35 Subpart B (35.100-.175) and Subpart R (35.1300-.1355) 105 CMR 120.211 and 120.225	Lead-Based Paint Poisoning Prevention in Certain Residential Structures MA Control of Radiation Occupational Dose Limitations and Surveys and Monitoring Lead-Based Paint Requirements and Definitions for All Programs	COMDINST 6260 series, Asbestos, Lead, and Radon in CG Housing; Procedure 13, Test for Radon; Procedure 14, Test for Drinking Water	Every five years for radon (last test conducted ___); annually for drinking water—lead and copper (last test conducted ___).
National Environmental Policy Act	40 CFR 1500-1508	Basic national charter for protection of the environment for federal agencies' actions, including decisions to acquire, establish, relocate, sell, dismantle, decommission, or close a facility, decommission/dispose of a vessel, conduct research, promulgate regulations, grant permits, and/or change operations	COMDTINST M16475.1D, National Environmental Policy Act Implementing Procedures and Policy for Considering Environmental Impacts	As needed

ASCC environmental regulations

Continued

Category	Regulatory reference	Description (of regulations/requirements)	Program (How ASCC complies)	Due date
Emergency Planning and Community Right to Know Act	105 CMR 670.000	Protect public health by providing and encouraging transmission of health and safety information concerning toxic and hazardous substances	COMDTINST M16455.10; COMDTINST M16478 series, Hazardous Waste Management Manual; COMDTINST 6260 series, Hazardous Communications for Workplace Materials	Annual reporting; Tier II reports due March 1

6

Objectives, Targets, and Programs

Objectives and targets serve as the vehicle for moving an organization from words to action. They provide a basis for improving environmental performance and fulfilling all the commitments articulated in its environmental policy.

ISO 14001:2004 Text	ISO 14001:1994 Text
4.3.3 Objectives, targets and programs The organization shall establish, implement and maintain documented environmental objectives and targets, at relevant functions and levels within the organization. The objectives and targets shall be measurable, where practicable, and consistent with the environmental policy, including the commitments to prevention of pollution, to compliance with applicable legal requirements and with other requirements to which the organization subscribes, and to continual improvement. When establishing and reviewing its objectives and targets, an organization shall take into	*4.3.3 Objectives and targets* The organization shall establish and maintain documented environmental objectives and targets, at each relevant function and level within the organization. When establishing and reviewing its objectives, an organization shall consider the legal and other requirements, its significant environmental aspects, its technological options and its financial, operational and business requirements, and the views of interested parties. The objectives and targets shall be consistent with the environmental policy, including the commitment to prevention of pollution.

Continued

Continued

ISO 14001:2004 Text	ISO 14001:1994 Text
account the legal requirements and other requirements to which the organization subscribes, and its significant environmental aspects. It shall also consider its technological options, its financial, operational and business requirements, and the views of interested parties. The organization shall establish, implement and maintain a program(s) for achieving its objectives and targets. Program(s) shall include a) designation of responsibility for achieving objectives and targets at relevant functions and levels of the organization, and b) the means and time-frame by which they are to be achieved.	*4.3.4 Environmental management program(s)* The organization shall establish and maintain (a) program(s) for achieving its objectives and targets. It shall include a) designation of responsibility for achieving objectives and targets at each relevant function and level of the organization; b) the means and time-frame by which they are to be achieved. If a project relates to new developments and new or modified activities, products or services, program(s) shall be amended where relevant to ensure that environmental management applies to such projects.

SIGNIFICANT CHANGES

The most noticeable change is the consolidation of two clauses from the 1996 standard—4.3.3 Objectives and targets and 4.3.4 Environmental program(s)—into one clause that addresses both of these related requirements. The last paragraph in clause 4.3.3 (1996), concerning consistency with the environmental policy, has been repositioned as the second paragraph (2004) with additional language:

- ISO 14001:2004 requires that objectives and targets are measurable where practicable. The 1996 standard did not address measurability.

- ISO 14004:2004 delineates all commitments embodied in the environmental policy. Although the original language stated that objectives and targets must be consistent with the environmental policy, only prevention of pollution was explicitly identified.

In addition, ISO 14001:2004 states that objectives and targets are to be established at *relevant* functions and levels. Language in the original standard required objectives and targets at *each* relevant function and level.

The language that has been retained pertaining to programs for achieving objectives and targets is unchanged. However, the final paragraph in ISO 14001:1996, clause 4.3.4, has been moved to clause 4.3.1 (see Chapter 8).

INTENT OF ISO 14001:2004

The environmental policy is the foundation upon which the environmental management system is built. It provides the framework for setting and reviewing environmental objectives and targets that, in turn, guide subsequent environmental management activities.

Before assessing the degree to which an organization's objectives and targets conform to the requirements of ISO 14001:2004, the distinction between these terms and their relationship to the environmental policy should be clarified:

- The environmental policy is a macro-level statement of an organization's intentions and principles vis-à-vis its overall environmental performance. It articulates *what* an organization wants to accomplish. An example of a policy statement is "conserve natural resources."

- Environmental objectives are overall environmental goals. More specific than the environmental policy, they express *how* an organization plans to fulfill its intentions. Examples of objectives that reflect the policy to conserve natural resources are "reduce water use" and "reduce energy use."

- Environmental targets are detailed performance requirements that must be met to achieve environmental objectives. They describe *how much* will be done to achieve stated objectives. One example of a target that fulfills the objective of reducing water use is "reduce water by 15 percent of the amount used last year."

Organizations are divided about the degree of difficulty that should accompany targets. Some believe that targets should be *stretch* targets; that is, they should require considerable effort to achieve. In their view, falling short of such targets is not viewed as failure. Rather, it is seen as successfully improving performance to the utmost degree. For example, an organization may establish a stretch target that requires a 20 percent reduction of *X* even though it knows that a 10 percent reduction is reasonable and attainable. Workers who might otherwise suspend efforts at reduction upon attaining 10 percent continue to strive and eventually attain a 15 percent reduction.

Other organizations, fearing that failure to achieve a stated target will be interpreted by third-party auditors as failure to fulfill this requirement of the standard, suggest that targets should be attainable. As a result, they typically establish more realistic goals for themselves.

Some organizations develop both. They have targets that must be met as well as targets that would be highly desirable but unlikely.

In making decisions about target achievability, organizations should be guided by the ISO 14001:2004 requirement that objectives and targets reflect the commitments embodied in the organization's environmental policy statement. Therefore, organizations should ensure that environmental objectives and targets address prevention of pollution, regulatory compliance, compliance with other requirements to which the organization subscribes, and continual improvement.

Objectives and targets also should be subjected to a reality check. They should reflect the constraints of current technology, available capital, and worker skills. The third paragraph of the clause tells an organization that when establishing its objectives and targets, it must take into account:

- Legal requirements
- Other requirements to which it subscribes
- Significant environmental aspects
- Technological options
- Financial requirements
- Operational requirements
- Business requirements
- Views of interested parties

This list of considerations means that every significant environmental impact does not have to be addressed by an objective and target. An organization is expected to consider the above-listed factors and make a rational decision about what it is able to pursue. Suppose, for example, that there is a new technology that could reduce a significant impact by 50 percent. In considering the use of this technology, the organization discovers that the purchase price is equal to its entire operating budget. It is legitimate for the organization to conclude that financial requirements preclude it from purchasing the technology.

Similarly, suppose a company has a contract to provide parts to an original equipment manufacturer (OEM). The OEM has provided the specification that the company must meet if it is to continue providing parts. A significant environmental aspect is associated with the parts in question. The OEM, however, refuses to allow the company to modify the specification in a manner that reduces the significant aspect. The company can conclude that the business requirement to retain the customer is sufficient reason not to establish objectives and targets related to this specific significant aspect.

An interested party is defined as a "person or group concerned with or affected by the environmental performance of an organization" (section 3.13). Information about the views of such individuals, informal groups, and formal institutions and associations must somehow be obtained. Several of the communication techniques presented in Tables 9.1, 9.2, and 9.3 (see Chapter 9, pages 143, 146, and 152) can assist this effort.

If it is acceptable to establish objectives and targets for selected significant aspects, how many objectives and targets are required? ISO 14001:2004 does not specify a number. It addresses the issue somewhat obliquely through two requirements:

- The phrase *relevant functions and levels* means that objectives and targets must be established at those points in an operation associated with significant aspects, regardless of where those points are located physically or in the organizational structure.

- Objectives and targets must reflect the commitments contained in the environmental policy. The commitment to prevention of pollution requires a focus on significant environmental aspects that have an adverse effect on the environment. An organization also must establish objectives and targets related to regulatory compliance, continual improvement and, where applicable, compliance with other voluntary requirements.

The need to establish objectives and targets designed to achieve the environmental policy suggests that ISO 14001:2004 intends an organization to generate several objectives and targets rather than just one. This is reinforced by the manner in which the clause is titled—*objectives* and *targets* are presented as plural words instead of as *objective(s)* and *target(s)* which is the form that ISO uses to indicate that either one or more than one is acceptable.

A program for achieving objectives and targets encompasses the planning and logistics that enable an organization to ensure a clear understanding of what is to be accomplished and how it will be done. ISO 14001:2004 requires such programs to address four components:

- *Responsibility.* Specific functions in an organization that are responsible for each stated objective and target must be identified. Moreover, clause 4.4.1 (Resources, roles, responsibility and authority) states that responsibility must be defined, documented, and communicated (see Chapter 11). Therefore, responsible individuals within identified specific functions must be designated.

- *Means.* There can be many different ways to achieve a specific target. One could reduce a significant environmental aspect, for example, by reducing production, although it is unlikely that organizations would select this approach. The program must explain how each objective and target will be accomplished.

- *Time frame.* The organization must determine the length of time in which specific objectives and targets are to be achieved. Some might be short-term (for example, substitute Y for X when the supply of X runs out next month). Others might be multi-year (for example, modify customer specifications to eliminate process step 5 as contracts come up for renewal). It is important that the time frame is realistic and progress is evaluated on a regular basis.

- *Progress.* Although there is no reference in clause 4.3.3 to monitoring progress in achieving objectives and targets, clause 4.5.1 (Monitoring and measurement) imposes this requirement (see Chapter 14). Identifying performance indicators should be an integral component of an organization's process for establishing objectives and targets. If it is unable to delineate either a specific characteristic that will be measured or an appropriate unit of measure for that characteristic, it is likely that a stated target is not clearly expressed.

EXAMPLES

U. S. Steel Gary Works
EMS Procedure 4.3.3—Objectives, Targets, and Programs
(Effective October 4, 2005)

1.0   Purpose

　　1.1   This procedure describes the development, implementation, and maintenance of environmental objectives, targets, and programs.

2.0 Scope

    2.1 Personnel responsible for the development, implementation, and maintenance of environmental objectives, targets, and programs use this procedure.

3.0 References

    3.1 ISO 14001:2004 Standard

    3.2 EMS Procedure 4.3.1—Environmental Aspects

    3.3 EMS Procedure 4.5.3—Nonconformity and Corrective and Preventive Action

    3.4 EMS Objectives and Targets Web page

4.0 Definitions

    4.1 An environmental objective is an overall environmental goal arising from the environmental policy that an organization sets for itself to achieve through a continuous improvement process. Environmental objectives are quantified where practicable.

    4.2 An environmental target is a detailed, continuous improvement performance requirement, quantified where practicable, that arises from the environmental objectives.

    4.3 Environmental programs are one or more projects whose sole purpose is to assist the business units in achieving their objectives and targets.

5.0 Responsibilities

    5.1 The following job positions have responsibilities in this procedure:

- Gary Complex Environmental Management System Steering Team

- Environmental Control ISO 14001 Steering Team

- Cross-functional teams (CFT)

- All employees

6.0 Procedure

    6.1 Development of Objectives and Targets

        6.1.1 Each significant environmental aspect, as determined by EMS Procedure 4.3.1, is evaluated by the CFT to determine if an objective and target can be assigned. Criteria considered during the development of objectives and targets shall include the following:

- Technological options/limitations

- Financial requirements

- Operational requirements

- Business requirements

6.1.2   Significant environmental aspects that have attained an acceptable level of environmental performance may be assigned Monitoring status.

6.1.3   Environmental aspects that have not been classified as significant may also be evaluated for the assignment of an objective and target using the criteria specified in 6.1.1 above. The EMR, CFT members, and ISO 14001 Coordinator may recommend an environmental aspect for consideration in assigning an objective and target.

6.1.4   The decision and rationale for not assigning an objective and target for any significant environmental aspect will be noted on the agenda of the Environmental Control ISO 14001 Steering Team meetings.

6.1.5   If the CFT determines that an objective and target is warranted for an environmental aspect, the CFT develops a proposed objective associated with the environmental aspect.

6.1.6   The CFT develops a proposed quantifiable target (where possible) to achieve the objective. A review of legal and other requirements associated with the significant environmental aspect is conducted to determine if numerical or narrative performance standards have been established for the aspect through regulations, permit conditions, voluntary agreements, or agreed orders. The CFT will establish a target level more rigorous than the performance standard contained in the regulation, permit condition, voluntary agreement, or agreed order. If no performance standard is provided, the CFT will develop a target for the aspect.

6.1.7 Proposed objectives and targets are submitted to the EMR for review, revision, and approval. The approved objectives and targets are recorded on the EMS Objectives and Targets Web page.

6.1.8 Approved objectives and targets are presented to the Gary Complex Environmental Management System (EMS) Steering Team at the next scheduled management review meeting. The Gary Complex EMS Steering Team reviews approved objectives and targets to ensure that they are consistent with the Gary Complex Environmental Policy and goals. Established objectives and targets are considered in the development of the annual business plan.

6.2 Environmental Program Development and Implementation

6.2.1 The business unit cross-functional teams are responsible for establishing environmental programs to achieve objectives and targets. However, no programs are needed for those significant aspects relegated to Monitoring status. Environmental programs must include:

- A designated person/organization with the responsibility for achieving the objectives and targets.

- The methods and resources employed for implementation of the environmental program.

- A time frame for completion of the environmental program, if applicable. If the environmental program is continuous, no completion date is required.

6.2.2 Where practicable, environmental projects will be developed utilizing the Gary Complex continuous improvement program, which, when implemented properly, provides a positive planning and progress tracking tool. This tool may then be utilized to document projects in order to achieve the objectives and targets.

6.2.3 Environmental programs that focus on preventive maintenance activities may utilize the Gary Complex PASSPORT System. The PASSPORT System is a mainframe database application that is used to generate work orders, track equipment history, and schedule maintenance and repair activities.

6.3   Objective, Target, and Program Review

6.3.1   Internal EMS auditors review the attainment of established objectives and targets through EMS audits. These reviews are conducted at any time at the discretion of the EMR. Significant environmental aspects that are assigned Monitoring status are evaluated annually. Ongoing nonconformance or adverse target performance trends may be addressed in accordance with EMS Procedure 4.5.3—Nonconformity and Corrective and Preventive Action.

6.3.2   The Environmental Control ISO 14001 Steering Team will review and revise the status of objectives and targets any time operations within a business unit are suspended or terminated. Objectives and targets associated with those operations will assume a status equivalent to those operations (suspended or terminated). Objectives and targets will be reinstated to active status within 30 days after operations resume.

7.0   Approval

7.1   Approval of this procedure by the Gary Complex Environmental Management System Steering Team is effected by the signature (on the Document Validation Form) of the Manager, Environmental Control that has been designated as the Environmental Management Representative.

7.2   Approved for use.

Manager, Environmental Control and Environmental Management Representative

Delaware North Companies Parks & Resorts
P1400.13—Sustainable Development
(Effective May 1, 2005)

As specified in the description of its environmental management system, environmental objectives and targets are established by individual GreenPath locations. In addition, DNC has established a procedure that requires all GreenPath locations to incorporate the principles of sustainable development into their operations and activities.

Policy

It is the policy of Delaware North Companies Parks & Resorts (DNC) to operate its businesses in a manner consistent with the principles of sustainable development.

Purpose

To incorporate the principles of sustainable development into DNC development projects, policies, procedures, and operations, including construction, remodeling, destruction, and disposal activities.

Procedure

Responsibility:

The General Manager at each GreenPath location, with input, as appropriate, from local staff, corporate personnel, and others, is responsible for ensuring that this policy is adopted and followed for all local construction and development projects.

Definition:

Sustainable development, as defined by the World Commission on Environment and Development (the Brundtland Commission), is "the capacity to meet the needs of the present without compromising the ability of future generations to meet their own needs."

Process:

The objective of this policy is to incorporate the principles of sustainable development into DNC programs, policies, procedures, and operations. Consistent with the visionary principles of DNC, the sustainable development principles include the following:

- Leadership: promote sustainable development through actions, policies, and programs
- Accountability: define and be held accountable for assigned roles in supporting sustainable development
- Integrated decision making: integrate sustainable development into corporate decision-making processes
- Informed decision making: provide the necessary knowledge, information, and learning opportunities to support the incorporation of sustainable development

- Results-based approach: take actions to ensure measurable progress toward sustainable development

- Shared responsibility and cooperation: work with colleagues, clients, communities, and business partners to achieve shared goals and objectives

- Environmental stewardship and compliance: meet or exceed federal environmental legislation and implement best practices

- Design and practice construction and remodeling projects using sustainable best practices, as deemed appropriate

- Utilize sustainable materials wherever practical, with consideration given to availability, durability, aesthetics, and cost

- Dispose of waste and excess material using the most practical sustainable means (reuse and recycle)

Required Documentation:

The general manager and/or other staff members with development responsibilities will be required to maintain documentation that substantiates conformance to this policy. Documentation may include: design documents, purchase orders, meeting minutes, and so on.

Coast Guard Air Station Cape Cod
Procedure 06—Objectives and Targets
(Effective February 1, 2001)

1.0 Purpose:

A systematic approach to improving environmental stewardship above and beyond what is required by law. Specific measurable goals will be established for categories of environmental impacts that ASCC can influence to effect environmental improvements. Improvements within these categories are defined according to specific aspects of environmental impacts (for example, emissions of heavy metals within air emissions).

2.0 Scope:

2.1 This procedure will include the review of all areas of Air Station Cape Cod that are under the ownership or operation of the USCG, including areas that are within the USCG's control and/or influence.

2.2 This procedure will include both USCG and civilian operations within these areas as well as all contracted services.

3.0 Procedure:

3.1 The Environmental Health and Safety Manager will assemble a team to establish initial objectives and targets. Team members should include, at a minimum, the USCG–ASCC environmental staff and command staff.

3.2 Per EPA's National Environmental Performance Track, a minimum of four (4) objectives will be set. A baseline and measurable quantities will be established in order to track actual improvements. Objectives may be based on the environmental aspects identified during the environmental aspects review (Procedure 01).

3.3 Using the EPA's National Environmental Achievement Track form, the team will identify objectives and targets. The determination of whether to establish objectives and targets may be based on:

- Ability of the organization to control or influence

- Severity of environmental impact

- Legal or regulatory concerns

- Public relations/stakeholder issues

3.4 The list of environmental objectives and targets will be periodically reviewed and kept up to date. The team will meet, at a minimum, on an annual basis to assess progress toward established targets. As appropriate, the team may amend objectives and targets (that is, establish new objectives and targets and close out targets that have been met). Environmental objectives and targets review sessions will be documented using the form provided in Appendix A (page 97).

3.5 Environmental aspects associated with facility changes will be identified in accordance with Procedure 05—New Chemical Review and Pharmacy System, and Procedure 06—Environmental Analysis Procedure. Each of these procedures makes provision for the review of environmental aspects associated with facility changes, and for update of the environmental aspects inventory as necessary.

3.6   Each updated list (or National Environmental Achievement Track application form) of objectives and targets will be assigned a revision number and date. Previous records will be retained in accordance with Procedure 03—Recordkeeping and Record Retention.

4.0   Responsibilities:

The USCG–ASCC EHS Manager is responsible for the implementation of this procedure. This includes the selection of the aspects review team and oversight of the team's activities.

5.0   Appendix:

A.   Environmental Objectives and Targets Review Documentation form (page 97)

6.0   Related Documentation:

National Environmental Policy Act

Procedure 01—Environmental Aspects Review

Procedure 03—Recordkeeping and Record Retention

7.0   Records:

Records generated by this procedure include:

- National Environmental Achievement Track(er)

- Environmental Objectives and Targets Review forms

APPENDIX TO COAST GUARD AIR STATION CAPE COD PROCEDURE 06

Meeting date:
Participants:
Agenda:
Action items:

Appendix A Environmental Objectives and Targets Review Documentation form.

7

Resources, Roles, Responsibility, and Authority

S uccessful transition from planning to implementation requires access to a variety of support systems from equipment and machinery to knowledge and expertise.

ISO 14001:2004 Text	ISO 14001:1996 Text
4.4.1 Resources, roles, responsibility and authority Management shall ensure the availability of resources essential to establish, implement, maintain and improve the environmental management system. Resources include human resources and specialized skills, organizational infrastructure, technology and financial resources. Roles, responsibilities and authorities shall be defined, documented and communicated in order to facilitate effective environmental management. The organization's top management shall appoint a specific management representative(s) who, irrespective of other responsibilities, shall have defined roles, responsibilities and authority for	*4.4.1 Structure and responsibility* Roles, responsibility and authorities shall be defined, documented and communicated in order to facilitate effective environmental management. Management shall provide resources essential to the implementation and control of the environmental management system. Resources include human resources and specialized skills, technology and financial resources. The organization's top management shall appoint (a) specific management representative(s) who, irrespective of other responsibilities, shall have defined roles, responsibilities and authority for

Continued

Continued

ISO 14001:2004 Text	ISO 14001:1996 Text
a) ensuring that an environmental management system is established, implemented and maintained in accordance with the requirements of this International Standard,	a) ensuring that environmental management system requirements are established, implemented and maintained in accordance with this International Standard;
b) reporting to top management on the performance of the environmental management system for review, including recommendations for improvement.	b) reporting on the performance of the environmental management system to top management for review and as a basis for improvement of the environmental management system.

SIGNIFICANT CHANGES

The original title of this clause—structure and responsibility—has been changed to better reflect the content of the clause.

The second paragraph (on resources) in the first edition of the standard has been repositioned as the first paragraph. The original wording required management to "provide" resources. The revision directs management to "ensure the availability" of resources. Moreover, "organizational infrastructure" has been added to the list of resources.

INTENT OF ISO 14001:2004

This clause addresses three distinct requirements—resources, duties, and oversight of the environmental management system.

ISO 14001:2004 requires that necessary resources are available to those responsible for creating, executing, and improving an environmental management system. Resources can take many forms. The need for resources such as technology and financial support varies from organization to organization and depends on the nature of a specific operation, the kind and number of significant environmental aspects associated with the operation, and the array of governing regulatory requirements.

The single most critical resource is the availability of employees at various levels within an organization. Creating procedures, training workers to follow them, and implementing them on a continuous basis are labor-intensive activities that require participation throughout an organization. It is unlikely that an environmental management system can be successfully implemented without worker involvement at all levels.

The resources required to design and initially implement an environmental management system are often different than those needed to maintain and improve it. Thus, attention paid to a system during its design phase and the type and amount of resources available for initial implementation often decline once conformity is achieved. High capital costs during initial implementation often are balanced by lower operating costs in subsequent years. Incorporating resource needs and allocation into every management review of an environmental management system (see Chapter 19) assures continuing and appropriate allocation of resources.

To ensure that individual duties are fulfilled and obligations met, it is important to understand the distinction between responsibility and authority. Within the context of an environmental management system, responsibility pertains to specific tasks or obligations with which one is charged; authority pertains to influence and power.

Individuals with responsibility do not necessarily have authority. For example, the environmental manager within a facility may have the responsibility for establishing an environmental awareness training program, yet lack the authority to require attendance by plant employees who report to an operations manager.

An effective environmental management system accommodates this difference in one of two ways. Individuals with assigned responsibilities may also be given authority to compel others in the organization to perform as instructed. Alternatively, there may be a clearly articulated chain of command to which individuals turn when the involvement of others must be obtained.

ISO 14001:2004 highlights the need for oversight in the requirement to appoint one or more specific management representatives. It is up to an organization to decide whether this position is most effectively filled by an individual, a small team, or a large committee.

Regardless of the number of people involved, the purpose of the management representative function is twofold. First, it guarantees that assigned responsibilities are accomplished and needed resources are available so that, once established, an environmental management system continues to conform to all requirements. Second, it provides a direct communication link to an organization's senior decision makers, thereby ensuring that top management is kept informed about the performance of their environmental management system and, by extension, their organization's environmental performance.

EXAMPLES

U. S. Steel Gary Works
EMS Procedure 4.4.1—Resources, Roles,
Responsibility, and Authority
(Effective October 4, 2005)

1.0 Purpose

    1.1 The purpose of this procedure is to define the roles, responsibilities, and authorities of personnel who perform environmental work activities and who implement, maintain, control, and evaluate the effectiveness of the Gary Complex Environmental Management System.

2.0 Scope

    2.1 This procedure applies to employees who manage, perform, and verify work activities affecting the environment.

3.0 References

    3.1 ISO 14001:2004 Standard

    3.2 EMS Procedure 4.2—Environmental Policy

    3.3 EMS Procedure 4.4.2—Competence, Training, and Awareness

    3.4 EMS Procedure 4.5.3—Nonconformity, Corrective and Preventive Action

    3.5 EMS Procedure 4.5.5—Internal Audit

    3.6 EMS Procedure 4.6—Management Review

4.0 Definitions

For the purpose of this procedure, the following definitions shall apply:

    4.1 The Gary Complex Environmental Management System Steering Team members are: the Gary Works General Manager

(Chairman of the Team), Plant Managers, Business Unit Division and Staff Managers, and the Environmental Management Representative (EMR).

4.2 The Environmental Control ISO 14001 Steering Team members are the Manager, Environmental Control, who has been designated as the Environmental Management Representative (EMR) and is chairman of the team, the Area Manager Environmental Technical Services, the Area Manager Environmental Compliance, the ISO 14001 Coordinator, and the Document Custodian.

4.3 Cross-functional team (CFT) members are: representatives from the business unit, staff organization, or relevant contractors, Environmental Compliance Managers, and/or Environmental Control Managers.

5.0 Responsibilities

5.1 The following job positions have responsibilities in this procedure:

- Environmental Management System Steering Team
- Cross-functional teams (CFT)
- Environmental Control ISO 14001 Steering Team
- Gary Complex management
- All employees and personnel working on behalf of the Gary Complex

6.0 Procedure

6.1 The Gary Complex Environmental Management System Steering Team meets at least annually, during the management review meeting, to ensure ongoing suitability, adequacy, and effectiveness of the Environmental Management System. Relevant information, performance data, and results presented during the meeting allow the Steering Team to thoroughly complete their evaluation of the EMS. Based on the information presented in the meeting, changes to the EMS will be made, if necessary. Meeting minutes will be documented and provided to Steering Team members. Members of the Steering Team are identified in 4.1 above. Other personnel attend the Steering Team meeting by invitation (see EMS Procedure 4.6).

6.2 Elements of the Gary Complex Environmental Management System are controlled and implemented under the guidance of the Environmental Control ISO 14001 Steering Team.

6.2.1 The Environmental Control ISO 14001 Steering Team and the cross-functional teams perform specific activities to facilitate implementation of the Gary Complex Environmental Management System (see 4.2 and 4.3 above).

6.3 Gary Complex management provides adequate resources and assigns trained personnel to:

6.3.1 Ensure that procedures and work instructions are implemented and followed to meet environmental performance requirements.

6.3.2 Conduct internal EMS audits by personnel independent of those having direct responsibility for the activity being performed (see EMS Procedure 4.5.5).

6.3.3 Implement appropriate corrective action when environmental performance is unacceptable and when audit results identify that corrective action is required (see EMS procedure 4.5.3).

6.4 During environmental awareness training, employees are made aware of their roles, responsibilities, and authorities to implement and maintain the Gary Complex EMS as an effective environmental management system.

7.0 Approval

7.1 Approval of this procedure by the Gary Complex Environmental Management System Steering Team is effected by the signature (on the Document Validation Form) of the Manager, Environmental Control that has been designated as the Environmental Management Representative.

7.2 Approved for use.

Manager, Environmental Control and Environmental Management Representative

Delaware North Companies Parks & Resorts
P1400.04—GreenPath Environmental Responsibilities
(Effective August 1, 2005)

Policy

Delaware North Companies' GreenPath locations shall define, document, and communicate environmental roles, responsibilities, and authorities to employees, contractors, and vendors, as appropriate.

Purpose

To identify the environmental roles, responsibilities, and authorities associated with positions affecting environmental activities at Delaware North Companies' (DNC) GreenPath operations.

Procedure

Responsibility:

Director of Environmental Affairs. The Director of Environmental Affairs is charged with the overall responsibility to implement the company's Environmental Management System (EMS). Acting under the direction of executive staff and in consultation with environmental consultants and regulatory agencies, the Director will interpret the EMS and environmental regulations and assist the operating locations in the management of the DNC EMS and the GreenPath locations' environmental programs.

The Director of Environmental Affairs has the responsibility for reporting environmental performance and EMS performance to appropriate top management.

Operations Manager (GreenPath Location President/General Manager). The Operations Manager is the Management Representative for the EMS.

The Operations Manager is responsible for the following:

- Reviewing and reporting environmental and EMS performance to top management, as deemed appropriate by the Operations Manager

- Endorsement and implementation of the DNC Corporate Environmental Policy at the operational level

- Coordinating, as needed, EMS activities with the Director of Environmental Affairs

Environmental Manager (Operations Manager or designees). The Environmental Manager at each GreenPath location carries the responsibility for environmental management and performance at the location. The EMS requires the Environmental Manager to undertake the following:

- Communicating and delegating legal and other environmental responsibilities and authorities as defined by the EMS to appropriate personnel

- Reviewing legal and other requirements to assure that such requirements are current

- Implementing the Corporate Environmental Policy and developing programs to communicate the Environmental Policy to all personnel

- Developing environmental objectives and targets for the location

- Implementing programs to ensure that environmental issues are identified and that environmental impacts are evaluated and given consideration in the evaluation of new projects

- Exercising authority to ensure that the EMS is implemented and maintained

- Exercising appropriate authority to ensure that EMS nonconformances are identified, addressed, monitored, and rectified

- Assigning and communicating environmental responsibilities and tasks to relevant personnel as defined by the EMS

- Allocating adequate resources and developing operational procedures for implementation of the EMS

- Ongoing evaluation of the effectiveness of the EMS to improve EMS performance

- Assisting personnel and employees with the implementation and monitoring of EMS objectives and targets

- Reviewing and completing existing and emerging environmental training obligations affecting location personnel

- Reporting environmental incidents that may occur to the Operations Manager and other affected management personnel and agencies

- Completing and forwarding records produced in support of the EMS in a prompt, legible, and accurate manner

- Completing environmental audits as required and forwarding audit results to the Operations Manager and management personnel for review

- Developing new EMS documentation and modifying existing EMS documentation to reflect changing operational and regulatory issues

- Ensuring that location emergency response planning activities address environmental preparedness and concerns

- Ensuring that a comprehensive management review of the EMS, including recommendations for improvement, is undertaken on an annual basis and is reported to the Operations Manager

- Responding to inquiries concerning location environmental management programs and issues from regulatory authorities and other interested parties

- Coordinating all of the above responsibilities in consultation with the Director of Environmental Affairs

All DNC staff. DNC GreenPath location managers and employees are responsible for the implementation of the environmental management programs at the location. The staff is required to undertake the following:

- Completing routine and nonroutine environmental monitoring activities in accordance with prescribed procedures, and collecting, storing, analyzing, and interpreting of relevant environmental data

- Performing work assignments in accordance with relevant work instructions and job procedures in compliance with the EMS

- Exercising authority to ensure that EMS nonconformances are identified, addressed, monitored, and rectified

- Reporting environmental incidents in accordance with regulatory requirements, community obligations, and corporate dictates

- Maintaining documents and records as required by the EMS and scheduling complete calibrations for all environmental equipment

- Familiarizing themselves with the environmental components associated with relevant work instructions and job procedures

- Reporting improvements and suggestions to improve the environmental components of work instructions and job procedures to management personnel

- Reporting noncompliance with the environmental components of work instructions and job procedures to management personnel

- Familiarizing themselves with the actual or potential environmental impacts of job activities and associated legal implications

- Reviewing work practices for environmental issues and associated impacts

- Attending environmental awareness training sessions

Training Matrix

GreenPath locations shall be guided by the following training matrix:

Part 1 of 3—General awareness training

Who	What—subject	When—schedule	Where	How	Why—objectives
Environmental Manager	GreenPath procedures, ISO 14001, EMS management	Upon being awarded the EM duties	On site or off site	The DNC Director of Environmental Affairs will provide	To ensure effective management of all GreenPath policies and procedures and ISO standards, and to ensure continuing environmental improvement at the facility
New employee	Environmental awareness	At hiring	Part of new-employee training	Scheduled, prepared, and given by Environmental Manager or designee, or Training Department	• Meet regulatory requirements • Instill sense of personal responsibility toward pollution prevention and continual environmental improvement
Contractor	Environmental awareness	First visit to facility or prior to beginning project, if deemed necessary	Part of site-specific training	Given by Environmental Manager, Maintenance Manager, or designee	• Meet regulatory requirements • Instill sense of personal responsibility toward pollution prevention • Meet location/project environmental expectations

Continued

Continued

Part 1 of 3—General awareness training

Who	What— subject	When— schedule	Where	How	Why— objectives
Suppliers— Written notification	GreenPath awareness	Selected suppliers as deemed appropriate by local management	By mail or e-mail at intervals deemed appropriate by local management	By mail or e-mail at intervals deemed appropriate by local management	• Meet regulatory requirements • Instill sense of personal responsibility toward pollution prevention • Meet location/project environmental expectations • Notice to offer environmentally friendly alternatives
Current employee	Environmental awareness	Annual	Annual Hazcom refresher class	Scheduled, prepared, and given by Environmental Manager or designee, supervisor, or Training Department	• Meet regulatory requirements • Instill sense of personal responsibility toward pollution prevention and continual environmental improvement • Gain commitment to environmental policy, objectives, and targets

Part 2 of 3—Training for operational controls

What— subject	Who— trainee	When— schedule	Where	How	Why— objectives
Operational control	Operating personnel	When assigned to department	Job site—part of new task training	Use existing process description	• Awareness of significant environmental requirements of new position

Part 3 of 3—Training for special operations

What— subject	Who— trainee	When— schedule	Where	How	Why— objectives
Hazardous waste management					
Resource Conservation and Recovery Act (RCRA) training and/or state-specific hazardous waste training	Selected operational staff	When newly assigned to position	On or off site	By internal DNC staff or outside consultant	• Meet regulatory and safety requirements
Hazwoper 24-hour training	Selected operational staff	Annual update	On or off site	By internal DNC staff or outside consultant	• Meet regulatory and safety requirements

Operating locations are authorized to develop additional site-specific training requirements.

Coast Guard Air Station Cape Cod

A description of organizational structure and departmental and individual responsibilities is contained in the environmental management system manual:

Organization

By identifying key players and their responsibilities, each person is made aware of what influence they will have with regard to environmental stewardship and how it will affect their workload. Specific job descriptions of top management, the EH&S department, and other key players' roles and responsibilities are located in Coast Guard Air Station Cape Cod's Organizational Manual (AIRSTAINST M5500.1 [series]). A basic overview of the EH&S department and job descriptions are also provided in this manual. The job descriptions provided below expand on the individual's role with regard to environmental stewardship. In any conflict between the organizational charts, the following is the leading authority.

The Environmental, Health, and Safety Department is responsible for all environmental issues per COMINST M5100 and safety issues relating to Hazmat/Hazwaste, public safety, health services, fire inspection, and facility safety.

EH&S Department Head

Under the direct supervision of the Executive Officer, the EH&S Department Head shall:

- Coordinate the activities of all facets of the department
- Supervise and direct:
    - Administrative Assistant/EMS Records Administrator
    - Environmental Protection Specialist
    - Facility Safety and Energy Manager
    - Environmental Management Systems Officer
    - Public Safety Officer
    - Recycling Coordinator
    - Hazmat/Hazwaste Manager for Support Department
    - Hazmat/Hazwaste Manager Aviation Engineer Department
    - Security Contractor

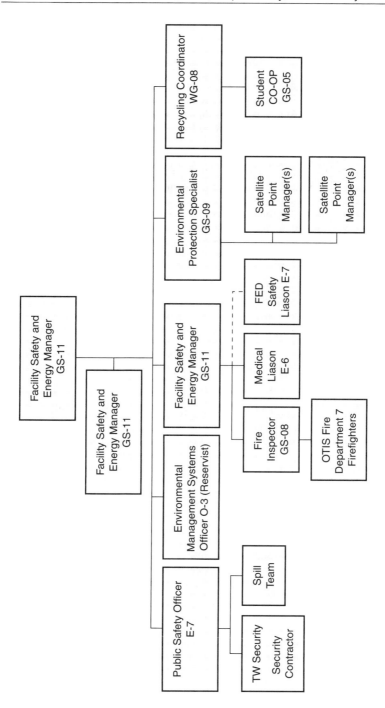

- Coop Interns

- Spill Team/Satellite Point Managers

• Manage the unit Environmental Compliance and Pollution Prevention Program. Stay abreast of all current environmental laws and regulations and evaluate impacts to the unit including the requirements and cost of implementation.

• Maintain effective safety awareness, accident prevention, and accident/injury reporting system; coordinate these programs with district, MLCANT, and Commandant.

• Advise the command staff on all matters affecting environmental, occupational health, and facility safety. Ensure that all management plans and reports are created, maintained, updated, and submitted as required.

• Serve as Aeronautical Engineering's prime unit for environmental compliance and pollution prevention, directly supporting the Aircraft Repair and Supply Center (ARSC) and efforts throughout the Coast Guard Aviation Program.

• Serve as Aeronautical Engineering's prime unit and as a resource to D1 for the implementation of ISO 14001 standards, Environmental Compliance, directly supporting ARSC.

• Serve as the unit's Environmental Compliance and Pollution Prevention Officer, reporting on the performance of the Environmental Management System to top management for review and as a basis for improvement of the Environmental Management System.

• Serve as the unit's OSHA compliance officer.

• Serve as the Coast Guard representative with the Joint Program Office (JPO) at the Massachusetts Military Reservation. The Under Secretary of Defense for Environmental Security established the JPO. This office coordinated with all tenants of the Reservation to efficiently and effectively address overlapping environmental concerns.

• Represent the Coast Guard on regional environmental committees: Standing Water Supply and Policy Group, Public Information Group, and MMR Environmental Committee.

- Maintain direct liaison with the 2300 base residents and three Town of Bourne schools for all environmental issues such as the Installation Restoration Project, Safe Drinking Water issues.

- Unit representative for all environmental public affairs issues.

- Monitor all functions of the Air Station (except aviation) for unsafe and unhealthy practices and recommend appropriate corrective actions.

- Assume overall responsibility for internal and external audits on the Environmental Management System and provide the command staff with recommendations for continuous improvement and to eliminate deficiencies.

- Report all mishaps to MLC-Atlantic in accordance with the Safety and Environmental Health Manual, COMDINST M5100.

- Assign an officer to investigate all class A- and B-level mishaps (that is, fatal mishaps and those involving high values of property damage).

- Serve as Chairman of the unit Environmental, Occupational Health, and Facility Committee and Pollution Prevention Committee.

- Serve as unit's Emergency Response Coordinator for hazardous material releases.

- Assume responsibility to assess unit's National Environmental Policy Act requirements.

- Represent the command to ensure that each department that uses hazardous material and/or generates hazardous waste designate in writing a name, both primary and alternate, for management of this material/waste. The designated personnel shall constitute the unit's safety committee.

- Serve as unit's Security Officer.

Administrative Assistant/EMS Records Administrator

Under the direction and supervision of the Department Head, the Administrative Assistant shall:

- Track and monitor the implementation and compliance of the environmental management system for ISO 14001.

- Maintain correspondence files and publication library.

- Track departmental schedules and activities.

- Provide assistance to Aviation Safety Department as directed through the EH&S Department Head.

- Maintain environmental training records.

- Maintain direct liaison with the base residents and Bourne schools for all environmental issues such as the Installation Restoration Project, Safe Drinking Water issues.

- Provide assistance in Environmental Public Affairs issues.

- Assist in annual environmental and safety audits.

- Attend and keep record of unit Environmental, Occupational Health, and Facility Safety Committee and Pollution Prevention Committee meetings.

Environmental Management System Officer

Under the direction and supervision of the EH&S Department Head, the Environmental Management System Officer shall:

- Provide assistance as directed by the EH&S Department Head in all aspects of environmental compliance issues.

- Coordinate and assist with internal and external environmental audits.

- Implement, track, and monitor compliance of the environmental management system in accordance with ISO 14001.

- Train personnel on implementation of and compliance with ISO 14001 policies and procedures.

- Draft, maintain, and amend procedures and other documentation related to the EMS.

- As directed by the EH&S Department Head, provide assistance with regard to environmental issues to other Coast Guard units.

Environmental Protection Specialist

Under the direction of the EH&S Department Head, the Environmental Specialist shall:

- Manage the unit Hazardous, Special, and Medical Waste Programs. Maintain all associated records required by the Resource Conservation and Recovery Act, Massachusetts Hazardous Waste Regulations, and Coast Guard Hazardous Waste Instruction.

- Represent the command to ensure that all departments that generate hazardous waste designate in writing a primary and alternate hazardous waste satellite point manager.

- Manage unit's Hazwaste collection, disposal, and minimization programs.

- Manage unit's Asbestos and Lead-Based Paint Abatement Program.

- Serve as the Contracting Officer's Technical Representative and/or inspect for hazardous waste disposal contract, release of hazardous materials, lead and asbestos abatement projects, pesticide applications, and other environmental contracts.

- Coordinate and conduct indoor firing range maintenance/cleaning activities for the First District including lead removal, disposal, and high efficiency particulate air (HEPA) filter replacements.

- Serve as unit's Assistant Emergency Response Coordinator for hazardous material releases.

Facility Safety and Energy Manager

Under the direction of the EH&S Department Head, the Facility and Energy Manager shall:

- Assume the duties of the Department Head, in his absence.

- Ensure that applicable OSHA and Coast Guard safety and health standards are applied to unit work practices, such as:

  - Ensure compliance with the unit's Facility Safety Plan

  - Ensure compliance with the unit's Respiratory Protection Plan

  - Coordinate defensive driver and motorcycle operator safety training

  - Utilize hazard abatement plans as necessary

  - Manage Hazcom training and confined space entry program

- Conduct training in accord with OSHA standards.

- Serve as Personal Protective Equipment Manager, ensuring proper practices and use of PPE.

- Ensure compliance with the Emergency Planning, Community, and Worker Right to Know Acts.

- Maintain effective safety awareness, accident prevention, and accident/injury reporting system; coordinate these programs with district, MLCLANT, and Commandant.

- Maintain OMSEP (Occupational Medical Surveillance and Evaluation Program).

- Provide technical assistance to all departments for additions, deletions, and changes to their hazardous material Authorized Use List (AUL). Maintain hazardous material database and maintain the master list of the unit's Material Safety Data Sheets.

- Review and approve all requests for hazardous materials not listed on the AUL prior to purchase.

- Manage the MISHAP Reporting System (MISREPS).

- Conduct annual facility safety stand-downs.

- Serve as Energy Manager, coordinating projects for energy conservation/efficiency.

Coop Intern

The Coop Intern is a joint effort between USCG Air Station Cape Cod and private continuing education institutions, that is, Mass Maritime and Cape Cod Community College. The program provides on-the-job training for students while enabling the EH&S Department to attend to details of its EMS. Under the direction of the EH&S Department Head and the supervision of the Environmental Protection Specialist or Facility Safety Specialist and Energy Manager, Coop Interns are assigned projects based on the needs of the EH&S department.

Fire Inspector

Under the direction and supervision of the EH&S Department Head, the Fire Inspector shall:

- Engage in the regulation, inspection, control, and abatement of fire hazards and promotion of fire prevention practices.

- Perform fire prevention visits to inspect residences, office work areas, warehouse, shops, commissary, Base Exchange, gas station, and air traffic and support operations. This includes military tactical aircraft armed with conventional weapons, large quantities of fuel, aircraft maintenance activities, munitions, refueling activities, and activities involving oxygen handling.

- Visually inspect and check installed fire prevention equipment.

- Install, inspect, and maintain firefighting appliances.

- Prepare and conduct classes in fire prevention/protection for flight line military, civilian personnel, and base residents.

- Conduct fire drills, identify incorrect procedures, and develop corrective action plan.

- Conduct annual fire safety stand-down.

Recycling Coordinator

Under the direct supervision of the EH&S Department Head, the Recycling Coordinator manages the Recycling Center at Air Station Cape Cod and ensures the daily operation of the Recycling Center: receiving, storing/consolidating, and disposal of recyclable material, universal waste, and compost material.

Medical Liaison

Under the direction and supervision of the EH&S Department Head the Health Services Technician shall:

- Serve as the Medical Waste Satellite Point Manager, responsible for reporting, record keeping, storage, packaging, labeling, transportation, and disposal of Coast Guard generated infectious waste.

- Serve as the unit's Food Service Sanitation Officer.

- Conduct weekly sanitation inspection in the food service area in conjunction with Coast Guard food service manual.

- Serve as unit's medical monitor.

- Provide training/assistance to occupational medical monitoring program. Serve as the unit's point of contact (POC) with district Safety and Environmental Health Officer. Report all updates to program manager.

- Assist in facility environmental health and safety inspections.

Satellite Point Managers

Under the direction of the Environmental Specialist, a Satellite Point Manager has the overall responsibility for the proper storage of regulated waste in the [Aeronautical Engineering Dept]. As such, he shall:

- Ensure that all hazardous waste within his work area is managed in accord with the following:

  - Air Station Cape Cod Hazardous Wastes Management Plan

  - COMDTINST M16478 USCG Hazardous Waste Management Manual

  - 310 Code of Massachusetts Regulation 30.00 Hazardous Waste Regulations

  - 40 CFR Parts 260 through 262

- Ensure that their respective department personnel are aware of their responsibility in accord with spill response procedures set forth in the Hazardous Material Spill Response AIRINST 11000 and the Spill Prevention Control and Countermeasure Plan (SPCC).

- When necessary, properly identify, package, mark, and label hazardous waste.

- Ensure that waste generated in the work activity is placed in designated, waste-specific container within Satellite Accumulation Points (SAP).

- Inspect SAP daily.

- Ensure that SAP maintains high housekeeping standards.

- Inspect above-ground storage tanks and secondary containment systems within respective area of operation weekly and document accordingly.

- When hazardous waste drum is filled, contact ASCC HWC for removal to the 90-day temporary storage facility.

- Ensure that the container is removed from the SAP within three days of being filled.

- Attend annual hazardous waste training for SAP management.

- Liaise with ASCC Hazardous Waste Coordinator concerning proper hazardous waste management and/or environmental protection.

AMO Liaison

In addition to the duties of Satellite Point Manager, acts as the Aviation Engineering Department's direct liaison to the EH&S Department for hazardous materials and hazardous waste management.

Spill Team

Under the direction of the Public Safety Officer, Spill Team members shall:

- Perform routine daily, weekly, and monthly inspections for both the storage facilities and spill response equipment, to include tank supports, foundations, and piping.

- Ensure that inventory records are maintained for all fuel storage tanks.

- Ensure that appropriate personnel are trained in spill response procedures.

- Be prepared to coordinate and direct spill containment and cleanup procedures.

- Coordinate with the Environmental Specialist for (reordering) supplies for spill response kit.

Public Safety Officer

Under the direction and supervision of the EH&S Department Head, the Public Safety Officer shall:

- Manage state policy and public safety officers to maintain good order and public safety of Air Station Cape Cod.

- Serve as the unit's Public Safety Officer.

- Assume responsibility to uphold and enforce the laws of the Commonwealth of Massachusetts.

- Manage private security contractor.

- Conduct annual public safety stand-downs.

- Serve as the unit's traffic safety officer.

- Serve as Emergency Response Coordinator.

TW Security Contractor

Under the direct supervision of the Public Safety Officer, maintain access control, good order, and public safety at Air Station Cape Cod. Oversee and manage security guards and provide patrol services for the protection of personnel, property, facilities, and land at Air Station Cape Cod.

8

Competence, Training, and Awareness

The end results of an environmental management system are only as good as the people involved. It is critical that workers understand the purpose of the system, are motivated to fulfill associated requirements, and possess the skills to accomplish assigned responsibilities.

ISO 14001:2004 Text	ISO 14001:1996 Text
4.4.2 Competence, training and awareness	*4.4.2 Training, awareness and competence*
The organization shall ensure that any person(s) performing tasks for it or on its behalf that have the potential to cause a significant environmental impact(s) identified by the organization is (are) competent on the basis of appropriate education, training, or experience, and shall retain associated records.	The organization shall identify training needs. It shall require that all personnel whose work may create a significant impact upon the environment, have received appropriate training.
The organization shall identify training needs associated with its environmental aspects and its environmental management system. It shall provide training or take other action to meet these needs, and shall retain associated records.	It shall establish and maintain procedures to make its employees or members at each relevant function and level aware of
	a) the importance of conformance with the environmental policy and procedures and with the requirements of the environmental management system;

Continued

Continued

ISO 14001:2004 Text	ISO 14001:1996 Text
The organization shall establish, implement and maintain a procedure(s) to make persons working for it or on its behalf aware of a) the importance of conformity with the environmental policy and procedures and with the requirements of the environmental management system, b) the significant environmental aspects and related actual or potential impacts associated with their work, and the environmental benefits of improved personal performance, c) their roles and responsibilities in achieving conformity with the requirements of the environmental management system, and d) the potential consequences of departure from specified procedures.	b) the significant environmental impacts, actual or potential, of their work activities and the environmental benefits of improved personal performance; c) their roles and responsibilities in achieving conformance with the environmental policy and procedures and with the requirements of the environmental management system, including emergency preparedness and response requirements; d) the potential consequences of departure from specified operating procedures. Personnel performing the tasks which can cause significant environmental impacts shall be competent on the basis of appropriate education, training and/or experience.

SIGNIFICANT CHANGES

The original title of this clause (training, awareness and competence) was reversed (competence, training and awareness) to increase emphasis on worker competence. The last paragraph in ISO 14001:1996, dealing with the expectation that workers must be competent on the basis of education, training, and/or experience, becomes the first paragraph in ISO 14001:2004.

The other two modifications of significance are contained in the reference to "any person(s)" performing tasks or working for the organization or on its behalf. First, "any" means that awareness training must be provided to all workers. An organization no longer has the flexibility to select trainees. Second, "working on behalf of" directs organizations to consider a broader array of workers than full-time employees. Temporary workers, contractors, and others working on behalf of an organization also must be included in any evaluation of worker competence.

INTENT OF ISO 14001:2004

This element addresses two areas of training: skills or competence training for workers who perform tasks that have the potential to cause a significant environmental impact and general awareness training for all workers.

Workers who can cause significant environmental impacts must be competent to perform assigned responsibilities. Competence—defined as the effective execution of required actions—can be attained through avenues other than training, such as formal education and/or experience. ISO 14001:2004 does not require training *per se*—it requires competence. Therefore, it is incumbent upon an organization's management to define competence and determine whether workers perform their jobs accordingly. In other words, an organization should determine the specific knowledge and skills that are necessary to properly perform any activity for which an actual or potential significant environmental impact has been identified, and ascertain whether workers who perform these activities possess such knowledge and skills.

Training needs must be identified for those workers whose on-the-job performance does not meet defined competence levels. This can take any form that is useful to an organization. Typical methods for delineating training needs are job descriptions, performance objectives, and personnel reviews.

Training needs also must be identified for workers who are required to hold a license or other similar credential. Some state and federal regulations may require training on a one-time basis while others may impose periodic follow-up training.

Once a training need is identified, an organization must take steps to ensure that affected workers are trained or otherwise instructed so they can perform as required. This requires an organization to reevaluate competence after training has been provided.

Management also should be cognizant of the specific activities in which temporary workers and contractors are involved. If those activities could result in significant environmental impact, management must require the same level of competence and accountability that it demands of its own employees. This does not necessarily place the burden of training on the contracting organization. As a condition of doing business, a company can require that contractors provide evidence of appropriate experience and ability.

Awareness training differs from competency or skills training. It is intended to emphasize the importance of conforming to the environmental management system and reinforce the environmental benefits of improved individual performance. Therefore, it is offered to a broad array of workers at all levels and from all functions in the organization, rather than being limited to workers whose jobs are associated with significant environmental impacts.

ISO 14001:2004 requires that an organization keep associated records. An organization is free to create records in any form that it finds useful. Records must, however, verify whether a worker is deemed competent or has a training need. Two types of records often substantiate these efforts:

- In many organizations, worker competence is determined by pairing an experienced worker with one who is new to the task at hand. The inexperienced worker learns through on-the-job instruction and, at some point, is recognized by the experienced worker as capable. Typically, the experienced worker or a supervisor signs an evaluation form that indicates that the new worker is able to perform a required task without intensive supervision. Written evaluations that reflect the abilities of workers trained through a buddy system are one example of records of employee competence.

- When an evaluation reveals that knowledge and/or skills are lacking, any documented deficiency can serve as a record of a training need. Once a training need is identified, a second record is required to show that the training need has been addressed. Records verifying that training has occurred can take a variety of forms, such as a certificate of attendance or an exam score. Participation in a training program does not necessarily guarantee worker competence. Only a reevaluation of on-the-job abilities offers evidence of worker competence.

EXAMPLES

U. S. Steel Gary Works
EMS Procedure 4.4.2—Competence, Training, and Awareness
(Effective October 20, 2005)

1.0 Purpose

    1.1 The purpose of this procedure is to describe the Gary Complex Environmental Management System (EMS) training requirements.

2.0 Scope

    2.1 This procedure applies to training for personnel whose work *may* create a significant impact on the environment and to ensure the competence of personnel whose work assignments (tasks) *can* cause significant environmental impacts.

3.0 References

    3.1 ISO 14001:2004 Standard

    3.2 EMS Procedure 4.4.6—Operational Control

    3.3 EMS Procedure 4.5.4—Control of Records

    3.4 EMS Procedure 4.5.5—Internal Audit

4.0 Definitions

For the purposes of this procedure, the following definitions shall apply.

    4.1 ISO 14001 Training Needs Web page—Identifies job positions whose work activities can cause significant environmental impacts and work instructions utilized to prevent those impacts.

    4.2 Competence—Refers to demonstrated ability to complete specified tasks on the basis of appropriate education, training, and/or experience.

5.0 Responsibilities

    5.1 The following job positions have responsibilities in this procedure:

        • Business units, staff groups, contractors/suppliers

- ISO 14001 Coordinator

- Cross-functional teams (CFTs)

- All employees

6.0 Procedure

6.1 ISO 14001 Awareness Training is developed by Environmental Control and is conducted in accordance with the requirements of this procedure for *all* Gary Complex and relevant contractor employees.

6.1.1 Employees receive ISO 14001 Awareness Training through Environmental Bulletins, posters, hardhat stickers, wallet cards, and videos. This training is recorded through various means and is verified by EMS internal audits.

6.2 Employees working for identified relevant contractors/ suppliers receive ISO 14001 Awareness Training provided by the contractor/supplier.

6.2.1 The contractor/supplier is responsible for maintaining a training record of ISO 14001 Awareness Training.

6.2.2 Environmental Control develops training materials to be used by contractors/suppliers for ISO 14001 Awareness Training.

6.3 The CFTs, including relevant contractors/suppliers, shall identify job positions whose work tasks *can* cause significant environmental impacts.

6.3.1 It is the responsibility of the business unit/staff organization or contractor/supplier to ensure that their employees are competent on the basis of appropriate education, training, and/or experience.

6.3.2 It is the responsibility of the business unit/staff organization and contractor/supplier to ensure that employees working in job positions associated with significant environmental aspects receive training on identified (Operational Control) work instructions annually.

6.4 Audits are conducted per the requirements of EMS Procedure 4.5.5—Internal Audit to ensure that the requirements of this procedure are met.

6.4.1   Effectiveness of training is evaluated during EMS audits focused on employee knowledge and understanding of environmental issues. These audits include general awareness issues, implementation of job responsibilities, and response to potential emergency situations.

7.0   Approval

7.1   Approval of this procedure by the Gary Complex Environmental Management System Steering Team is effected by the signature (on the Document Validation Form) of the Manager, Environmental Control that has been designated as the Environmental Management Representative.

7.2   Approved for use.

Manager, Environmental Control and Environmental Management Representative

Delaware North Companies Parks & Resorts
P1400.04—GreenPath Environmental Responsibilities
(Effective August 1, 2005)

Training is addressed in the procedure on environmental responsibilities, which appears in its entirety in Chapter 7. Only that portion of the procedure that directly addresses training is reproduced here.

Procedure

Responsibility:

Environmental Manager (Operations Manager or designees). The Environmental Manager at each GreenPath location carries the responsibility for environmental management and performance at the location. The EMS requires the Environmental Manager to undertake the following:

• Reviewing and completing existing and emerging environmental training obligations affecting location personnel

All DNC staff. DNC GreenPath location managers and employees are responsible for the implementation of the environmental management programs at the location. The staff is required to undertake the following:

• Attending environmental awareness training sessions

Training Matrix

GreenPath locations shall be guided by the following training matrix:

Part 1 of 3—General awareness training

Who	What—subject	When—schedule	Where	How	Why—objectives
Environmental Manager	GreenPath procedures, ISO 14001, EMS management	Upon being awarded the EM duties	On site or off site	The DNC Director of Environmental Affairs will provide	To ensure effective management of all GreenPath policies and procedures and ISO standards, and to ensure continuing environmental improvement at the facility
New employee	Environmental awareness	At hiring	Part of new-employee training	Scheduled, prepared, and given by Environmental Manager or designee, or Training Department	• Meet regulatory requirements • Instill sense of personal responsibility toward pollution prevention and continual environmental improvement
Contractor	Environmental awareness	First visit to facility or prior to beginning project, if deemed necessary	Part of site-specific training	Given by Environmental Manager, Maintenance Manager, or designee	• Meet regulatory requirements • Instill sense of personal responsibility toward pollution prevention • Meet location/project environmental expectations

Continued

Continued

Part 1 of 3—General awareness training

Who	What—subject	When—schedule	Where	How	Why—objectives
Suppliers—written notification	GreenPath awareness	Selected suppliers as deemed appropriate by local management	By mail or e-mail at intervals deemed appropriate by local management	By mail or e-mail at intervals deemed appropriate by local management	• Meet regulatory requirements • Instill sense of personal responsibility toward pollution prevention • Meet location/project environmental expectations • Notice to offer environmentally friendly alternatives
Current employee	Environmental awareness	Annual	Annual Hazcom refresher class	Scheduled, prepared, and given by Environmental Manager or designee, supervisor, or Training Department	• Meet regulatory requirements • Instill sense of personal responsibility toward pollution prevention and continual environmental improvement • Gain commitment to environmental policy, objectives, and targets

Part 2 of 3—Training for operational controls

What—subject	Who—trainee	When—schedule	Where	How	Why—objectives
Operational control	Operating personnel	When assigned to department	Job site—part of new task training	Use existing process description	• Awareness of significant environmental requirements of new position

Part 3 of 3—Training for special operations

What—subject	Who—trainee	When—schedule	Where	How	Why—objectives
Hazardous waste management					
Resource Conservation and Recovery Act (RCRA) training and/or state-specific hazardous waste training	Selected operational staff	When newly assigned to position	On or off site	By internal DNC staff or outside consultant	• Meet regulatory and safety requirements
Hazwoper 24-hour training	Selected operational staff	Annual update	On or off site	By internal DNC staff or outside consultant	• Meet regulatory and safety requirements

Operating locations are authorized to develop additional site-specific training requirements.

Coast Guard Air Station Cape Cod
Procedure 04—Training Procedure
(Effective May 31, 2004)

1.0 Purpose:

To identify the process of assuring environmental training of U.S. Coast Guard Air Station Cape Cod (USCG–ASCC) employees.

2.0 Scope:

2.1 This procedure effects both USCG and civilian employees whose work may create a significant impact upon the environment at ASCC.

3.0 Procedure:

3.1 The training requirements of this organization are budget driven. Each department is required to review its training needs and submit a proposal to the Comptroller department for funding prior to each fiscal year. It shall be noted that environmental training is considered an important component of job responsibilities and qualifications at ASCC. Required environmental training receives funding priority and all efforts will be made to arrange for funding of optional/job enhancement environmental training as deemed appropriate by department heads and Comptroller.

3.2 The Comptroller department initiates the process via a memorandum regarding fiscal year budget development and execution. This memorandum is distributed to all department heads annually on or about September.

3.3 Department heads develop budget submissions to justify and effectively use ASCC's funds. Department heads make use of the spreadsheet provided as Appendix A to justify their request.

3.4 EH&S develops its training request based on the following criteria:

- Regulatory requirements
- Budget
- CG policy and ASCC's operating objectives
- Past certifications
- Annual refresher requirements

- Job enhancement

- Personnel turnover

3.5   Department heads submit the completed spreadsheet to the Training and Education department for administrative review.

3.6   The Training and Education department in turn submits the spreadsheet to the Comptroller department for funding approval.

3.7   Subsequently the Comptroller department issues an "Approved Spend Plan for (the) Fiscal Year."

3.8   Once funding is granted, the EH&S department will meet after budget approval to:

- Identify the training to be accomplished for the upcoming year (this includes, but is not limited to, new arrivals, initial training, and annual refresher training)

- Identify individuals to attend specified training and/or what training the staff will provide to the unit.

3.9   New personnel assigned to the EH&S Department, Spill Team, or EH&S departmental related responsibilities are quickly taken into account and acclimated.

3.10 Once the training agenda is determined for the fiscal year, the EH&S Department will meet quarterly to schedule and provide for budgeted environmental training. Training review sessions will be documented using the form provided as Appendix B.

3.11 Individuals within the EH&S department coordinate attending their specified training. If training is required for a member outside of the EH&S department, the Environmental Protection Specialist coordinates for the training with the member(s).

4.0   Responsibilities:

Department heads are responsible for their respective department personnel training and continuation of qualifications. Department heads may coordinate with the EH&S department in providing and assuring environmental compliance and training.

The EH&S Manager is responsible for providing for environmental training to ASCC in support of its EMS and other environmental compliance practices/operations.

The Administrative Assistant is responsible for maintaining environmental training records of personnel whose work may create a significant impact upon the environment and maintaining copies of the fiscal year training budget.

Individuals are responsible for ensuring that copies of course completion or certificates are submitted to the Administrative Assistant for proper filing.

5.0 Appendixes:

Spread Plan Worksheet for (the) FY

6.0 Related Documentation:

Procedure 03—Record Keeping and Record Retention

SPCC Section 14, Training

7.0 Records:

Records generated by this procedure include:

- Fiscal Year Purchase Order and Budget Worksheet

- Spend Plan Worksheet for (the) FY

- Approved Spend Plan Worksheet for (the) FY

Coast Guard Air Station Cape Cod
Procedure 18—New Arrivals/Check-In
(Effective February 4, 2004)

1.0 Purpose:

To identify the process of assuring that new personnel arriving at ASCC are made aware of the EMS and their responsibilities with regard to environmental compliance.

2.0 Scope:

2.1 This procedure affects both USCG and civilian employees newly arriving at ASCC for duty.

3.0 Procedure:

3.1 When a member reports onboard at ASCC, among other things he is provided with a check-in sheet. (See Appendix A.) The new member is to be guided by the check-in sheet and meet with all personnel listed on the sheet. This benefits the member in meeting ASCC personnel and providing him with the necessary information to perform his duties and live as a responsible resident at the station. Similarly, department heads are made aware of new members.

3.2 Per the check-in sheet, newcomers are required to meet with the EH&S Department Head. During this meeting, the new member is made aware of the EMS, the AUL (see Procedure 08), his responsibilities toward environmental stewardship and compliance, and any other pertinent information relative to his job function. Further, an environmental training record will be established for the new member as deemed necessary by his job responsibilities and he is added to the roster for consideration of any necessary or required environmental training (see Procedure 04).

3.3 The newcomer has 14 days to complete the check-in process.

3.4 Once the initial meeting is complete, the EH&S Department Head signs the check-in sheet and the member may carry on to the next department head.

4.0 Responsibilities:

The Administration Department is responsible for the implementation of this procedure as well as maintaining the records of new arrivals' completed check-in sheets.

Department heads are responsible to meet with new arrivals and share relevant information.

The EH&S Manager is also responsible to ensure that new arrivals are made aware of the EMS and other pertinent environmental information.

The Administrative Assistant is responsible for creating (environmental) training records for all newcomers assigned positions that may have a significant impact on the environment.

Individuals are responsible for ensuring that they meet with all personnel listed on the check-in sheet in the allotted time. They are to return the completed check-in sheet to the Administration Department.

5.0   Appendixes:

    A. Check-in Sheet

    B. New Arrival Discussion Checklist

6.0   Related Documentation:

Procedure 03—Record Keeping and Record Retention

Procedure 04—Training

Procedure 08—Procurement Guidelines for Supplies and Authorized Use List

7.0   Records:

Records generated by this procedure include:

- Check-in Sheet

9
Communication

Sharing of information and exchange of ideas among all organizational functions and levels are critical for implementation and improvement of an environmental management system. Equally important are strategies for communication between an organization and a diverse array of external parties.

ISO 14001:2004 Text	ISO 14001:1996 Text
4.4.3 Communication With regard to its environmental aspects and environmental management system, the organization shall establish, implement and maintain a procedure(s) for a) internal communication between the various levels and functions of the organization b) receiving, documenting and responding to relevant communication from external interested parties. The organization shall decide whether to communicate externally about its significant environmental aspects and shall document its	*4.4.3 Communication* With regard to its environmental aspects and environmental management system, the organization shall establish and maintain procedures for a) internal communication between the various levels and functions of the organization; b) receiving, documenting and responding to relevant communication from external interested parties. The organization shall consider processes for external communication on its significant environmental aspects and record its decision.

Continued

Continued

ISO 14001:2004 Text	
decision. If the decision is to communicate, the organization shall establish and implement a method(s) for this external communication.	

SIGNIFICANT CHANGES

The only changes are found in the last paragraph. The somewhat ambiguous directive to "consider processes for external communication" has been replaced with a clearer instruction to decide whether to communicate externally. A new requirement states that when an organization decides to communicate externally, it must institute an explicit method to accomplish that communication.

INTENT OF ISO 14001:2004

Two procedures are required by this clause. To establish effective procedures, it is necessary to understand what is meant by the term *communication*. As used here and elsewhere in the standard, it connotes two distinct but related activities—sharing of information by an individual, group, or organization and understanding of that information by its intended audience.

Distributing information is not synonymous with communicating. An organization can provide written information to all employees. This does not ensure, however, that employees will actually read the document or understand what the document means if they do read it.

Internal Communication

The procedure for internal communication (see paragraph [a]) requires that an organization establish a process for sharing information among the levels and functions comprising its organizational structure. Think of *level* as a position of rank with assigned control and authority (for example, middle management) and *function* as a group of related actions that contribute to a larger accomplishment (for example, the health and safety department). ISO 14001:2004 uses these terms to indicate that the environmental management system must be understood throughout the organization in which it is implemented.

Conventional organizational structure suggests that internal communication typically occurs between headquarters and facilities; senior, mid-level, and lower-level managers and workers; employees and contractors. However, an organization will identify levels and functions based on its own configuration and hierarchy.

External Communication

The procedure for external communication (see paragraph [b]) is reactive. It does not require an organization to seek opportunities for sharing information. Rather, it directs an organization to respond when individuals or groups external to the organization have a relevant query. Examples of external parties are regulatory agencies, community residents, civic associations, trade associations and industry groups, members of the financial sector, stockholders, environmental interest groups, and members of print, radio, and broadcast media.

An organization will define for itself what it considers *relevant*. However, the dictionary definition—relating to or bearing upon the matter at hand—suggests that any external inquiry related to "the environment" should be considered relevant.

Any relevant external request for information must be documented by the organization to which the request is made. Such requests will take different forms—the most common are letter, e-mail, fax, telephone request, and personal conversation. To be effective, a procedure should offer direction for documenting the array of methods by which an organization is likely to be contacted.

The requirement to respond does not mean that an organization must provide any and all information requested by an external party. Different kinds of information will be available to different external entities. The response to a regulatory agency, for example, is likely to contain information that may be deemed inappropriate for dissemination to a local community group or private citizen.

It is up to an organization to determine what information will be provided and what information is confidential. It is acceptable to respond to a request for confidential information by explaining that it is the organization's policy not to publicly disclose the information being sought.

The final paragraph focuses on proactive external communication. Although ISO 14001:2004 does not require an organization to voluntarily share information about its significant environmental aspects, it encourages decision makers to consider the advantages and disadvantages of doing so.

It is a good idea to address this issue as a standing agenda item during management review. This allows an organization to consider, on a periodic basis, whether to reaffirm or change its position. An added benefit is that since the management review must be documented, the requirement to document the decision about external communication is achieved.

An organization that chooses to share information about its significant environmental aspects must establish and implement one or more methods for accomplishing external communication. Environmental communication is not synonymous with environmental reporting. Although organizations often view a printed report as an appropriate vehicle, different audiences are likely to respond to other methods.

The approach selected for external communication should reflect what the organization wants to accomplish—it can inform, persuade, consult with, or otherwise engage an audience—and with whom it will be communicating. Tables 9.1, 9.2, and 9.3 describe written, verbal, and other communications approaches and tools, respectively, and the strengths and weaknesses of each.

Table 9.1 Written communications approaches and tools.

Technique	Description	Strengths	Weaknesses	Keep in mind
Web sites	Electronic communication medium, accessible to all online external and internal interested parties. Can include downloadable reports, educational material, or links to Web sites where users can provide feedback to the organization.	Offer great potential to reach out to many people on many issues (and to offer tailored information). Easy to update, with potential to effect two-way communication.	Companies often put brochure ware on their Web sites, which misses the opportunity for interactivity (for example, video, real data, e-mail feedback).	Keep technical computer requirements to a low level—not everybody has the latest computer hardware. Need not be expensive. Answers to frequently asked questions can be provided on the Web site, with a phone number provided for more detailed inquiries.
Environmental or sustainability reports	Comprehensive presentation of commitment and performance on a number of key issues. Extracts or summaries of these reports can be included in other communications of the organization, for example financial reports.	Opportunity to address multiple issues in depth. Basic approach for building trust and credibility. Creates internal transparency about all relevant issues of an organization.	Hard work to produce and can be difficult to update frequently. May provide information in a form that does not permit comparison with similar organizations.	Address external and internal interested parties' interests. Include difficulties and failures as well as successes.

Continued

Continued

Technique	Description	Strengths	Weaknesses	Keep in mind
Printed material (Reports, brochures, and newsletters)	*Report or brochure—* A brief summary of the facility or specific project of interest, key issues, and how people can participate. *Newsletter—*Periodic update of facility activities. Informs and maintains links with interested parties.	Can cover a single issue if necessary. Inexpensive and quick to produce. Informs large numbers of people. Newsletters can be effective for both external and internal interested parties.	Can be misinterpreted. Only basic information given. No direct feedback. May be difficult to distribute in remote areas.	Issues must be researched. Use basic language. Use photos and maps. Be objective. Include contact name, telephone number, and address.
Product or service information labels or declarations	Description of the significant environmental issues associated with a product or service. In case of products, it can be attached to product or available separately.	Can inform customers about the environmental attributes of a product or service.	May cause confusion because information is presented in brief form.	Form and content of environmental product labels may conform to the requirements of ISO 14020 series.
Posters/ displays	A description of a project, highlighting issues and set up in a public place.	Provides general information at relatively low cost. Reaches many that may not participate otherwise.	Information giving, rather than receiving.	Keep to main points. Use photos and maps. Update regularly. Advertise the location of the display. Provide contact name and number.

Continued

Technique	Description	Strengths	Weaknesses	Keep in mind
Letters	Letters on specific issues to and from named individuals.	Can address particular interested parties' needs. Quick and easy to produce.	Can be overly formal. Generally poor way to communicate complex information.	Reading level of recipients. Make one argument well.
Media/ newspaper feature articles	Explains features of a facility or project.	Can reach a large audience. Convenient for the public. Good vehicle for education.	May be edited by the paper so that only part of the story is told. In remote areas or developing countries, not necessarily widely available.	Local media and nationwide media may require different approaches, style, and level of detail.
Media/ news releases	Information is prepared and distributed to the media for its use.	An effective and cheap way to get publicity and interest.	Media will not cover unless the story is deemed newsworthy. May be edited to meet guidelines.	Avoid misrepresenting the organization's environmental performance.
Media/ advertising	Paid-for promotional material, for example, a straight ad in a newspaper, or sponsorship of a section (such as the environment page of the regional paper).	Reaches a large audience.	Can be expensive. May have limited lifespan. Limited opportunity to describe complex issues.	Audience profile of publication/program within which the advertisement appears.

Source: ISO FDIS 14063, Environmental management—Environmental communication—Guidelines and examples. Geneva: International Organization for Standardization, 2005.

Table 9.2 Verbal communications approaches and tools.

Technique	Description	Strengths	Weaknesses	Keep in mind
Public meetings	A way to present information and exchange views. Addresses specific agenda or project aspect. Consists of presentations and question-and-answer sessions or formal, timed testimony.	Seen as 'legitimate' consultation. Information provided to large number of people. Costs are low. People usually willing to attend.	Interactions can be limited. Does not ensure that all views are heard. May become an emotional shouting match. Vocal minority may dominate.	Often best to use after smaller activities (interviews, focus groups) to know what the interested parties' reactions will be in advance. Advertise the meeting well. Staff needs proven experience. Use an independent chairperson and/or a facilitator/mediator if possible.
Interested party interviews/personal contact	Talking with people in their homes, offices, or a neutral location.	Two-way exchange of information. People feel they have been heard. Specific issues can be addressed. An honest talk may build trust. Interviews help identify key issues and concerns and establish relationships.	Difficult to identify all interested parties. Time-constraining. Non-community feel. May be threatening for some. May sometimes be culturally inappropriate.	Identify individuals who represent the types of interested parties who could be or are being affected by a specific activity. Accept that some people may want professional representation. Often good to include influential interested parties. Meet at a location that is convenient for interested parties.

Continued

Continued

Technique	Description	Strengths	Weaknesses	Keep in mind
Focus groups	Meeting with a small group of interested parties with a similar background (for example, government officials or residents) to discuss a particular topic.	Allows a free exchange of ideas because participants feel comfortable being with their peers. Often a consensus can be reached about the most important issues.	Time-consuming to conduct focus groups with all important interested parties.	Often best used after some initial interviews with interested parties to identify the main issues that may be raised.
Surveys	Questionnaire used with interested parties (may be conducted by an independent organization if deemed necessary) to gather demographic information from the respondents and indicate their issues and concerns.	Helpful to use when a company is planning to establish itself in a community or if a major change in operations is being considered. Also good to update on some regular basis (for example, every two years).	Surveys may be labor-intensive depending on the complexity of the questionnaire, the way questions are asked (personally or via Web for example), the number of persons in the sample, and the number and size of the geographical locations chosen.	Surveys can be conducted door to door or over the telephone. They may also be written or be performed over the Internet.

Continued

Technique	Description	Strengths	Weaknesses	Keep in mind
Open houses, information days, site visit, videos	Open houses are usually held at a central, public spot and provide a chance for people to ask questions and discuss issues. Information days can be combined with site visits to give the public a chance to see a facility firsthand and ask questions. Videos can be used at any of these events to explain facility operations.	Allows for direct interaction. Provides opportunity to correct misinformation and explore issues. Can be useful for reaching both external and internal interested parties.	Are more giving than receiving. Can be expensive, require many staff hours. Rely on staff knowledge and skills.	Must be well advertised. Staff must be well briefed. Project manager should be present. Issues raised must be recorded. Staff should not be defensive but be listening actively to interested parties' comments.
Workshops, conferences, dialogue events	Workshops, conferences, and dialogues are opportunities for a range of interested parties to discuss ideas, concerns, and issues.	They can be very productive and helpful in reaching consensus on issues with high priority.	They can be time-consuming to organize to ensure that a good mix of interested parties is present.	It is usually most effective to host such an event after either interviews or focus groups to provide information on the type of issues that may be raised.

Continued

Technique	Description	Strengths	Weaknesses	Keep in mind
Media/radio interviews	Short programs usually aimed at discussing or responding to narrow or focused issues.	Avenue to reach many people.	It is not possible to control the questions that will be asked. Unless the radio station permits listeners to phone in, it is difficult to have any type of exchange.	Keep messages sharp, clear, and simple. Give these interviews if some major decision is being considered that would be of interest to the broader community.
Citizen advisory groups or community liaison groups	Group made up of people from outside the organization with various interests and expertise that meet periodically to give advice on environmental issues from an interested-party point of view.	Investigate issues, put forward suggestions. Two-way exchange of information. Shows that the organization is willing to work with people. Helps maintain the visibility of the organization in the community.	Can have limited power. May not represent all interests, different levels of expertise. Information not always passed on to community. Advisory group members may become out of touch with those they represent.	Must represent full range of interests. The role and authority of the group must be clearly defined. Should have predetermined lifespan. Members must communicate with the community.

Continued

Technique	Description	Strengths	Weaknesses	Keep in mind
Help desk	Phone advice and information available to interested parties about the environmental and other aspects of products.	Provides opportunity for interested parties to ask questions and receive responses about products.	Calls may cover any subject. Callers may not always listen carefully to answers and may therefore misinterpret responses.	Staff must be well informed about environmental aspects of the organization's activities, products, and services. If responding to difficult questions, it is sometimes better to offer to get back to the caller or to send a written response.
Presentation to groups	Talks to interested groups, usually held at the group's regular meeting place. A short presentation is followed by a question-and-answer session. May be used for internal or external groups.	Groups can be targeted. Information can be tailored to meet group needs and may be passed to others. The host group may do some of the work (inviting people). Useful for indigenous communities.	Potential for hostile audience reaction. If used alone can fail to reach sections of the community.	Use it to develop working relationships. Do not exclude nonsupportive groups. Provide written material to be considered before meeting. Leave written material to be taken home.

Continued

Technique	Description	Strengths	Weaknesses	Keep in mind
Interested party dinners/ sustainable business dinners	Series of group meetings bringing together different interested parties either to launch a report or discuss sustainability.	Participants benefit from sharing their views (for example, enjoying a meal). Firsthand interested parties' views obtained. Constructive atmosphere in which to discuss sustainability.	Difficulties in selecting guests and steering conversation to sustainability.	Can be of different sizes, for example, large meetings with regional and local interested parties or small meetings with less than 10 participants.
Theatre presentations	Use of a theatrical format to present environmental infor-mation to internal or external interested parties.	Can attract attention of interested parties. Can reach interested parties who may not read written materials.	It may be difficult to develop presentations that are appropriate for groups with varying levels of knowledge, understanding, and interest.	Presentations must be well done, lively, and must avoid preaching to the audience.

Source: ISO FDIS 14063, Environmental management—Environmental communication—Guidelines and examples. Geneva: International Organization for Standardization, 2005.

Table 9.3 Other communications approaches and tools.

Technique	Description	Strengths	Weaknesses	Keep in mind
Cooperative projects	Projects carried out jointly by an organization and groups of interested parties.	Can build trust and cooperation through working together to achieve a mutual goal.	Interested parties may have unrealistic expectations about the input and resources that an organization can provide.	In developing cooperative projects be sure to define clearly the project goals, and the roles, responsibilities, and resources to be provided by each participant.
Sustainability agreement	An agreement reached by an organization and a community to mutually commit to sustainable development.	Assists in building relationships between a community and an organization that will foster environmental communication and interaction. Benefits can include having the organization recognized as a leader committed to improving quality of life and the environment.	Time and resources are needed to maintain community relationships.	If an organization fails to meet its commitment, its reputation may suffer because of the visibility of the agreement.

Continued

Technique	Description	Strengths	Weaknesses	Keep in mind
Art exhibitions	Display of artworks organized around environmental themes.	Encourages involvement of external and/or internal interested parties who may not be attracted by more conventional approaches.	May be time-consuming to organize.	Exhibitions should be available for viewing during hours when people have time to attend, for example, evenings and weekends.

Source: ISO FDIS 14063, Environmental management—Environmental communication—Guidelines and examples. Geneva: International Organization for Standardization, 2005.

EXAMPLES

U. S. Steel Gary Works
EMS Procedure 4.4.3—Communication
(Effective September 7, 2005)

1.0 Purpose

    1.1   The purpose of this procedure is to describe the processes for managing internal and external communications on the Environmental Management System and other environmental issues at the Gary Complex.

2.0 Scope

    2.1   This procedure applies to employees who are involved in internal and external communications on the Environmental Management System and other environmental issues at the Gary Complex.

3.0 References

    3.1   ISO 14001:2004 Standard

    3.2   EMS Procedure 4.3.1—Environmental Aspects

    3.3   EMS Procedures 4.2 through 4.6

    3.4   Environmental Control Plantwide Communication Plan

    3.5   External Communication Log (Exhibit I)

4.0 Definitions

    4.1   Internal communication occurs within the Gary Complex, and possibly throughout the U. S. Steel Corporation, on matters related to the Environmental Management System and other environmental issues.

    4.2   External communication occurs between Gary Complex Management and outside individuals/organizations (regulatory authorities, community organizations, customers, contractors, media, and so on) on the Gary Complex Environmental Management System and other environmental issues.

5.0 Responsibilities

    5.1   The following job positions have responsibilities in this procedure:

- Environmental Management Representative (EMR)

- Environmental Control Managers

- Gary Complex Managers

- U. S. Steel Public Affairs

6.0 Procedure

  6.1 Internal Communications

  6.1.1 Gary Complex Management provides internal communications to ensure that employees at each relevant level and function receive information on environmental aspects, the Gary Complex EMS, and other environmental issues. This communication may occur through, but is not limited to, the following:

  - Training on relevant Level III Work Instructions

  - Environmental Bulletins

  - Electronic mail

  - Newsletters and other written (electronic or paper copy) memos, letters, and documents (for example, APEX Newsletter)

  - Electronic bulletin boards/Target Vision

  - Business and area manager meetings, and crew/team meetings

  - Internal audits and Environmental Preventive Corrective Action Requests.

  - Daily Report of Operations (DRO)

  - Gary Works intranet environmental Web page at location: http://www.xxx

  - Gary Complex Environmental Management System Steering Team meetings

  - Environmental Control ISO 14001 Steering Team meetings

  6.1.2 Employees may communicate their environmental concerns and issues to the appropriate level of management by contacting their supervisor and/or

Environmental Compliance Manager. Responses to concerns and issues may be facilitated through appropriate personnel, which may include the following: the Environmental Control Department, the business unit or staff group cross-functional team, or when necessary, the EMR.

6.1.3 The Environmental Control Plantwide Communication Plan provides a listing of various methods used for communicating environmental information within the Gary Complex, and when applicable, corporatewide. The plan identifies the report, the frequency of communication, the person responsible for the communication, and the method of communication. The Manager, Northwest Indiana Environmental Affairs is responsible for this plan.

6.2 External Communications

6.2.1 The Gary Complex provides information about the EMS and environmental issues to outside individuals and organizations through various means. This communication may occur through, but is not limited to, the following:

- Contractor orientation training

- Environmental information included in contract documents

- Scheduled contractor meetings

- Project-specific line-up meetings

- Issue-specific public meetings

- Environmental Bulletins

- Television and print media

6.2.2 Gary Complex management receives communications from outside individuals or organizations on the Gary Complex EMS or other environmental issues and refers them to the EMR.

6.2.3 The EMR or designee prepares responses to relevant external communication involving the Gary Complex

EMS and other environmental issues. A record of receiving and responding to the communications, the actions taken, and the decisions reached is documented in the External Communication Log or in issue-specific files of a Technical Services Manager.

6.2.3.1 The EMR or designee shall consult with the Public Affairs Department when responses involve media requests for information and/or other communications.

6.2.3.2 The EMR or designee shall consult with the U. S. Steel Legal Department and/or Environmental Affairs when responses involve legal issues.

6.2.3.3 The EMR or designee must approve any correspondence to regulatory agencies regarding environmental issues.

6.2.3.4 The EMR or designee may issue communications on the Gary Complex EMS or other environmental issues without solicitation by outside individuals/organizations.

6.2.4 If it is deemed necessary to respond to relevant external communications during phone conversations, discussions, or meetings, a record of the issues or responses and decisions reached must be recorded in the External Communication Log or in issue-specific files of a Technical Services Manager.

7.0 Approval

7.1 Approval of this procedure by the Gary Complex Environmental Management System Steering Team is effected by the signature (on the Document Validation Form) of the Manager, Environmental Control that has been designated as the Environmental Management Representative.

7.2 Approved for use.

Manager, Environmental Control and Environmental Management Representative

Delaware North Companies Parks & Resorts
P1400.07—GreenPath Communications
(Effective August 5, 2005)

Policy

Delaware North Companies' GreenPath locations shall maintain procedures for internal GreenPath communications and for receiving, documenting, and acting on communications pertaining to environmental issues with external parties.

Purpose

To describe the procedures and responsibilities for internal GreenPath communications and for receiving, documenting, and responding to relevant communication from external interested parties.

Procedure

Responsibility:

The Environmental Manager, or designee, at each operating location is responsible for internal and external communications related to GreenPath and the location's environmental activities and issues, including addressing and documenting routine incoming and outgoing environmental communications with external parties as described in number 3 of the Process section, below.

Under some circumstances, the responsibility for communications with external parties under various operating conditions may fall to others, as shown in number 2 of the Process section, below.

Policy:

The Environmental Manager, or designee, at each operating location will establish and maintain a procedure for receiving, documenting, and responding to relevant information and requests from interested external parties.

Definitions:

External party—Persons not employed by DNC, including contractors, other business units of Delaware North Companies, government agencies, media, local interest groups, and families of DNC employees.

Internal party—Persons employed by DNC.

Process:

External Communications

1. The Environmental Policy Statement established for DNC is made available to all external parties upon request.

2. Responsibilities for environmental communications with external parties under normal, abnormal, and emergency operations are as follows:

Communication responsibility

External party	Normal operations	Abnormal operations	Emergency operations
Contractor	Environmental Manager/ designee	Environmental Manager/ designee or Unit Manager	Environmental Manager/ designee or Area Emergency Coordinator
Other Delaware North operating location	Environmental Manager/ designee	Environmental Manager/ designee or Unit Manager	Environmental Manager/ designee or Area Emergency Coordinator
Governmental agency	Environmental Manager/ designee	Environmental Manager/ designee or Unit Manager	Environmental Manager/ designee or Area Emergency Coordinator
Media	Environmental Manager/ designee	Media and Public Relations	Media and Public Relations
Local interest group	Environmental Manager/ designee	Media and Public Relations	Media and Public Relations
Employee family member	Environmental Manager/ designee	Media and Public Relations	Media and Public Relations

3. The Environmental Manager/designee is responsible for ensuring that incoming and outgoing environmental communications to interested external parties are addressed and documented in the Environmental Filing System.

- Communications requiring documentation are those that may affect environmental policies and activities and/or have legal or regulatory consequences.

- These communications will be documented on the External Communication Record form. This form may have related documentation attached to it.

- Copies of the documentation of these communications will be filed in a file designated for them, so that they can be reviewed and considered as part of the annual aspects review and subsequent objectives and targets formulation.

4. The Environmental Manager/designee, in consultation with the Director of Environmental Affairs is also responsible for:

   - Managing the preparation and submission of reports on environmental performance, as required by regulations

   - Receiving and responding to questions concerning environmental performance reports, environmental incidents, and so on, submitted by government agencies or other external parties

   - Reporting environmental incidents in accordance with regulatory requirements

   - Seeking environmental approval for new or proposed activities from relevant statutory authorities

5. The significant environmental aspects of GreenPath locations will be made available to the public upon request. The Environmental Manager is authorized to communicate the significant environmental aspects in writing. The analysis of aspects will not be communicated with requesting parties.

Internal Communications

1. The Environmental Manager/designee will ensure that GreenPath information is communicated to DNC associates.

2. The goal of communicating GreenPath to DNC associates is to promote awareness and support of the environmental policy and the environmental management system.

3. The local Environmental Manager will develop a GreenPath Internal Communication Plan.

> • The GreenPath Internal Communication Plan will be reviewed, and updated if necessary, at least annually.

4. The format, frequency, and subject matter of information to be communicated to DNC associates will be determined by the Environmental Manager and/or local management, and may be based on the following:

   • Number of associates

   • Seasonality of operations

   • Physical layout of operations (single-building operation, large geographic area)

   • Complexity of operations and environmental issues

   • Local communication/media technology

5. Subjects of internal communication may include:

   • Significant environmental aspects

   • Environmental management plans

   • Environmental successes and failures

   • The link between associates' environmental duties and the DNC environmental policy statement

   • DNC environmental initiatives

Required documentation:

• F1400.07—External Communication Record form

• GreenPath Internal Communication Plan

Coast Guard Air Station Cape Cod

Air Station Cape Cod has not documented its communication procedures. Internal communication occurs through a variety of methods, including "all hands" meetings, base cable television channel, e-mail, and in-briefs for all new members.

As a member of EPA's National Environmental Performance Track, ASCC is required to submit an annual report to EPA, which is publicly available on the Performance Track Web site. Reports must describe activities conducted to interact with the community on environmental issues and to report publicly on environmental performance.

ASCC's 2004 annual report identified a number of such activities, including:

- Member, Massachusetts Military Reservation Senior Management Board and Civilian Military Advisory Council

- Member, Cape Cod Community College Environmental Advisory Board

- Partner with local communities and Barnstable County Extension Program to conduct household hazardous waste collection events

- Partner with Senior Environmental Corporation to staff the base recycling center on Saturdays to promote recycling in the base community

- Presentations to federal agencies and local government officials on the benefits of implementing an environmental management system and participating in the National Environmental Performance Track program

- Provision of intern positions for environmental students from Massachusetts Maritime Academy and Cape Cod Community College

ASCC interacts with community members through town meetings, news releases, local community cable access channel, and newsletters. ASCC also makes its Performance Track Annual Performance Report available to the public through its Web site.

10

System Documentation

A clear understanding of the intent and structure of an environmental management system is essential for successful execution. Delineating system components and explaining how they work together to create a single, effective approach assists in the transition from planning to practice.

ISO 14001:2004 Text	ISO 14001:1996 Text
4.4.4 Documentation The environmental management system documentation shall include a) the environmental policy, objectives and targets, b) description of the scope of the environmental management system, c) description of the main elements of the environmental management system and their interaction, and reference to related documents, d) documents, including records, required by this International Standard, and	*4.4.4 Environmental management system documentation* The organization shall establish and maintain information, in paper or electronic form, to a) describe the core elements of the management system and their interaction; b) provide direction to related documentation.

Continued

Continued

ISO 14001:2004 Text	ISO 14001:1996 Text
e) documents, including records, determined by the organization to be necessary to ensure the effective planning, operation and control of processes that relate to its significant environmental aspects.	

SIGNIFICANT CHANGES

Changes to this clause are largely for purposes of clarification. ISO 14001:1996 focused on the need to describe the elements of the environmental management system. Other documentation requirements were addressed in different clauses.

ISO 14001:2004 uses this clause to restate the documentation requirements from other clauses in the standard. Reference to a documented environmental policy is found in clause 4.2, objectives and targets in clause 4.3.3, and scope of the environmental management system in clause 4.1.

The revised language informs an organization that documentation must include those documents and records that it needs to successfully implement its environmental management system, in addition to those documents specified in the standard.

The reference to paper or electronic format has been removed. However, section 3.4 defines a document as "information and its supporting medium," and notes that media include "paper, magnetic, electronic or optical computer disc, photograph or master sample, or a combination thereof." Thus, either paper or electronic documentation continues to be acceptable.

INTENT OF ISO 14001:2004

Documentation of an environmental management system can take any form that is useful to an organization. ISO 14001:2004 does not require a single manual, nor does it dictate the kinds of information that should be maintained. Rather, the level of detail should be sufficient to describe the various parts of the environmental management system and how its parts work together.

Documentation does not have to be unique to the environmental management system. Documents created for another purpose can be used. For example, an organization might have in place a procedure for internal communication. Rather than creating a new procedure, an organization can use its existing communication procedure to fulfill the requirement imposed by clause 4.4.3.

Environmental management system documentation can also be integrated with documentation developed for other internal management systems. For example, an organization might combine its quality system (such as ISO 9001:2000) and environmental management system into a single system. In such a situation, documentation would address requirements imposed by both guiding standards.

Most organizations create four levels of documents:

• *System description.* An umbrella document, often in the form of a manual, that provides an overview of the environmental management system and describes how each element of ISO 14001:2004 is being achieved.

The majority of organizations present the environmental management system description, required by paragraph (c), in the form of a manual that is organized to reflect the clause numbers that appear in ISO 14001:2004 (see U. S. Steel Gary Works example at the end of this chapter). However, any method of organization is acceptable. Table 10.1 provides an example of an alternative format.

• *Procedures.* Provide interdepartmental guidance about how the system is implemented. This includes all procedures specified in ISO 14001:2004 plus any additional procedures deemed necessary by an organization (see Chapter 11).

• *Work instructions.* Provide detailed information for individuals. They explain how to perform specific duties by identifying the steps needed to carry out a task, the knowledge and skills required for each step, and the tools, equipment, and materials required for each step.

• Records, reports, and other similar accounts and measures of environmental performance (see Chapter 17).

Table 10.1 EMS manual organized by activity.

Section	Activities	Clauses
I	Scope	4.1
II	Management system	
	A. Policy	4.2
	B. Objectives and goals	4.3.3
	C. Resources	4.4.1
	D. Responsibility and structure	4.4.1
	E. Communication	4.4.3
III	Support activities	
	A. Documentation	4.4.4, 4.4.5
	B. Training	4.4.2
	C. External requirements	4.3.2
	D. Internal requirements	4.4.6
	E. Calibration of equipment	4.5.1
	F. Records	4.5.4
IV	Special considerations	
	A. Environmental aspects and impacts	4.3.1
	B. Emergency preparedness and response	4.4.7
V	Control and improvement	
	A. Monitoring environmental performance	4.5.1
	B. Evaluating regulatory compliance	4.5.2
	C. System audits	4.5.5, 4.5.3
	D. Management review	4.6

EXAMPLES

Selected portions of this documentation appear elsewhere for clarity (for example, environmental policies are presented in Chapter 3). The value of seeing all components of an environmental management system description in context outweighs the minor inconvenience imposed by redundancy.

U. S. Steel Gary Works
EMS Procedure 4.4.4—EMS Documentation
(Effective September 28, 2005)

1.0 Purpose

    1.1 The purpose of this procedure is to describe the development and maintenance of the Gary Complex Environmental Management System (EMS) documentation.

2.0 Scope

    2.1 This procedure applies to the Gary Complex Environmental Management System, the requirements of which are described in the Gary Complex EMS Manual, Procedures, and Work Instructions.

3.0 References

    3.1 ISO 14001:2004 Standard

    3.2 The Gary Complex Environmental Management System Manual

    3.3 The Gary Complex Environmental Management System Procedures 4.2 through 4.6

    3.4 The Gary Complex EMS Documentation Diagram—Exhibit I (page 172)

    3.5 Environmental Requirement Notice (ERN)(70100062FRM)— Exhibit II (page 173)

4.0 Definitions

For the purpose of this procedure, the following definitions shall apply.

    4.1 The Gary Complex Environmental Management System Manual (Level I Documents) describes and summarizes the Gary Complex EMS and is the major basis for compliance with the ISO 14001:2004 standard.

    4.2 The Gary Complex Environmental Management System Procedures (Level II Documents) provide the procedural requirements for the Gary Complex EMS and are consistent with the ISO 14001:2004 standard.

    4.3 Environmental Management Practices (EMPs) are Level III documents used by Environmental Control (and other business units or staff groups, as applicable) to provide specific instructions on environmental compliance requirements.

    4.4 Standard Operating Procedures (SOPs) are Level III documents and provide detailed instructions for the operation of work elements and the control of work activities for process control and environmental control (if applicable) in manufacturing and support activities.

4.5 Standard Maintenance Procedures (SMPs) are Level III documents and are detailed work instructions covering the predictive, preventive, and routine maintenance activities for process control and environmental control (if applicable).

4.6 Safe Job Procedures (SJPs) provide Level III work instructions per 4.4 above and include safety-related requirements.

4.7 Operations Manuals and/or Operating Plans, used for reference purposes, describe the operation of a process or facility and provide guidance for development of detailed work (operating) instructions.

4.8 Environmental Requirement Notice (ERN) is a Level IV document and is used as notification of new or revised environmental requirements (Exhibit II, page 173).

5.0 Responsibilities

5.1 The following job positions have responsibilities in this procedure:

- Environmental Control ISO 14001 Steering Team

- Cross-functional teams (CFTs)

- Business unit area managers

6.0 Procedure

6.1 The ISO 14001 section on the Gary Works Environmental Control home page (www.xxx.com) is the location for various EMS documents. Documents contained on the Web page provide links (when applicable) to supporting EMS documentation. These include the Environmental Preventive/Corrective Action Request (EPCAR) System, Environmental Incident Reporting System, Q5 Audits and Inspection Management System, and process flow diagrams.

6.2 Gary Complex Environmental Management System Manual (Level I Manual)

6.2.1 The EMS scope and activities are described in this manual. The Level I Manual is located on the ISO 14001 Web page under EMS Documents.

6.2.2 The Gary Complex EMS Manual is reviewed annually by the EMR or designee and is revised when required.

Revisions to the previous edition are noted by an asterisk "*" in the left-hand column.

6.3   The Gary Complex Environmental Management System Procedures (Level II Procedures)

   6.3.1   Gary Complex Environmental Management System Procedures provide the interdepartmental requirements needed for an effective environmental management system and are modeled after the ISO 14001 standard. The Level II Procedures are located on the ISO 14001 Web page under EMS Documents.

   6.3.2   EMS Procedure format includes:

Section	Title
1.0	Purpose
2.0	Scope
3.0	Reference
4.0	Definitions
5.0	Responsibilities
6.0	Procedure
7.0	Approval

     6.3.2.1   Section 1.0 contains a clear statement of the procedure intent.

     6.3.2.2   Section 2.0 defines the personnel, organizations, functions, or items affected by the procedure.

     6.3.2.3   Section 3.0 identifies other applicable procedures, documents, and applicable exhibits.

     6.3.2.4   Section 4.0 is a list of unique or special words and terms appropriate to the procedure.

     6.3.2.5   Section 5.0 identifies job positions with responsibilities specified in the procedure.

     6.3.2.6   Section 6.0 is a detailed description of the specific requirements.

6.3.2.7 Section 7.0 contains the signature of the Manager, Environmental Control (EMR) who, representing the EMS Steering Team, officially approves (by signature) the procedures.

6.3.3 The Environmental Control ISO 14001 Steering Team is responsible for developing, reviewing, and maintaining Gary Complex Environmental Management System Procedures, including additions, deletions, and/or changes.

6.3.4 The Gary Complex EMS Procedures are reviewed annually by the EMR or designees and revised when necessary. Revisions to the previous edition will be noted with an asterisk "*" in the left-hand column.

6.3.5 The ISO 14001 Coordinator or designee is responsible for distributing and controlling the Gary Complex Environmental Management System Procedures.

6.3.6 The Gary Complex EMS Procedures are controlled electronically except for the signature copy (paper copy), which is retained by the EMS Document Control Custodian.

6.4 Work Instructions (Level III Documents)

The following work instructions may be found on the Gary Complex Document Management System (www.xxx.com).

6.4.1 Environmental Management Practices (EMPs) are signed (approved) by the ISO 14001 Coordinator or designee. Other managers may approve the practice if identified in the approval section of the practice.

6.4.2 Standard Operating Procedures (SOPs) are signed (approved) by the business unit area manager or designee. Other managers may approve the procedure if identified in the approval portion of the procedure.

6.4.3 Standard Maintenance Procedures (SMPs) are signed (approved) by the business unit area manager or designee. Other managers may approve the procedure if identified in the approval portion of the procedure.

6.5   Level IV documents consist of the following:

   6.5.1   Forms/logs used to record environmental related data/information.

      6.5.1.1   Environmental Regulatory Notice (ERN) is a form used as notification of new or revised environmental requirements. The Area Manager, Environmental Technical Services is responsible for approval and distribution of ERNs.

   6.5.2   Tables are used to communicate necessary environmental related information. Tables that support the EMS located on the ISO 14001 Web page include: Significant Environmental Aspects, Objectives, Targets, Programs and Process Controls, EMS Training Requirements, and the EMS Internal Audit Schedule.

   6.5.3   Environmental Records are any records, electronic or hard copy, that demonstrate conformance with the EMS. Environmental Records are identified on the Environmental Records Retention Schedule (Exhibit III of EMS Procedure 4.5.4—Control of Records).

6.6   Documents of external origin include operating manuals or plans, permits, agreements, or other documents that are used for reference and/or provide guidance for the development of detailed work instructions.

6.7   To assist the reader in understanding the Gary Complex Environmental Management System, an EMS Documentation Diagram is attached (Exhibit I).

7.0   Approval

   7.1   Approval of this procedure by the Gary Complex Environmental Management System Steering Team is effected by the signature (on the Document Validation Form) of the Manager, Environmental Control that has been designated as the Environmental Management Representative.

   7.2   Approved for use.

   Manager, Environmental Control and Environmental Management Representative

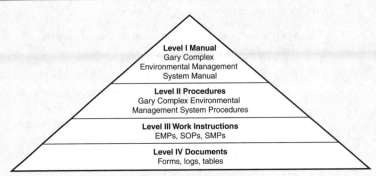

EMS documentation diagram

Gary Complex Environmental Related Work Instructions (Level III Documents)

- *Environmental Management Practices (EMPs)* are documents used by the Environmental Control Division (and other business units, as applicable) to provide specific instructions on environmental compliance requirements. EMPs are issued and controlled by the Environmental Control Department.

- *Standard Operating Procedures (SOPs)* provide detailed instructions for the operation of work elements and the control of work activities for process control and environmental control (if applicable) in manufacturing and support activities. SOPs are issued and controlled by the originating business unit and/or staff organization.

- *Safety Operating Procedures (SOPs)* are standard operating procedures that also contain safety-related issues.

- *Standard Maintenance Procedures (SMPs)* are detailed work instructions covering the predictive, preventive, and routine maintenance activities for process control and environmental control. SMPs are issued and controlled by the originating business unit and/or staff organization.

Gary Complex Environmental Related Level IV Documents

- *Forms/logs.* Forms and logs (for example, Environmental Requirement Notices [ERNs]) are used and completed by the user to provide information. Forms and logs must have a unique identification number and revision date and are controlled by the issuing organization.

- *Tables.* A table contains information employees use to complete a task and are controlled by the issuing organization. Tables must have a unique identification number, issue date, and, if applicable, a revision date. When applicable, paper copies are stamped in red ink indicating that the copy is controlled.

Exhibit I   EMS Procedure 4.4.4.

EMS PROCEDURE 4.4.4—
ENVIRONMENTAL REQUIREMENT NOTICE

1.0   Purpose

State purpose for notification: "This provides notification of a (regulatory or other) requirement that may impact operations at facilities that . . ."

2.0   Background

Provide background of requirement:

* Provide the status of requirement, proposed rule, final rule, consent decree item, agreed order item, voluntary agreement, and so on.

* Provide a summary of the requirement

* Provide critical compliance dates

3.0   Impact on Operations

Preliminary evaluation of significance of requirement:

* List potentially affected operations

* Summarize potential impacts to operations

* Evaluate current compliance status with requirement

4.0   Compliance Performance

Provide an evaluation of current compliance performance of the affected operations/process equipment using the requirements (above) as the compliance standard: "The (affected operations/ process equipment) is currently in (compliance or noncompliance) with the regulatory requirement."

5.0   Recommendations

Provide recommendations (action items) to ensure compliance with requirement:

* No action required, current compliance status is satisfactory

* Develop Compliance Action Plan

* Modifications to equipment and/or work practices

* Conduct evaluations to determine compliance approach

Exhibit II   EMS Procedure 4.4.4.   *Continued*

Continued

Action Items	Responsibility	Target completion date(s)
1)		
2)		
3)		
4)		

6.0 Responsibility for Compliance

Identify the position titles that are responsible for ensuring compliance with the requirement.

7.0 Contact

Identify environmental control manager(s) assigned the responsibility for compliance with the requirement.

8.0 Approval

Approved for distribution and use.

_____

Area Manager
Environmental and Program Services

9.0 Notice Distribution

Environmental
Compliance Manager: _____ Date: _____

Business Unit Manager: _____ Date: _____

10.0 Returned To

Area Manager
Environmental and
Program Services: _____ Date: _____

11.0 Action Item Completion

Action item number	Completion date
1	
2	
3	
4	

Exhibit II EMS Procedure 4.4.4.

U. S. Steel Gary Works
Gary Complex Level I System Manual
(Effective November 8, 2005)

This Level I Manual summarizes the Gary Complex Environmental Management System (EMS) through descriptions of Level II EMS administrative procedures.

The manual was reviewed by the EMS Steering Team and approved by the Manager, Environmental Control who was designated as the Environmental Management Representative. Approval is denoted by the presence of the EMR's signature on an accompanying Document Validation Form.

_____ (signed)

Manager, Environmental Control and Environmental Management Representative

Environmental Management System Scope

The U. S. Steel Gary Complex consists of the integrated operations of Gary Works in Gary, Indiana, the East Chicago, Indiana Tin and Pickling facilities, and the finishing and support operations at the Midwest Plant in Portage, Indiana. Combined, the Gary Complex manufactures various forms of steel. The processes include coke making and by-product recovery, ironmaking and sintering, steel slabs, hot and cold rolled steel sheet, galvanized steel, tin plate and tin-free steel, and black plate products.

Excluding RCRA Corrective Action, all other activities related to production, operation, and environmental management are subject to the ISO 14001:2004 standard.

Definitions:

1. *EMS* is an acronym for the Environmental Management System

2. *EMR* is an acronym for Environmental Management Representative

3. *CFT* is an acronym for cross-functional team

4. *Gary Complex* refers to the Gary Works Facility, the East Chicago Tin and Pickle Facilities, and the Midwest Plant.

5. *Gary Complex EMS Steering Team* comprises the Gary Works General Manager (chairman of the team), plant managers, business unit and staff managers, and the EMR. The EMS Steering Team is equivalent to what the ISO 14001:2004 standard refers to as "top management."

6. *Environmental Control ISO 14001 Steering Team* comprises the Manager, Environmental Control (also the EMR and chairman of the team), the Area Manager, Environmental Technical Services, the Area Manager, Environmental Compliance, the ISO 14001 Coordinator, and the EMS Document Custodian.

7. Environmental Control ISO 14001 intranet Web page is used to organize and maintain EMS information and documentation. This Web page is located at www.xxx.

Environmental Management System

4.1 General Requirements (No EMS Procedure)

4.2 Environmental Policy (See EMS Procedure 4.2)

The Gary Complex EMS Steering Team (top management) defined, documented, implemented, approved, and maintains the Gary Complex Environmental Policy. The Gary Complex Environmental Policy is contained in EMS Procedure 4.2—Environmental Policy. The Environmental Policy is posted throughout the Gary Complex and is available on the Gary Complex intranet site and USS Web site. All Gary Complex employees receive training on the Environmental Policy.

4.3 Planning

4.3.1 Environmental Aspects (See EMS Procedure 4.3.1)

The Gary Complex maintains EMS Procedure 4.3.1 (Environmental Aspects) to identify the environmental aspects of its activities, products, or services that can have impacts on the environment.

Process flow diagrams, the Environmental Aspect Inventory, and evaluation worksheets are utilized in aspect evaluations to determine which environmental aspects have significant impacts on the environment. Environmental aspect information is available on the Environmental Control ISO 14001 Web page.

4.3.2 Legal and Other Requirements (See EMS Procedure 4.3.2)

The Gary Complex maintains EMS Procedure 4.3.2 (Legal and Other Requirements) that describes the process of identifying legal and other requirements applicable to the Gary Complex.

Identified requirements are documented on the List of Legal and Other Requirements. The list is reviewed at least annually to ensure its accuracy. This list is an exhibit to the EMS procedure, available on the Environmental Control ISO 14001 Web page.

4.3.3   Objectives, Targets, and Programs (See EMS Procedure 4.3.3)

The Gary Complex maintains documented environmental objectives, targets, and associated programs for significant and selected environmental aspects. Objective, target, and program information is maintained on the Environmental Control ISO 14001 Web page. Conformance with established objectives, targets, and programs is evaluated through quarterly internal EMS audits.

4.4   Implementation and Operation

4.4.1   Resources, Roles, Responsibility, and Authority (See EMS Procedure 4.4.1)

The Gary Complex defines, documents, and communicates the roles, responsibilities, and authorities necessary for employees to effectively implement and maintain the EMS. The Gary Complex provides the resources (technological, financial, and human— including specialized skills) essential for establishing, implementing, and controlling the EMS. Roles, responsibilities, and authorities are contained in EMS Level II Procedures available on the Environmental Control ISO 14001 Web page.

4.4.2   Competence, Training, and Awareness (See EMS Procedure 4.4.2)

The Gary Complex identifies the training needs for all Gary Complex employees and for applicable contractor/ supplier personnel. Environmental Management System training features the following topics:

• Gary Works Environmental Policy

- Roles and responsibilities

- Benefits of following established procedures

- Emergency response

- Level III Work Instructions for significant environmental aspects

Required training for personnel whose work assignments (tasks) can cause significant environmental impacts are located on the Training Needs section of the Environmental Control ISO 14001 Web page.

4.4.3   Communication (See EMS Procedure 4.4.3)

The Gary Complex maintains EMS Procedure 4.4.3 (Communication) to ensure that EMS information is effectively communicated throughout the Gary Complex and that relevant external communications are properly managed. These communications are recorded in the electronic ISO 14001 External Communication Log.

4.4.4   Documentation (See EMS Procedure 4.4.4)

The Gary Complex maintains a procedure that describes the various environmental management system documents. EMS documentation includes:

- EMS Manual (Level I Document) that describes conformance to the requirements of the ISO 14001:2004 Standard.

- EMS Procedures (Level II Documents) that provide the requirements needed for an effective EMS.

- Work Instructions (Level III Documents) that provide detailed information and requirements for a specific work activity.

- Forms, logs, and tables (Level IV Documents). Forms and logs are used to record information about an activity and/or process. Tables provide requirements and/or necessary information.

Many EMS documents are located on the Environmental Control ISO 14001 Web page.

4.4.5   Control of Documents (See EMS Procedure 4.4.5)

The Gary Complex maintains EMS Procedure 4.4.5 (Control of Documents) to create, modify, establish responsibilities for, and control all documents that are required by the Gary Complex EMS. This ensures that EMS documents are managed in accordance with the Gary Complex requirements.

4.4.6   Operational Control (See EMS Procedure 4.4.6)

The Gary Complex identifies the operations and activities associated with significant environmental aspects to ensure that they are performed in accordance with Gary Complex requirements. Operational Control work instructions are identified on the Training Needs section of the Environmental Control ISO 14001 Web page.

4.4.7   Emergency Preparedness and Response (See EMS Procedure 4.4.7)

The Gary Complex maintains EMS Procedure 4.4.7 (Emergency Preparedness and Response) and the Integrated Contingency Plan (ICP), which identify the potential for and response to accidents and emergencies in order to prevent and mitigate the associated environmental impacts.

The ICP serves as the primary emergency-planning document at the Gary Complex. Selected sections of the ICP are available on the Environmental Control Web site.

4.5   Checking and Corrective Action

4.5.1   Monitoring and Measurement (See EMS Procedure 4.5.1)

The Gary Complex maintains EMS Procedure 4.5.1 (Monitoring and Measurement) that defines how the key environmental characteristics of Gary Complex operations/activities are monitored and measured. Monitoring and measuring includes recording information to track environmental performance. Calibration and maintenance records, for equipment monitoring key characteristics, are appropriately retained. Monitoring and measurement information is maintained on the Objectives and Targets section of the Environmental Control ISO 14001 Web page.

4.5.2 Evaluation of Compliance (See EMS Procedure 4.5.2)

The Gary Complex maintains EMS Procedure 4.5.2 (Evaluation of Compliance) that describes the methods utilized to determine compliance with the Gary Complex legal and other requirements. Evaluation of compliance includes daily monitoring of environmental performance, internal EMS audits, and periodic USS corporate environmental audits. A compliance summary for the Gary Complex is maintained on the Environmental Control Daily Report of Operations (DRO) on the Gary Works home page.

4.5.3 Nonconformity, Corrective Action, and Preventive Action (See EMS Procedure 4.5.3)

The Gary Complex maintains EMS Procedure 4.5.3 (Nonconformity, Corrective Action, and Preventive Action) that defines the responsibility and authority for handling and investigating nonconformances, takes action to mitigate any impacts caused by the nonconformance, and effects preventive/corrective action. Environmental Preventive/Corrective Action Requests (EPCARs) are used to document implemented preventive/corrective actions. EPCARs are available on the Gary Works home page.

4.5.4 Control of Records (See EMS Procedure 4.5.4)

The Gary Complex maintains EMS Procedure 4.5.4 (Control of Records) for the management of environmental records. Environmental Record Control Custodians are appointed to help ensure that environmental records are managed in accordance with the EMS Procedure. A list of environmental records is maintained as an exhibit to the EMS procedure, available on the Environmental Control ISO 14001 Web page.

4.5.5 Internal Audit (See EMS Procedure 4.5.5)

The Gary Complex maintains EMS Procedure 4.5.5 (Internal Audit) that defines a comprehensive audit program. EMS audits provide a systematic examination of conformance with the requirements of the Gary Complex Environmental Management System. Internal audit information is available in the EMS Audits section of the Environmental Control ISO 14001 Web page.

4.6 Management Review(See EMS Procedure 4.6)

The Gary Complex maintains EMS Procedure 4.6 (Management Review) that describes the management review process for the Gary Complex. Management review is conducted to ensure the continuing suitability, adequacy, and effectiveness of the EMS. The ISO 14001 Coordinator maintains management review meeting minutes.

Delaware North Companies Parks & Resorts
P1400.01—GreenPath Introduction and Summary
(Effective September 1, 2005)

Policy

The environmental programs of Delaware North Companies (DNC) are collectively managed within a process and philosophy we call GreenPath.

Purpose

Section 1.0 Introduction

The Environmental Management System policies and procedures have been developed to conform to the standards of ISO 14001, the Environmental Management System Standard established by the International Organization for Standardization (ISO). The manual describes the core elements of the DNC Environmental Management System (EMS) and describes where additional related documentation can be found.

ISO 14001 identifies EMS requirements, which assist an organization in developing an environmental policy and environmental objectives to respond to an organization's significant environmental aspects. DNC has based GreenPath and our EMS on ISO 14001 to accomplish the following:

- Implement, maintain, and improve environmental management activities at designated DNC GreenPath operations

- Assure conformance with DNC environmental policies and with other environmental requirements to which our organization subscribes, including National Park Service (NPS) and other client requirements

- Demonstrate such conformance to other interested parties
- Seek certification/registration of the EMS by external accrediting organizations

The EMS established by DNC is a tool to assist management with efforts to control environmental performance. The EMS is reviewed periodically to identify opportunities for improvement.

Section 2.0 Environmental Policy

The corporate Environmental Policy is the foundation for the EMS at each GreenPath location. The Environmental Policy summarizes the intentions and principles of our organization with respect to environmental management, and commits DNC to continual environmental improvement, pollution prevention, compliance with relevant environmental regulations and laws, and consistency with other environmental requirements subscribed to by our organization. Additionally, the Environmental Policy forms the basis for the establishment of environmental objectives and targets.

The Director of Environmental Affairs is responsible for the implementation of the Environmental Policy and a periodic review to ensure continued relevance. The Environmental Policy is posted in prominent locations throughout our operating locations, is available to the public, and is included in the EMS policies and procedures.

Procedure

Section 3.0 Manual Administration

The Environmental Management System policies and procedures summarize the core components of the DNC environmental program. The EMS policies and procedures are reviewed periodically to ensure continued relevance and are modified to reflect changes to work practices at each operating location. Administration of the EMS policies and procedures is the responsibility of the Director of Environmental Affairs and the President/ General Manager, or a designee, at each operating location. (For the purpose of this manual, the on-site person responsible for local environmental issues will be referred to as the Environmental Manager.) Final approval of the manual is the responsibility of the Director of Environmental Affairs.

The EMS policies and procedures are implemented and maintained by the Director of Environmental Affairs through the use of controlled online procedures, which can be found on the DNC portal by accessing "The GreenPath Community" at www.xxx. Hard copies may be printed and used in the field, but they are considered uncontrolled documents. Users of uncontrolled copies of the EMS policies and procedures are to refer to controlled online procedures to ensure accuracy.

Section 4.0 Environmental Management System Components

A. Planning

Legal and Other Requirements. Process for identification, access, and evaluation of legal and other requirements applicable to environmental issues at each operating location is in place. The procedures ensure that legal and other requirements are periodically reviewed for compliance and accuracy.

The primary environmental legal requirements that apply to the operating locations are implemented through permits issued by local, state, and federal regulatory agencies. The operating location Environmental Managers ensure regulatory compliance with these permits through periodic communication with personnel at the regulatory agencies (for example, permitting and licensing process, on-site visits). The Environmental Managers identify other regulatory issues that may apply to operating locations by:

- Subscribing to publications that summarize current and proposed regulations

- Attending environmental association meetings and/or seminars that address regulatory issues

- Online search of environmental Web sites, including regulatory agency Web sites

- Other appropriate means

The Environmental Manager is responsible for evaluation and review of legal and other requirements. The Director of Environmental Affairs shares information with operations personnel and works in concert with DNC corporate staff as necessary to prioritize action items and track emerging regulatory issues.

A procedure that describes how Environmental Managers identify legal and other requirements and a summary of the applicable environmental regulatory issues are in the Environmental Management Procedures as P1400.03.

Environmental Aspects. ISO 14001 defines an environmental aspect as "an element of an organization's activities, products or services which can interact with the environment."

A procedure has been established and maintained to identify environmental aspects related to DNC activities, products, and services.

Environmental aspects are developed from standardized protocols, prioritized within the EMS, and kept up to date. Environmental aspects aid in identifying significant environmental issues at operating locations and are considered in setting environmental objectives and targets.

P1400.02, included in the EMS policies and procedures, describes the environmental aspect identification process in additional detail.

Objectives and Targets. Each GreenPath location maintains documented environmental objectives and targets. Objectives and targets are established and reviewed to consider legal and other requirements, significant environmental aspects, technological options, financial, operational, and business requirements, and views of interested parties. Environmental objectives and targets are consistent with the Environmental Policy.

Environmental Management Programs. Each GreenPath location maintains procedures for achieving established objectives and targets. The procedures designate responsibility for achieving objectives and targets and identify the means and time frames by which objectives and targets are to be achieved.

The Director of Environmental Affairs and/or operating location Environmental Managers develop and maintain procedures to achieve established environmental objectives and targets. The procedures accommodate new or modified activities and specify roles, responsibilities, and time frames for achievement of objectives and targets.

As new processes or services are implemented at each operating location, the Director of Environmental Affairs and/or operating location Environmental Managers evaluate the need for additional environmental management procedures. If required, additional environmental management procedures will be established that identify the actions to be taken, to whom the actions are assigned, and the time frame in which the actions need to be accomplished.

Environmental Managers and the Director of Environmental Affairs monitor environmental management activities to ensure that the established objectives and targets are met. Results are evaluated to confirm achievement of environmental objectives and targets.

Management procedures established to achieve objectives and targets are maintained as controlled documents and are kept on file by local environmental managers.

B. Implementation and Operation

Structure and Responsibility. Environmental Managers/designees at each operating location are responsible for ensuring that employees are aware of their responsibilities for implementation of the EMS.

Resources required to implement and control the EMS are made available by DNC management. These resources include, but are not limited to, human resources, knowledge of specialized skills, technology, and financial resources.

Environmental duties for personnel responsible for the EMS and environmental accountabilities are summarized in the EMS policies and procedures in P1400.04.

Training, Awareness, and Competence. Operating location employees and contractors performing tasks that could have a significant impact on the environment must demonstrate job performance competence. Competence is based on appropriate levels of education, training, and/or experience. If necessary, local procedures are established and maintained to identify and complete training requirements. Both legal and operational training needs are addressed.

A training needs matrix has been developed to summarize the types of training required to adequately complete job responsibilities identified in the EMS. This matrix is included in the EMS policies and procedures as P1400.04.

Communication. The EMS addresses both internal and external communications. EMS communications at DNC GreenPath locations involve proactive communications, as well as organized processes for receipt, documentation, and response to inquiries pertaining to environmental issues.

Internal communications include EMS training per the EMS policies and procedures and EMS performance reporting to top management, as well as other communication necessary to implement and maintain the EMS. EMS performance reporting and communication are accomplished through written report from the Environmental Managers to top operations executives and through the annual management review of the EMS. Communication with operations personnel is handled through press releases, company newsletters and publications, payroll notices, and meetings.

Communication with outside parties includes responses to individual inquiries and dissemination of the Environmental Policy to interested parties upon request. P1400.07, External Communications, is included as part of the EMS policies and procedures.

Environmental Management System Documentation. The Director of Environmental Affairs is responsible for the establishment of the EMS and periodic review of the system to ensure continued relevance.

This document, P1400.01, describes the core elements of DNC's environmental programs, and describes where additional related documentation can be found. Documentation developed to support the EMS includes environmental policies, EMS procedures, environmental management programs, forms, and related documents. The EMS policies and procedures are electronically controlled on the DNC Web site. Other related documents are available in the director's office files and in appropriate operating location departments.

Document Control. EMS documents are clearly named, legible, dated, readily identifiable, maintained in an orderly manner, and retained for an identified time period. Procedures ensure that documents are available, revised, reviewed, and current.

Obsolete external documents are retained as required by government/company regulations. Obsolete internal documents (for example, procedures, programs) are retained in hard copy form in files as necessary. Electronic copies of obsolete internal documents are not retained. Additionally, procedures are maintained concerning the creation and modification of EMS documents.

P1400.08 addressing document control is included in the EMS policies and procedures.

Operational Control. Environmental Managers at each operating location are responsible for identification of operations and activities associated with significant environmental aspects identified for the location. The Environmental Managers ensure that employees are aware of their environmental responsibilities.

Documented procedures are in place to cover situations where the absence of such documentation could compromise the Environmental Policy or other environmental performance objectives.

A basic written operational control procedure for hazardous waste management is included as P1400.05 in the EMS policies and procedures. Each location is authorized to create its own site-specific hazardous waste management plan. Other operational controls are maintained at DNC operating locations.

Emergency Preparedness and Response. Each GreenPath location maintains procedures to identify the potential for accidents/emergency situations and has plans to respond to these situations. Based on these plans, DNC has developed programs to prevent such events from occurring and to mitigate environmental impacts from any occurrences. These plans are reviewed/revised as necessary and tested periodically, as practicable. When needed, the plans address emissions to air, land, and water, and impacts to site-specific ecosystems.

The Environmental Manager at each GreenPath location is responsible for periodically reviewing the emergency preparedness and response programs to ensure continued applicability. The programs may consider abnormal operating conditions that could occur, and establishes roles, responsibilities, and authorities assigned to personnel that respond to emergencies.

C. Checking and Corrective Action

Monitoring and Measurement. DNC maintains procedures to monitor and measure key operational characteristics that can significantly impact the environment. Operational control procedures are used to control, monitor, and/or measure performance of the EMS. Information is collected to track performance of relevant operational controls and conformance with environmental objectives and targets.

Each DNC GreenPath location maintains a documented procedure describing the periodic evaluation of compliance with relevant environmental laws and regulations. This is included in the EMS policies and procedures as P1400.10.

Nonconformance and Corrective and Preventive Action. Procedures exist to respond to nonconformances with the requirements of the EMS. The procedures address mitigation of environmental impacts and completion of corrective and preventive measures as required by the magnitude of the impacts encountered. Changes to the existing EMS from implemented corrective and/or preventive actions are recorded.

P1400.06 addressing nonconformance and corrective and preventive actions is included in the EMS policies and procedures.

Records. DNC GreenPath locations maintain procedures for identification, maintenance, and disposition of EMS records. These procedures focus on records needed to implement and operate the EMS and on accomplishment of environmental objectives and targets.

Records are legible, identifiable, and traceable to the activities, products, or services associated with the activity. Records are stored safely, are readily retrievable, and have established retention times. The records are maintained to demonstrate conformance with regulatory requirements and other standards, including NPS and ISO 14001 standards. Training records and the results of audits and reviews are included in EMS records.

P1400.09, Records Management Procedures, is included in the EMS policies and procedures.

Environmental Management System Audit. DNC maintains programs and procedures for auditing the EMS. Audits evaluate compliance with ISO 14001 and NPS requirements and are reporting tools used to update the top operations executive at each operating location on the status of the EMS.

Audits are scheduled periodically to ensure that the entire EMS is covered on an annual basis. Audits focus on the environmental importance of the activities and results from previous audits. Audit procedures cover audit scope, frequency, methodology, reporting, responsibilities, and requirements for conducting audits.

Audits are performed by the Director of Environmental Affairs, operating location employees, and/or by outside persons. Auditing methods ensure that audits are accomplished in an impartial and objective fashion.

P1400.11 addresses EMS audits undertaken by DNC operating locations. This procedure is included in the EMS policies and procedures.

D. Management Review

Top management at each DNC GreenPath location reviews and evaluates the EMS on both a formal and an informal basis. The EMS audit process represents a formal component of the EMS management review. EMS audits consider:

- Results from past EMS audits

- Consistency with the Corporate Environmental Policy

- Progress toward objectives and targets

- EMS scope in light of changes to location operations

- Identified concerns among relevant interested parties

Results from auditing activities are documented, and necessary actions are noted and implemented.

Informal reviews of the EMS are ongoing. Environmental projects are updated and discussed with top management as required. Nonroutine, emergency environmental situations are reported to top management for immediate evaluation.

P1400.12 addresses management review activities undertaken at DNC operating locations. This procedure is included in the EMS policies and procedures.

Coast Guard Air Station Cape Cod
Environmental Management System
(Effective May 6, 2003)

Table of Contents

Overview. 189
Environmental Policy Statement 190
Definitions 190
Organization. 192
Legal Requirements 193
Environmental Aspects and Impacts 194
Objectives and Targets 194
Environmental Programs 194
Documentation 194
Training, Awareness, and Competence. 195

Overview

Coast Guard Air Station Cape Cod was commissioned August 29, 1970, and is located on the Military Reservation in Massachusetts along with three Department of Defense counterparts. It is the second-largest unit in the U.S. Coast Guard, with 1.9 million square feet of building space encompassing over 1400 acres of land. In addition, Air Station Cape Cod serves as the single largest local housing authority within the Coast Guard and is responsible for the administration, maintenance, and well-being of 690 family housing units and over 2200 residents of the military housing community, serving all four of the armed services. The population generally consists of 300 active duty personnel, 2000 family members in the area, 230 civilians, and three elementary schools.

The Station's primary mission is search and rescue, which involves protection of life and property in the offshore areas from the Canadian border to Long Island. The Station also plays a major role in maritime law enforcement, fisheries enforcement patrols, marine environmental protection, international ice patrols, drug interdiction, and logistics support for many offshore lighthouses in New England.

Air Station Cape Cod's environmental philosophy is simple: it makes economic sense, is ethically responsible, and is applicable to both operational forces as well as the housing community. The environmental program's roots can be traced to a cultural change beginning in 1993 and continuing today. The Station's environmental program concentrates on three main areas of emphasis: hazardous material and waste minimization, recycling and affirmative procurement, and natural resource protection.

In summary, Air Station Cape Cod is a model federal facility for environmental awareness, improvement, and compliance integrated into the performance of our operations. From abatement of asbestos-containing building materials, removal of lead-based paint and mini blinds, to the replacement of all polychlorinated biphenyl (PCB)–oil-filled equipment, Air Station Cape Cod practices a holistic approach to environmental responsibility. Our success is due to the dedicated efforts of the staff and the cultural change we have enacted in all our operations. Environmental concern is the standard and not the exception. We are committed to continuously improving our process and operating a leaner, cleaner, greener Air Station.

Environmental Policy Statement

As the world's premier maritime service and steward of our nation's marine environment, our goal is to manage the land, sea, and air resources under our cognizance in an environmentally responsible manner. The preservation of marine biodiversity and the prevention of marine ecosystem degradation from land-based activities, including our own, is central to our environmental efforts.

We will comply with all applicable environmental regulations. Operations shall be planned and executed to reduce or eliminate the potential for pollution and waste of the Earth's limited resources. We will work aggressively, in partnership with federal, state, and local agencies, environmental interest groups, and private industry, to provide for long-term environmental quality and improvement. Our environmental program will focus on marine emergency preparedness, marine transportation management, environmental law, environmental justice, pollution response, and internal programs of compliance and restoration.

Our goal is to be the world's leader in maritime environmental stewardship. Protecting the environment is inherent in every mission and operation at Air Station Cape Cod. The leadership of all personnel at Air Station Cape Cod is expected to execute this policy.

Definitions

Continual improvement—The process of enhancing the environmental management system to achieve improvements in overall environmental performance in line with the organization's environmental policy. (Note: The process need not take place in all areas of activity simultaneously.)

Environment—Surroundings in which an organization operates, including air, water, land, natural resources, flora, fauna, humans, and their interrelation. (Note: Surroundings in this context extend from within an organization to the global system.)

Environmental aspect—Element of an organization's activities, products, or services that can interact with the environment.

Environmental impact—Any change to the environment, whether adverse or beneficial, wholly or partially resulting from an organization's activities, products, or services.

Environmental Management System—The part of the overall management system that includes organizational structure, planning activities, responsibilities, practices, procedures, processes, and resources for developing, implementing, achieving, reviewing, and maintaining the environmental policy.

Environmental Management System audit—A systematic and documented verification process of objectively obtaining and evaluating evidence to determine whether an organization's environmental management system conforms to the environmental management system audit set by the organization and for communication of the results of this process to management.

Environmental Management System manual—Describes the environmental management system in accordance with the stated environmental policy, objectives, and applicable standards.

Environmental objective—Overall environmental goal, arising from the environmental policy, that an organization sets itself to achieve, and which is quantified where practicable.

Environmental performance—Measurable results of the environmental management system, related to an organization's control of its environmental aspects, based on its environmental policy, objectives, and targets.

Environmental Policy—Statement by the organization of its intentions and principles in relation to its overall environmental performance, which provides a framework for action and for the setting of its environmental objectives and targets.

Environmental target—Detailed performance requirement, quantified where practicable, applicable to the organization or parts thereof, that arises from the environmental objectives and needs to be set and met in order to achieve those objectives.

Hazardous material—A material that has one or more of the following characteristics: (1) a flash point below 140°F, closed cup, or is subject to spontaneous heating, (2) a threshold limit value below 500 ppm for gases and vapors, below 500 mg/m^3 for fumes, and below 25 mppcf (million particles per cubic foot) for dust, (3) a single dose oral LD_{50} below 50 mg/kg, (4) is subject to polymerization with the release of large amounts of energy, (5) is a strong oxidizing or reducing agent, (6) causes first-degree burns to skin from short duration exposure or is systematically toxic through skin contact, or (7) in the course of normal operations, may produce dusts, gases, fumes, vapors, mists, or smokes that have one or more of the above characteristics.

Hazardous Materials Response (Hazmat) Team—An organized group of employees, designated by the employer, who are expected to perform work to handle and control actual or potential leaks or spills of hazardous substances requiring possible close approach to the substance. The team members perform responses to releases or potential releases of hazardous substances for the purpose of control or stabilization of the incident.

Interested party—Individual or group concerned with or affected by the environmental performance of an organization.

Prevention of pollution—Use of processes, practices, materials, or products that avoid, reduce, or control pollution, which may include recycling, treatment, process changes, control mechanisms, efficient use of resources, and material substitution.

Procedures—Describes what activities are, who does them, and when, where, and why they are performed.

Significant—Determined by the USCG–ASCC as important in the consideration of the organization's environmental policy and in accordance with agreed-upon criteria.

Records—Documents, chronicles, archives, worksheets, or checklists that keep an account of and provide objective evidence of activities being carried out stemming from the Environmental Management System.

Waste—Any material resulting from industrial, commercial, mining, or agricultural operations, or from community activities, that is discarded, or is being accumulated, stored, or physically, chemically, thermally, or biologically treated prior to being discarded, recycled, or discharged.

Organization

By identifying key players and their responsibilities, each person is made aware of what influence they will have with regard to environmental stewardship and how it will affect their workload. Specific job descriptions of top management, the EH&S department, and other key players' roles and responsibilities are located in Coast Guard Air Station Cape Cod's

Organizational Manual (AIRSTAINST M5500.1 [series]). A basic overview of the EH&S department and job descriptions is also provided in this
manual. The job descriptions provided below* expand on the individual's
role with regard to environmental stewardship. In any conflict between the
organizational charts, the following is the leading authority.

Legal Requirements

In order to ensure compliance with state and federal rules and regulations,
a complete list of all regulations that are relevant for each division has been
generated. By compiling this list, each supervisor is aware of what they
must comply with. It also improves communication for other employees
that would otherwise not be aware of regulations.

Occupational Safety and Health Act

Clean Air Act

Clean Water Act

Comprehensive Environmental Response, Compensation, and
Liability Act

The Federal Insecticide, Fungicide, and Rodenticide Act

Medical Wastes Tracking Act of 1988

The Noise Control Act of 1972

The Ocean Dumping Reform Act of 1988

The Radiation Control for Health and Safety Act

Resource Conservation and Recovery Act (as enforced by 310
CMR 30)

Safe Drinking Water Act

The Toxic Substance Control Act

National Environmental Policy Act

Federal Facilities Compliance Act

Above Ground Storage Tank Regulations

Underground Injection Well Program

---

* This section is presented in its entirety in Chapter 7 (see pages 112–22);
therefore, it is not reproduced here.

Air Installation Compatible Use Zone (Air Force Instruction)

Cross Connection Control Program (310 CMR 22.22)

B-Well

Consumer–Patient Radiation Health and Safety Act

Emergency Planning and Community Right to Know Act

Environmental Aspects and Impacts

Procedures have been established to identify the environmental aspects of Air Station Cape Cod's activities that can be controlled or at a minimum can have an influence, in order to determine those that have or can have significant impacts on the environment. The aspects related to significant impacts will be considered in setting environmental objectives (see Procedure 01).

Objectives and Targets

Concurrent with procedures addressing environmental aspects and impacts, procedures also have been developed for addressing objectives and targets at each relevant function and level within the organization. The objectives and targets have been made consistent with the environmental policy (see Procedure 06).

Environmental Programs

The Environmental Management Programs are the actual methods that are used to achieve the objectives and targets. Each environmental program details the objective and how the target will be reached. Each program is named and how it relates to the environmental policy is described. Then the target is specified along with the time frame in which it should be reached. The responsible parties and the action to be taken are listed. The implementation of these programs provides details of how each goal was reached (see Procedure 06).

Documentation

An important part of the Environmental Management System is documentation. Documentation can be broken into three components: a description of the Environmental Management System—the policy, procedures, and environmental records; a record of aspects, objectives, targets, and training records; and document retention policy and document control.

Air Station Cape Cod has developed a core document, the Environmental Management System (this document) with all necessary information for each division. Each department then has its own manual, as appropriate, with associated documents (procedures and work practices) for that division only.

Document record keeping and retention is addressed in Procedure 03 and document control is addressed in Procedure 07.

Training, Awareness, and Competence

Procedures have been established to identify the organization's training needs to make employees at relevant functions and levels aware of the importance of conformance with the environmental policy and procedures, significant environmental impacts, their roles and responsibilities in achieving conformance, and the consequences of departure from specified operating procedures (see Procedure 04).

11

Control of Documents

To encourage a focus on effective environmental management and improved environmental performance, ISO 14001:2004 imposes relatively few requirements for documents. Once an organization determines what documents will be necessary, it is important to handle them in a manner that ensures they are appropriate for their intended purpose and available where needed.

ISO 14001:2004 Text	ISO 14001:1996 Text
4.4.5 Control of documents	*4.4.5 Document control*
Documents required by the environmental management system and by this International Standard shall be controlled. Records are a special type of document and shall be controlled in accordance with the requirements given in 4.5.4.	The organization shall establish and maintain procedures for controlling all documents required by this International Standard to ensure that
The organization shall establish, implement and maintain a procedure(s) to	a) they can be located;
a) approve documents for adequacy prior to issue,	b) they are periodically reviewed, revised as necessary and approved for adequacy by authorized personnel;
b) review and update as necessary and re-approve documents,	c) the current versions of relevant documents are available at all locations where operations essential to the effective

Continued

Continued

ISO 14001:2004 Text	ISO 14001:1996 Text
c) ensure that changes and the current revision status of documents are identified,	functioning of the environ-mental management system are performed.
d) ensure that relevant versions of applicable documents are available at points of use,	d) obsolete documents are promptly removed from all points of issue and points of use or otherwise assured against unintended use;
e) ensure that documents remain legible and readily identifiable,	e) any obsolete documents retained for legal and/or knowledge preservation purposes are suitably identified.
f) ensure that documents of external origin determined by the organization to be necessary for the planning and operation of the environ-mental management system are identified and their distribution controlled, and	Documentation shall be legible, dated (with dates of revision), and readily identifiable, maintained in an orderly manner and retained for a specified period. Procedures and responsibilities shall be established and maintained concerning the creation and modification of the various types of document.
g) prevent the unintended use of obsolete documents and apply suitable identification to them if they are retained for any purpose.	

SIGNIFICANT CHANGES

ISO 14001:2004 goes beyond ISO 14001:1996 in identifying documents that are subject to control. Both versions refer to control of all documents required by the standard; however, ISO 14001:2004 also mandates control of documents required by the system. In other words, if an organization creates a document that is not required by ISO 14001:2004 (for example, a procedure for establishing objectives and targets), that document is subject to the same controls as the procedures delineated in the standard.

ISO 14001:2004 also imposes control over documents of external origin. When originally published, ISO 14001:1996 addressed only those documents that were created by an organization.

Mention of dates, the manner in which documents are maintained, and retention period has been eliminated.

INTENT OF ISO 14001:2004

By definition, a document is information and its supporting medium (Section 3.4). Media include paper; magnetic, electronic, or optical computer disc; photograph or master sample; or a combination thereof. Records comprise a specific form of documentation and therefore are subject to a different set of controls (see Chapter 17).

All records are documents, but not all documents are records. A document typically explains what must be done; a record provides information to prove that something was done. For example, a procedure that describes how to monitor stack emissions is a document; a form on which the volume of a particular emission gets noted provides the supporting record and proves that the procedure was implemented.

ISO 14001:2004 states that all documents required by the standard must be controlled. Those documents are:

- Scope of the environmental management system

- Environmental policy

- Environmental aspects and impacts

- Environmental objectives and targets

- Roles, responsibilities, and authorities

- Relevant communication from external interested parties

- Decision regarding external communication about significant environmental aspects

- Description of the main elements of the environmental management system

- Operational control procedures (see Chapter 16)

These documentation requirements are generally viewed as minimal. An organization needs to determine the kind and amount of documentation necessary to effectively manage and maintain its environmental management system. An organization is likely to document far more. Most, for example, document legal requirements even though ISO 14001:2004 contains no requirement to do so.

When an organization creates such additional documents, they also are subject to control. ISO 14001:2004 specifically states that, in addition to documents required by the standard, documents required by the environmental management system must be controlled. As a result, all descriptions, procedures, instructions, reports, and forms that an organization deems necessary to implement and maintain its system must be controlled.

Unlike the original standard, ISO 14001:2004 imposes requirements for two categories of documents—those created by an organization and those of external origin. Internal documents, that is, those created by an organization, are subject to clearly defined limits concerning approval, issue, revision, and revocation.

External documents, created by others and brought into an organization for some purpose, are subject to somewhat different controls. An organization cannot revise nor reissue such documents, for example, so the constraints pertaining to internal documents do not apply. Instead, the distribution of external documents within an organization must be controlled.

Increasingly, organizations rely on electronic documents because of the ease and speed with which revisions can be provided to workers. Unlike documents in paper format, which must be physically removed from points of use and replaced, electronic documents always reflect the current version because there is only one "location" (the computer) at which documents are available. Cautionary notations that appear on printed versions reinforce this. At U. S. Steel Gary Works, for example, controlled documents contain the following statement on every page when printed: "Printed copies are uncontrolled copies and are valid for training or reference for 24 hours."

Despite this, organizations are often challenged to maintain conformity with document control requirements. The integrity of an electronic format relies on workers' willingness to access needed documents only through a computer. Nonconformities arise when workers rely on printed copies that exceed their authorized time limit in lieu of printing another current copy.

Both U. S. Steel Gary Works and Delaware North Companies Parks & Resorts maintain their environmental management system documentation in an electronic format. Coast Guard Air Station Cape Cod employs a paper format. The documents presented throughout this book were current at the time of publication and provide examples of how organizations in three different sectors choose to implement ISO 14001:2004. Registration and surveillance audits have affirmed that the procedures are appropriate and effective. Revision to any of these documents subsequent to their inclusion here does not detract from their illustrative value.

EXAMPLES

U. S. Steel Gary Works
EMS Procedure 4.4.5—Document Control
(Effective June 16, 2004)

1.0 Purpose

    1.1 The purpose of this procedure is to describe Gary Works' system to control the preparation, approval, distribution, revision, and maintenance of documents that relate to the requirements of the Gary Works Environmental Management System.

2.0 Scope

    2.1 This procedure applies to documents issued and controlled by Environmental Control as well as documents identified for Core Competence Training Requirements on the Significant Aspect Data Matrix.

3.0 References

    3.1 ISO 14001:1996.

    3.2 EMS Procedure 4.4.4—EMS Documentation

    3.3 EMS Procedure 4.5.3—Records

    3.4 Master List of Documents—Exhibit I

    3.5 Master List of Locations—Exhibit II

    3.6 Master List of Forms/Logs—Exhibit III

    3.7 Master List of Tables—Exhibit IV

    3.8 Documentation Validation Form—Exhibit V (page 207)

    3.9 Environmental System Document Request—Exhibit VI

    3.10 Significant Aspect Data Matrix—Exhibit VII

4.0 Definitions

For the purpose of this procedure, the following definitions shall apply.

4.1 *Master lists*—A master list is a mechanism for identifying the current revision status of EMS documents that are readily available in order to preclude the use of invalid or obsolete documents. This may be either hard copy or may reside in a controlled data file of a computer. Refer to Exhibits I, II, III, and IV.

4.2 *Controlled copy*—A document that is current at the time of issuance and will be updated as revisions are made.

4.3 *Uncontrolled copy*—A document that is current at the time of issuance and will not be updated as revisions are made. A photocopy of a controlled copy is an uncontrolled document.

    4.3.1 Controlled documents, printed from Gary Works' intranet, are uncontrolled copies that can be used for training and reference for 24 hours after the time of printing.

4.4 *EMS Document Control Custodian*—A person appointed by the EMR who is responsible for overseeing EMS document control activities for documents issued by Environmental Control.

4.5 *Business unit/staff group Document Control Custodian*—A person appointed by business unit/staff group management who is responsible for overseeing document control activities for documents issued by the business unit/staff group.

4.6 *EMS Document Validation form 70100011 FRM Exhibit V* (page 207)—A document that is recommended for use under the following situations:

- Approval of new or revised procedures

- Review of procedures

- Documenting that employees have been contacted/trained on procedures

- Acknowledgment of receipt of a new or revised procedure and the destruction of the old document

- Deletion of an obsolete document

5.0 Responsibilities

    5.1 The following job positions have responsibilities in this procedure:

- Manager, Environmental Control/Environmental Management Representative (EMR)

- ISO 14001 Coordinator

- Gary Works managers

- EMS Document Control Custodian

- Business unit/staff group Document Control Custodian

6.0 Procedure

6.1 Gary Works employees may request changes to the Level I EMS Manual or Level II EMS Procedures by completing the EMS Document Request form (Exhibit VI) and submitting it to the ISO 14001 Coordinator.

6.1.1 The ISO 14001 Coordinator reviews the request for new, revised, or deleted Level I or II documents, including corresponding drafts or notes, with the EMR.

6.1.2 The EMR approves or rejects new, revised, or deleted Level I or II document requests.

6.1.2.1 Approved requests are processed according to the requirements of EMS Procedure 4.4.4.

6.1.2.2 Drafts of new or revised documents are not controlled.

6.1.2.3 Rejected requests are returned to the employee requesting the new, revised, or deleted document with an explanation of the rejection.

6.1.3 The Gary Works Environmental Management System Steering Team agrees with or rejects the updated Level I or Level II documents.

6.1.3.1 Changes to the Level I Manual and Level II Procedures are noted with an asterisk "*" in the left-hand column.

6.1.3.2 Agreed-to requests for new or revised Level I or II documents are signed by the EMR.

6.1.3.2.1 If an entire Level I or II document is deleted, the signature copy

is retained according to the
requirements of EMS Procedure
4.5.3—Records.

6.1.3.3 Rejected requests are processed according to
6.1.2.3 above.

6.1.4 The ISO 14001 Coordinator issues the updated document
on the Gary Works intranet.

6.1.5 When exhibits to EMS Procedures are revised after
the revision date, it is not necessary to update the EMS
Procedure unless procedure elements are affected by the
exhibit change. When the EMS Procedure is updated,
the exhibits will be updated.

6.1.6 Gary Works EMS Manual and Gary Works EMS
Procedures are controlled on the Gary Works intranet.
The only paper copy and its associated Document
Validation form is retained by the EMS Document
Control Custodian(s).

6.2 Gary Works employees make requests for new, revised, or
deleted Level III work instructions directly to the responsible
manager.

6.2.1 The responsible manager approves or rejects the request
for new, revised, or deleted Level III documents.

6.2.2 Approved requests for new, revised, or deleted Level III
documents are processed by the responsible manager.

6.2.2.1 Drafts of new or revised documents are not
controlled. Draft versions of new documents
are valid for use for a period of ninety (90) days
from date of issue. These documents must be
finalized within the ninety-day period.

6.2.2.2 Revisions to documents are identified with an
"*" in the left-hand column.

6.2.2.3 Changes to procedures that have no influence
on the purpose of the document may be
completed without changing the revision date
or identifying the change with an "*" and with
the signature (approval) of the responsible
manager.

6.2.2.4   The signature copy of deleted documents is retained according to the requirements of EMS Procedure 4.5.3.

6.2.2.5   For Level III documents issued by Environmental Control, the EMS Document Control Custodian(s) will destroy obsolete or outdated controlled copies with the exception of the signature copy, which will be filed according to appropriate record retention requirements.

6.2.2.6   For Level III documents issued by business units/staff groups that are identified on the Significant Aspect Data Matrix, the business unit/staff group Document Control Custodian will destroy obsolete or outdated controlled copies with the exception of the signature copy, which will be filed according to appropriate record retention requirements.

6.2.3   Rejected requests for new, revised, or deleted Level III documents are returned to the employee making the request with an explanation for the rejection.

6.2.4   The responsible manager or designee ensures that the draft document (new or revised) is reviewed for correctness and effectiveness by the appropriate affected area(s) personnel.

6.2.5   The new document or document revision is approved by the appropriate level of management as identified in the Approval section of the document.

6.2.6   For documents issued by Environmental Control, the EMS Document Control Custodian(s) releases new or revised Level III documents, updates the applicable master list of documents, and distributes copies to the appropriate locations, when applicable.

6.2.7   The EMS Document Control Custodian(s) control Environmental Management Practices on the Environmental Control Web site on the Gary Works intranet.

6.2.8   For documents issued by the business unit/staff group that are identified on the Significant Aspect Data

Matrix, the business unit/staff group Document Control Custodian releases new or revised documents, updates the applicable master list, and distributes copies to the appropriate location, when applicable.

6.2.8.1 Paper copies of controlled documents are stamped "Copy Controlled" on each page in red ink.

6.3 The ISO 14001 Coordinator, or designee, will create or revise forms/logs or tables.

6.4 The EMS Document Control Custodian will:

6.4.1 Release new or revised forms/logs and tables.

6.4.2 Distribute copies to appropriate locations.

6.4.3 Update the appropriate master list.

6.4.4 Destroy all obsolete or invalid forms/logs and tables from area locations.

6.4.5 Issue paper copies of controlled EMS documents that are stamped "Copy Controlled" in red ink.

7.0 Approval

7.1 Approval of this procedure by the Gary Works Environmental Management System Steering Team is effected by the signature (on the Document Validation form) of the Manager, Environmental Control that has been designated as the Environmental Management Representative.

7.2 Approved for use.

Manager, Environmental Control and Environmental Management Representative

**EMS PROCEDURE 4.4.5—
ENVIRONMENTAL MANAGEMENT SYSTEM
DOCUMENT VALIDATION FORM**
(Effective March 12, 2000)

Date_____

Division/dept: _____   Area: _____

Document number: _____   Document title: _____

❑ Newly issued or revised document. (Please review with appropriate
   personnel.)

_____

❑ Document due for review

   ❑ Needs revision (as indicated)   ❑ No changes required   ❑ Delete

Acknowledgments:

❑ Employees who were contacted/trained on this document

❑ Employees who participated in the development, review, or revision
   of this document

❑ Employees acknowledging receipt of a new or revised document and
   the destruction of the old document

Print name	Signature	Check #	Department

Approvals:

The aforementioned document has been reviewed and approved by:

_____   _____   _____
Print name   *Signature*   *Title*

_____   _____   _____
Print name   *Signature*   *Title*

_____   _____   _____
Print name   *Signature*   *Title*

Exhibit V   EMS Procedure 4.4.5.

Delaware North Companies Parks & Resorts
P1400.08—GreenPath Document Control
(Effective August 4, 2005)

Policy

Delaware North Companies' GreenPath locations shall maintain procedures for controlling all documents subject to this procedure, including internally and externally prepared documents.

Purpose

To describe the procedures and responsibilities for control of documentation related to the Environmental Management System (EMS).

Procedure

Responsibility:

The Director of Environmental Affairs is responsible for the preparation, revision, removal, and management of documents associated with the corporate Environmental Management System.

The Environmental Manager/designee is responsible for the preparation, revision, removal, and management of documents associated with the Environmental Management System at each operating location.

Policy:

DNC maintains procedures to control Environmental Management System documents to ensure that documents can be located, are reviewed and revised as necessary, are maintained as current, and are managed properly when obsolete.

Process:

"Documents" may include policies, procedures, guidelines, descriptions, operations and maintenance manuals, and other types of communications, correspondence, and/or notices that are designed to be permanent, official, and authoritative. Documents are expected by their designers/creators to be official and unchangeable, except by the creator or other authorized personnel.

- Copies of the EMS may be downloaded, printed, and/or saved electronically but are considered "uncontrolled." The online procedures should always be referred to as the only current and official version of the EMS.

- Documents are reviewed as required or as otherwise indicated.

- Retention times for controlled documents are identified in the Controlled Document List.

2. Current versions of EMS documents are maintained online as electronic controlled copies. EMS hard copy documents are uncontrolled documents.

    - Users of uncontrolled documents must review the electronic EMS controlled copy to ensure accuracy.

    Employees access the EMS documents on the GreenPath Community Web site at www.xxx.

3. The Director of Environmental Affairs and Environmental Managers/designees update EMS documents to maintain the system as current. The document number located in the header of each document identifies EMS documents.

Preparation of a New Document

Director of Environmental Affairs (corporate), Environmental Manager/designee (operating locations):

1. Creates and names new document. Identifies document retention time frame.

2. Reviews and revises document, as required.

3. Includes revisions to the new document, as required.

4. Assigns a controlled-document number to the new document.

5. Forwards document to other operating location personnel or DNC personnel for review, if appropriate.

Designated Operating Location Personnel

6. Review document and make additional changes, as required. Return document to the Director of Environmental Affairs or Environmental Manager/ designee.

Director of Environmental Affairs (corporate), Environmental Manager/designee (operating locations):

7. Reviews and approves the new document, as appropriate.

8. Assigns date to the new document. Includes document on the Document Control Matrix and in the electronic files. Includes the document in EMS Manual.

9. Sends uncontrolled copy of the new document to the registrar, if necessary.

Revision of an Existing Document

Director of Environmental Affairs (corporate), Environmental Manager/designee (operating locations):

1. Makes changes to controlled document.

2. Assigns controlled document revision number to draft document. Types document revision.

3. Forwards draft document to other DNC personnel for review, if appropriate.

Operating location staff:

4. Reviews draft document and makes additional changes, if necessary. Returns document to Environmental Manager for review.

Director of Environmental Affairs (corporate), Environmental Manager/designee (operating locations):

5. Reviews and approves the revised draft document.

6. Assigns date to the revised document. Adds revised document to the electronic files. Modifies the EMS online document to include the revision.

7. Removes and retains, if necessary, hard copy of the revised document in department files.

8. If requested, sends uncontrolled copy of the revised document to the registrar.

Removal of an Obsolete Document

Operating location staff:

1. Discusses removal of obsolete document with the Director of Environmental Affairs or Environmental Manager/designee, as appropriate.

Director of Environmental Affairs (corporate), Environmental Manager/designee (operating locations):

2. Approves removal of obsolete document from the Controlled Document List.

3. Removes document from the Controlled Document List and the electronic files. Retains hard copy of the removed document in department files, as appropriate. Stores obsolete documents in the environmental files, if necessary.

4. If required, sends the registrar notification regarding removal of the document from the Controlled Document List.

Management of an External Document

(An external document is any document from a source as described in the External Communication procedure.)

Director of Environmental Affairs (corporate), Environmental Manager/designee (operating locations):

1. Reviews and approves the external document.

2. Forwards the external document to affected operating location staff, if appropriate.

Operating location staff:

3. Reviews the external document and returns it to the Director of Environmental Affairs or the Environmental Manager/designee.

Director of Environmental Affairs (corporate), Environmental Manager/designee (operating locations)

4. Adds new document to the hard copy office files.

Required Documentation

• Current copy of the Document Control Matrix

Coast Guard Air Station Cape Cod
Procedure 07—Document Control Procedure
(Effective February 1, 2001)

1.0   Purpose:

To identify procedures to ensure that the most current versions of relevant documents of the EMS are available at all appropriate locations and that obsolete documents are not inappropriately referenced.

2.0   Scope:

2.1   This procedure affects documents created and/or maintained for the EMS.

3.0   Procedure:

3.1   At a minimum, Coast Guard documents are marked with a date and revision number.

3.2   The EMS manual and procedures will be marked with the following header:

USCG–ASCC			Page
(Title of procedure)	Prepared by:	Date created:	Procedure no.
	Approved by:	Revision date:	Revision no.

3.3   When a revision to any of the EMS documents is made, the date and revision number, author, and approving entity shall be updated accordingly. Except for the SPCC plan, revisions may not be handwritten/penciled in. Revisions to the SPCC are governed by 40 CFR.

3.4   Revisions will be distributed to all controlled copy holders and accompanied with an explanation and acknowledgment receipt. An example of the acknowledgment receipt is provided as Appendix A (page 214).

3.5   The acknowledgment receipt form is to be signed by the recipient indicating that they have received the referenced enclosure and understand the changes/new requirements. The acknowledgment receipt is to be returned to the EH&S

department. The acknowledgment will be logged in the Master Distribution list.

3.6   Specifically for emergency contact numbers/notification lists, the document will be hand delivered and replaced by EH&S personnel. In this instance, an acknowledgment receipt is not required. However, the member delivering the document shall note this accordingly in the Master Distribution list. (An example of the Master Distribution list is provided in Appendix B.) Other EMS documents may be distributed in this same manner; however, the emergency contact numbers/ notification list must be hand delivered and replaced by EH&S departmental personnel.

3.7   There is no additional requirement to archive executed acknowledgment receipts once logged in the Master Distribution list.

3.8   Except for the Environmental Policy Statement, copies of controlled documents of the EMS may be made provided they are clearly marked indicating that the document is a copy, will not be given wide distribution or posted, and are removed/ destroyed when a revision is issued.

3.9   Copies of the originally executed current Environmental Policy Statement may be made, posted, and distributed throughout ASCC.

4.0   Responsibilities:

4.1   All revisions to EHS documents will be made and distributed through the EH&S department.

4.2   The Administrative Assistant will establish and maintain a list of all controlled documents, their revision number and dates, and recipients. Appendix B provides a copy of the Master Distribution list.

4.3   The Administrative Assistant will log all acknowledgment receipts as they are received and follow up/investigate missing acknowledgment receipts and assist with corrective action.

5.0   Appendixes:

A.   Acknowledgment receipt

B.   Master Distribution list

Kindly acknowledge receipt and understanding of the enclosure by signing below and returning to the EH&S department (attention Administrative Assistant).

Document: *(for example, Document Control Procedure 07)*

_____   _____
Name (print and sign)   *Date*

Appendix A   Acknowledgment receipt.

12

Operational Control

T he way in which day-to-day activities are carried out contributes substantially to an organization's efforts to lessen or eliminate adverse effects on the environment.

ISO 14001:2004 Text	ISO 14001:1996 Text
4.4.6 Operational control	*4.4.6 Operational control*
The organization shall identify and plan those operations that are associated with the identified significant environmental aspects consistent with its environmental policy, objectives and targets, in order to ensure that they are carried out under specified conditions by	The organization shall identify those operations and activities that are associated with the identified significant environmental aspects in line with its policy, objectives and targets. The organization shall plan these activities, including maintenance, in order to ensure that they are carried out under specified conditions by
a) establishing, implementing and maintaining a documented procedure(s) to control situations where their absence could lead to deviation from the environmental policy, objectives and targets, and	a) establishing and maintaining documented procedures to cover situations where their absence could lead to deviations from the environmental policy and the objectives and targets;
b) stipulating the operating criteria in the procedure(s), and	b) stipulating operating criteria in the procedures;

Continued

Continued

ISO 14001:2004 Text	ISO 14001:1996 Text
c) establishing, implementing and maintaining procedures related to the identified significant environmental aspects of goods and services used by the organization and communicating applicable procedures and requirements to suppliers, including contractors.	c) establishing and maintaining procedures related to the identifiable significant environmental aspects of goods and services used by the organization and communicating relevant procedures and requirements to suppliers and contractors.

SIGNIFICANT CHANGES

ISO 14001:1996 focused on operations and activities, with explicit reference to maintenance activities. ISO 14001:2004 focuses only on operations.

The original standard also included a reference to suppliers *and* contractors, implying that they constitute two separate groups. The revised language refers to suppliers *including* contractors, thereby suggesting that they constitute one group.

From an implementation standpoint, this change is negligible. In the United States, suppliers are viewed as those who provide goods to an organization and contractors as those who provide services. ISO 14001:2004 does not provide a definition for either term; however, ISO 9000:2000 supports the U.S. connotation by defining a supplier as an "organization or person that provides a product" (definition 3.3.6). It does not define *contractor*.

INTENT OF ISO 14001:2004

The primary purpose of this clause is to ensure that every task or activity for which a significant environmental aspect has been identified is performed in a manner that controls, reduces, or eliminates associated environmental impacts. Thus, an organization is directed to identify and plan the operations that are associated with its significant environmental aspects.

Although ISO 14001:2004 does not define *operations*, the term encompasses every function and its supporting processes, and by extension the tasks and actions associated with those processes, performed by an organization's employees as well as its contractors and suppliers.

Functions common to many companies include:

- Manufacturing

- Assembly

- Storage (materials, product)

- Packaging

- Delivery

- Maintenance

- Marketing

- Sales

- Purchasing

- Research and development

- Safety

Individual processes within such functions, as well as others that might be unique to an organization, must be examined and environmental aspects associated with those processes identified. Any function, process, task, or other activity for which an environmental aspect is determined to be significant is subject to control.

Operational control is not limited to significant environmental aspects. Consistency with the environmental policy indicates a need to consider controls that help an organization meet its commitment to comply with legal requirements and other requirements to which it subscribes. Consistency with objectives and targets prompts consideration of controls necessary to achieve stated environmental performance goals.

The approaches selected by an organization to control its operations should reflect the nature of the aspect of interest, the media affected by its impact, the purpose of the control, and the abilities of those workers responsible for applying the control. Forms of operational control include use of technology and equipment, procedures and work instructions, and contracts and agreements.

This is the only clause in ISO 14001:2004 that refers to documented procedures; however, documentation is required only when the lack of documentation results in a disparity between workers' actions and outcomes and the directives imposed by an organization's environmental policy, objectives, and targets. Thus, an operational control procedure could be communicated to workers through demonstration or on-the-job training as long as the criteria for performing the procedure are explained and understood. Even something as simple as color coding can impose control. Blue bins might be used for paper recycling and gray bins for metal shavings. A painted floor area can designate the location for hazardous waste collection containers.

Although there is a tendency to think of operational control in relation to an organization's employees, its operations also can be affected by suppliers and contractors with which it does business. The significant environmental aspects associated with such entities must be identified and the operations with which significant aspects are associated must be controlled.

Environmental aspects associated with goods purchased from suppliers typically are identified in conjunction with an organization's efforts to identify its own environmental aspects (see Chapter 4). This is because all incoming items that are used in conjunction with an operation—such as products, parts, materials, energy—are recognized as actual or potential contributors to its effect on the environment.

Environmental aspects associated with the services provided by contractors typically emerge when an organization evaluates worker competence (see Chapter 8). Any person performing a task for or on behalf of an organization that has the potential to cause a significant impact must be competent to perform that task properly. Therefore, both contractors and employees performing such tasks should be identified and evaluated.

Once it has identified the significant environmental aspects associated with suppliers and contractors, an organization is positioned to establish appropriate controls. These often are communicated to suppliers through contracts and agreements and to contractors through procedures, work instructions, and training.

EXAMPLES

Each organization has numerous operational control procedures. For illustrative purposes, the procedures that address hazardous waste have been selected.

U. S. Steel Gary Works
EMS Procedure 4.4.6—Operational Control
(Effective October 20, 2005)

1.0 Purpose

    1.1 This procedure describes the activities and responsibilities for controlling operations associated with significant environmental aspects at the Gary Complex.

2.0 Scope

    2.1 This procedure applies to employees involved in identifying activities and operations associated with significant environmental aspects, establishing and maintaining procedures for the control of operations, and communicating relevant procedures and requirements to contractors/suppliers.

3.0 References

    3.1 ISO 14001:2004 Standard

    3.2 EMS Procedure 4.3.1—Environmental Aspects

    3.3 EMS Procedure 4.3.3—Objectives, Targets, and Programs

    3.4 EMS Procedure 4.4.1—Resources, Roles, Responsibility and Authority

    3.5 EMS Procedure 4.4.2—Competence, Training, and Awareness

    3.6 EMS Procedure 4.4.4—EMS Documentation

    3.7 EMS Procedure 4.5.3—Nonconformity, Corrective Action, and Preventive Action

4.0 Definitions

    4.1 (None)

5.0 Responsibilities

    5.1 The following job positions have responsibilities in the procedure:

- Cross-functional teams (CFT)

- Business unit/staff organization management

- Contractors/suppliers

- Environmental Control ISO 14001 Steering Team

- All employees

6.0 Procedure

    6.1 Identification of Significant Aspect Associated Elements

        6.1.1 The cross-functional team (CFT) identifies operations, activities, and position titles that are associated with significant environmental aspects as specified in EMS

Procedures 4.3.1—Environmental Aspects and 4.4.2—
Competence, Training, and Awareness, section 6.3.

6.2 Operations and Maintenance Work Instructions

6.2.1 The Environmental Control ISO 14001 Steering Team
identifies contractors/suppliers whose work activities
are associated with significant environmental aspects
as identified in EMS Procedure 4.3.1—Environmental
Aspects.

6.2.2 Business unit/staff organization and relevant contractor/
supplier management establishes and maintains
documented procedures for the control of operations,
including maintenance activities that are related to
significant environmental aspects in their area of
responsibility. These procedures, where applicable,
stipulate operating criteria.

6.2.3 If a performance deviation from the Gary Complex
Environmental Policy occurs, an investigation is
conducted in accordance with EMS Procedure 4.5.3—
Nonconformity, Corrective Action, and Preventive
Action.

7.0 Approval

7.1 Approval of this procedure by the Gary Complex Environmental Management System Steering Team is effected by the
signature (on the Document Validation form) of the Manager,
Environmental Control that has been designated as the Environmental Management Representative.

7.2 Approved for use.

Manager, Environmental Control and Environmental
Management Representative

Waste Characterization and Classification Guidance
(Effective October 27, 2005)

1.0 Purpose:

1.1 USS Gary Works has established and implemented a Waste
Characterization and Classification Program (WCCP). The purpose of this document is to ensure the proper implementation

of the WCCP, by ensuring the identification, characterization, and classification of waste materials generated at Gary Works. Implementation of these procedures will result in the proper handling, storage, and disposition of waste materials in accordance with applicable environmental regulations. This procedure has been developed to assist Gary Works personnel in the proper characterization and classification of waste materials generated at the plant.

2.0 Scope:

    2.1 This procedure applies to all personnel whose job activities result in the generation of waste materials during production, maintenance, housekeeping, and/or cleanup activities.

3.0 References: None

4.0 Definitions:

The following are definitions of key terms used in this document:

    4.1 *Characterize*—The acquisition and testing of representative samples of a waste stream to determine its characteristics in order to ascertain its proper handling and disposition.

5.0 Responsibilities:

    5.1 Each business unit manager is responsible for ensuring the implementation of this procedure in the business unit. The Environmental Control Department will provide assistance and evaluate the business unit performance with respect to this procedure.

6.0 General Procedures:

    6.1 Waste Characterization and Classification Procedure

        6.1.1 If a business unit conducts, or plans to conduct, any production, maintenance, housekeeping, or cleanup activity that results, or will result, in the generation of a waste material, other than refuse, and guidance concerning the proper handling and disposition of the waste material has not been previously provided by the Environmental Control Department, the following procedure shall be implemented.

            6.1.1.1 A business unit representative will contact the Environmental Solid Waste Compliance

Manager at Environmental Control, extension 3383, if there are any questions concerning the proper handling and disposition of the waste material.

6.1.1.2　If the waste material has already been characterized and classified, the Environmental Solid Waste Compliance Manager will notify the business unit representative that the waste has been characterized and reiterate the proper method for handling and disposing of the waste material.

6.1.1.3　If the waste material has not been characterized and classified, the Environmental Solid Waste Compliance Manager will arrange for the collection and analysis of representative samples of the waste material for characterization. The uncharacterized materials will be held in a secure location within the appropriate business unit until characterization and disposition method has been verified. The sample collector will submit the waste material sample to the laboratory assigned by the Environmental Solid Waste Compliance Manager using a chain of custody form to assure consistency with the pilot plant sample.

6.1.1.4　The laboratory will submit the analytical results and the required quality assurance/quality control (QA/QC) package to the Environmental Solid Waste Compliance Manager.

6.1.1.5　Upon receipt of the analytical results and QA/QC package, the Environmental Solid Waste Compliance Manager will classify the waste, select a disposal option, and submit to the appropriate agency a formal request for approval of on-site or off-site disposal of the waste material.

6.1.1.6　Upon receipt of the agency's notification, the Environmental Solid Waste Compliance Manager will notify the business unit representative of the proper method for handling and disposing of the waste material. If the process or raw materials involved in generating the waste change, the business unit must notify the Environmental Solid Waste Compliance Manager. If the change is substantial, a new sample must be collected and the characterization process repeated. The above procedure from initial notification of the Environmental Control Department to receipt of the agency's notification may require a minimum period of 90 days.

6.1.1.7 Record keeping: The Environmental Solid Waste Compliance Manager will ensure that all pertinent information and data concerning the waste material is input to the Gary Works Management Information System database and maintains all records.

7.0 Practice Approval:

7.1 Approved for Principle and Practice.

ISO 14001 coordinator

Hazardous Waste Shipping/Disposal Guidance
(Effective October 27, 2005)

1.0 Purpose:

1.1 This Environmental Management Practice (EMP) provides guidance for U. S. Steel, Gary Works personnel who are responsible for the off-site shipment of hazardous waste that has been generated at Gary Works.

2.0 Scope:

2.1 This procedure applies to all personnel who are responsible for preparing shipments of hazardous waste for off-site disposal.

3.0 References:

3.1 USS Environmental Practice, "Waste Characterization and Classification Guidance." 70100015EMP

4.0 Definitions:

    4.1 *Hazardous waste*—Wastes that are classified as hazardous in accordance with Environmental Management Practice 70100015EMP.

5.0 Responsibilities:

    5.1 Each business unit manager is responsible for ensuring that these guidelines are followed within each business unit.

    5.2 The Environmental Control Department will provide assistance as necessary to ensure the appropriate shipment and disposal of hazardous waste.

6.0 General Practice:

    6.1 Waste Classification: Classification of waste disposal type (hazardous or nonhazardous) must be determined for proper disposal. Wastes are characterized in accordance with 70100015EMP. The characterization/approval status of wastes can be determined by contacting the Environmental Control Department (extension 1234).

    6.2 Containerization, Labeling, Marking: Collected hazardous waste must be placed in appropriate containers that display the proper labels and markings. The Hazardous Waste Shipping Information Table provides waste-specific information on containers, labels, and marking. For more information on containerization, labeling, and marking of hazardous waste containers, contact the Environmental Control Department at extension 1234.

        6.2.1 Accumulation Times: Hazardous wastes may be accumulated on-site no longer than ninety (90) days.

    6.3 Manifesting: Each shipment of hazardous waste must be accompanied by a Uniform Hazardous Waste Manifest (U.S. EPA Form 8700-22 manifest). Each hazardous waste manifest must be signed and dated in the Generator's Certification section by an authorized U. S. Steel manager. Blank Uniform Hazardous Waste Manifests can be obtained from the Environmental Control Department at extension 1234.

    The manifest system is designed to provide a record of the waste from "cradle to grave." The following summarizes manifest activity:

- The manifest is initiated by the generator (for example, Gary Works) who must retain one copy for records, send another copy to the office of solid waste management of the appropriate state agency, and provide the remaining copies to the transporter.

- The transporter signs the manifest accepting the waste, retaining one copy for their records, and provides the remaining copies to the designated treatment or disposal facility.

- The designated treatment or disposal facility signs the manifest acknowledging receipt of the waste and retains one copy of the manifest for their records. The designated facility also forwards a finalized copy to the generator within forty-five (45) days from the date of shipment. If the finalized copy has not been received within the 45 days, the generator must file an Exception Report with the appropriate agency. (Note: It is Gary Works' policy that if the finalized copy has not been received within thirty-five (35) days, the generator should contact the disposal facility and, if necessary, the transporter, to determine the reason and to find out if the shipment reached its intended destination.)

The following is a list of the information items that are required to be completed on the Uniform Hazardous Waste Manifest (Indiana version), in accordance with federal and state regulations.

6.3.1 Generator's Section

Item 1. Generator's twelve (12) digit U.S. EPA identification number and unique five (5) digit manifest document number assigned by the generator.

Item 2. Page number—total number of pages in manifest.

Item 3. Generator's name and mailing address of location where returned manifest forms will be managed.

Item 4. Generator's telephone number where an authorized agent of the company can be reached.

Item 5. First transporter's company name.

Item 6. U.S. EPA twelve (12) digit identification number of the first transporter.

Item D. Telephone number of the first transporter.

Note: If shipment is to be handled by two transporters, then items 7, 8, and 8D must also be completed.

Item 9. Name and site address of facility designated for receipt/disposal.

Item 10. U.S. EPA twelve (12) digit identification number of the designated facility.

Item H. Telephone number of designated facility.

Item 11. U.S. Department of Transportation Description including Proper Shipping Name, Hazard Class, and Identification Number. (Fill in items 11a, 11b, 11c, and 11d as necessary for additional hazardous wastes.)

Item 12. Number and type of containers.

Item 13. Total quantity of hazardous waste.

Item 14. Unit weight or volume of hazardous waste.

Item I. Waste number.

Item K. Handling codes for wastes listed on the manifest.

Item 15. Special handling instructions and additional information.

Item 16. Generator's certification including printed or typed name and signature of generator (or generator's authorized agent) and date.

6.3.2 Transporter's Section (This section to be completed by the transporter/shipper.)

6.3.3 Facility Section (This section to be completed by an authorized representative of the facility receiving the waste.)

6.3.4 Land Disposal Restriction Forms and One-Time Notifications: Certain hazardous wastes are restricted from disposal in landfills without prior treatment. Generators of hazardous wastes are required to notify treatment/storage/disposal facilities of the restriction status of each waste shipment. A Land Disposal Restriction (LDR) form (Land Ban form) must accompany each hazardous waste manifest unless a one-time notification for compliance with the Land Disposal Restriction certification requirements has been provided. Specific language addressing the one-time notification is as follows: "No further notification is necessary until such time as the waste or facility change, in which case a new notification must be sent and a copy placed in the generator's file." (Note: Any new waste streams generator will need a new one-time LDR notification for that particular waste stream.) LDR forms may vary according to hazardous waste contractor. The Environmental Control Department coordinates completion of the Land Disposal Restriction form with the contractor. For information regarding manifests, hazardous waste contractors, and Land Disposal Restriction forms, contact the Environmental Control Department at extension 1234.

6.3.5   Emergency Response Guide: The U.S. Department of Transportation requires a copy of the appropriate Emergency Response Guide (ERG) page for each hazardous waste line item on the manifest to be attached to the manifest during shipment. A copy must also remain with the generator as well. (Note: Listing the ERG number on the manifest alone does not meet compliance.)

6.4   Pre-Transportation Inspection Items: Several key items are related to each shipment of hazardous waste. In order to ensure that the hazardous waste is appropriately manifested and ready for shipment, it is recommended that the USS management representative who is to sign the Generator's Certification inspect the shipment for these key items before it leaves the plant. The following is a list of the items that should be present. If there are any questions regarding the following items, please contact the Environmental Control Department. Pre-Transportation Checklist (For use with Hazardous Waste Shipping Information Table [70100001TBL])

1. Appropriate containerization

2. Labeling

3. Marking

4. Manifest—noting each required item as listed in section 5.3 above

5. Land Disposal Restriction form

6. Verify that the vehicle is a licensed hazardous waste transport vehicle

7. Verify that transport vehicle is placarded for hazardous waste

7.0 Practice Approval:

7.1 Approved for Principle and Practice.

ISO 14001 coordinator

Delaware North Companies Parks & Resorts
P1400.05—GreenPath Hazardous Waste Management
(Effective August 8, 2005)

Policy

All Delaware North Companies (DNC) locations that generate hazardous wastes shall comply with all relevant laws and regulations pertaining to the storage and disposal of such wastes.

Purpose

Describe the process for identifying, handling, tracking, collecting, accumulating, and recycling/treatment/disposal of hazardous waste generated from all activities at DNC GreenPath operating locations, including procedures for release, response, and investigation.

This procedure applies to all DNC GreenPath operations generating or otherwise involved in the management of hazardous waste.

Procedure

Responsibility:

The operating location Environmental Manager or designee, in cooperation with the operation's management, shall develop, implement, train, practice, and monitor hazardous waste management activities in compliance with government regulations and DNC and local operating unit requirements.

Local operating units may develop site-specific hazardous waste programs that meet or exceed P1400.5.

Policy:

Through proper management of materials and prompt response to releases, DNC operating locations shall minimize hazards to human health and the environment from any sudden or gradual release of hazardous material or hazardous waste constituents into the air, soil, or water.

Definitions:

Disposal—The act of depositing, interring, or otherwise discarding waste as a final action after use has been achieved or is no longer intended.

Generator—An employee or department that produces a material designated as a hazardous waste by state and/or federal definitions, either through the performance of a prescribed process or by accident.

Hazardous waste—Any discarded material exhibiting the characteristics of a hazardous waste or listed as a hazardous waste according to applicable state and federal regulations.

Hazardous waste transporter—Licensed hazardous waste hauler contracted to transport hazardous wastes along public roadways.

Incompatible materials—Materials unsuitable for commingling with other materials where the commingling might result in explosion, violent chemical reaction, fire, extreme heat, formation of a toxic substance, or other condition that might endanger human health or the environment.

Nonroutine wastes—Hazardous wastes generated in a nonrecurring fashion, including, but not limited to, off-specification materials, out-of-date hazardous materials, damaged products, spill containment, debris residue, sludge, tank, bottoms, and unidentified materials.

Release—Any unplanned/improper spilling, leaking, pumping, pouring, emptying, discharging, dumping, or disposing of hazardous material into the environment.

Routine wastes—Hazardous wastes generated on an ongoing basis, generally characterized as production wastes, for example, used solvent rags, paint waste, batteries, spent aerosol cans, waste oils, and oil-contaminated debris.

Waste accumulation area—Staging/consolidation point for hazardous waste generated from activities at DNC operating locations.

Process:

Environmental Manager or designee shall:

1. Identify specific training requirements for employees required to handle or otherwise manage hazardous waste

2. Arrange for required hazardous materials/waste training for affected personnel

3. Develop and maintain training programs and training records to address applicable hazardous waste training record keeping requirements for DNC GreenPath location personnel

4. Determine, based on knowledge of the material or material sampling and analysis, whether materials are subject to regulation as hazardous waste

5. Review proposed projects to ensure adequate planning for hazardous waste management issues

6. Establish and maintain hazardous waste collection processes to address both production requirements and regulatory constraints

7. Conduct weekly inspections (or at intervals mandated by regulations) of facilities to ensure compliance with applicable hazardous waste management procedures

8. Develop waste segregation guidelines and records in concert with storage and disposal facility regulatory requirements, and promulgate segregation, labeling, and hazardous waste handling requirements among affected employees

9. Maintain supplies such as drums, bags, spill containment materials, sampling equipment, labels, tools, and personal protective equipment required for hazardous waste management activities

10. Package, schedule, stage, and coordinate hazardous waste transport activities, both on-site and off-site, to address applicable Department of Transportation (DOT) and Environmental Protection Agency (EPA) requirements

11. Establish and maintain department regulatory reference library

12. Research emerging hazardous waste management issues affecting compliance, and develop recommendations in response to new and proposed regulations

13. Manage systems, procedures, products, raw materials, processes, and so on, to facilitate pollution prevention and waste minimization and, wherever practical, pursue recycling/reuse of materials on-site

14. Administer inspection/audit program to ensure adherence to waste protocols and compliance with hazardous waste management requirements

15. Develop and maintain documents, records, and plans related to hazardous waste, as required by law

16. Secure required licenses, permits, and registrations and prepare and forward applicable hazardous waste fees and taxes

17. Manage visits from representatives of governmental agencies as follows:

    • Upon arrival at the operating location, ascertain the purpose of the visit and immediately notify the top operations executive or, if absent, his/her delegated authority and other appropriate staff, as required (nonroutine, emergency response, special investigation, and so on).

    • Escort governmental agency representatives at all times during the visit.

18. Participate in maintenance planning activities to ensure compliance with hazardous waste laws and regulations

19. Develop and maintain emergency procedures to ensure that emergency situations involving hazardous waste are dealt with appropriately

Generators of hazardous waste (operations personnel) shall:

1. Become familiar with hazardous materials, emergency response, fire, health and safety, and hazardous waste policies, procedures, manuals, and other related data, as is appropriate for each individual job classification.

2. Immediately notify the Environmental Manager when new sources/types of hazardous waste are to be generated.

3. Supply data to the Environmental Manager concerning hazardous materials to be managed as hazardous waste. (Note: Identifying data may include the manufacturer of the materials, hazardous class, MSDS data, and so on.)

4. Segregate and distribute hazardous wastes into containers established for receipt of each specific waste stream, as directed by the Environmental Manager or other DNC personnel.

5. Maintain waste collection stations so as to comply with established handling procedures (labeling, closed containers, housekeeping, and so on).

6. Review waste-handling practices on an ongoing basis to ensure that hazardous waste is not commingled with regular trash and is not allowed to collect within the workplace.

7. Respond to hazardous materials or hazardous waste releases in accordance with operating location procedures.

8. Immediately notify the Environmental Manager when representatives from government agencies arrive at the facility and retain representatives in the operating location's reception area until the Environmental Manager arrives.

Training Department (where applicable) shall:

1. Provide initial and ongoing OSHA Hazcom training for all employees, to include instruction on hazardous waste management

2. Maintain records documenting employee participation in all environmental training programs

3. Review emerging regulations for new training requirements affecting DNC employees, provide guidance to the Environmental Manager as required, and develop in-house programs or identify training opportunities to satisfy new requirements

DNC and operating location Purchasing Departments shall:

1. Ensure that liability insurance, indemnification, and hold-harmless clauses are part of agreements with hazardous waste contractors

2. Support requests from DNC operating locations for hazardous waste supplies and service contracts

Procedures:

These procedures are divided into three parts:

A. Routine Hazardous Waste

B. Nonroutine Hazardous Waste

C. Spills or Other Unplanned Releases of Hazardous
   Materials/Waste

A. Routine Hazardous Waste

Generators of hazardous waste shall:

1. Ensure that personnel have attended required training courses
   before handling hazardous materials and/or hazardous wastes

2. Notify the Environmental Manager prior to initiation of a new
   waste-generating process when it becomes apparent that a waste
   stream will be created from hazardous materials

3. Provide the Environmental Manager with information describing
   the volumes, types, and processes generating the waste, to
   include MSDS data related to the waste stream, as required

4. Dispose of hazardous wastes at waste collection station;
   leave head space when filling a closed-top drum with liquid
   hazardous waste

5. Segregate hazardous wastes into containers established for receipt
   of each specific waste stream; ensure that wastes are deposited
   within the correct waste container, rather than outside the
   container or on the floor

6. Keep waste containers closed except for receipt/removal of
   hazardous waste

7. Observe grounding and bonding requirements when transferring
   waste flammable liquids

8. Ensure that waste containers are properly labeled, as directed
   by the Environmental Manager

9. Dispose of hazardous wastes generated in the workplace
   immediately upon generation of the waste

10. Review waste-handling practices to ensure that hazardous wastes
    are not commingled or improperly disposed of in the regular trash

Environmental Manager shall:

1. Establish and monitor waste collection stations:

   • Develop waste stream segregation guidelines in accordance
     with regulatory/treatment, storage, and disposal facility
     requirements

- Provide labeled containers for collection of hazardous waste

- Service waste collection stations regularly to avoid overflow of containers

- Maintain waste containers as closed, except for receipt or removal of hazardous waste

- Inspect waste collection stations on an ongoing basis to ensure proper handling of hazardous wastes

- Replace damaged waste containers; maintain inventories of new containers

- Oversee hazardous waste–handling practices to ensure proper segregation of hazardous waste; notify responsible parties in the event of observed improper waste handling

- Support hazardous waste management activities at outlying facilities

- Instruct generators in handling procedures for hazardous waste, as required

2. Transfer hazardous waste to the waste accumulation area:

- Consolidate/containerize hazardous waste in accordance with applicable requirements

- Maintain records/logbooks for hazardous waste, as required

- Work with transporters to affix completed labels to shipping containers prior to off-site transport, in accordance with applicable DOT and EPA requirements

- Segregate salvageable/recyclable materials from hazardous waste; manage recyclable materials and solid wastes as required

- Monitor waste accumulation area for out-of-date drums, improper waste segregation, off-spec containers, incorrect labeling, and so on; effect proper housekeeping in the waste accumulation area

3. Arrange for recycling/treatment/disposal of hazardous waste off site:

- Schedule transportation of the hazardous waste utilizing approved hazardous waste haulers and treatment, storage, and disposal facilities whenever possible

4. Prepare a Uniform Hazardous Waste Manifest for shipment of the hazardous waste, in accordance with applicable state and federal regulations

- Complete Land Disposal Restriction forms, as directed by the facility, to facilitate receipt of the shipment; retain copies for filing with hazardous waste manifest copies

- Supervise loading of hazardous waste onto transport vehicles; ensure that manifest entries match the waste shipment

- Track hazardous waste manifest receipt copies, ensure that receipt copies are returned within prescribed time frames, and follow up on the late receipt copies, as required

B. Nonroutine Hazardous Waste

Generators of hazardous waste shall:

1. Notify the Environmental Manager as to the nature, types, and quantities of nonroutine hazardous waste generated; request assistance from the Environmental Manager to identify unknown materials

2. Request containers from the Environmental Manager for receipt of hazardous waste

3. Keep waste containers closed except for receipt/removal of hazardous waste

4. Ensure that proper labeling is maintained on containers, as directed by the Environmental Manager

5. Follow applicable procedures for handling, labeling, and storing hazardous waste.

Environmental Manager or designee shall:

1. Establish and maintain labeled containers and/or containment capability for receipt of nonroutine hazardous waste

2. Pick up and transport nonroutine hazardous waste in response to production demands; stage hazardous waste in the waste accumulation area

3. Monitor nonroutine waste collection stations for compliance with applicable waste handling requirements; instruct generators in handling procedures for hazardous waste, as required

4. Follow all applicable procedures

C. Spills or Other Unplanned Releases of Hazardous Materials/Waste

Incidental Releases of Hazardous Materials or Waste That Can Be Absorbed, Neutralized, or Otherwise Controlled at the Time of Release

Generators of hazardous waste shall:

1. Notify the Environmental Manager as to the type, amount, location, and status of the release

2. Consult with the Environmental Manager for direction/approval to clean up the release

3. Use available spill-containment media to contain and clean up the release. Note: Cleanup personnel must be trained on emergency response procedures prior to engaging in containment/cleanup activities.

4. Contact the Environmental Manager for assistance in disposal of the material and the materials used to contain the spill

Environmental manager or designee shall:

1. Assist in containerization and removal of the spilled materials

2. Review incident with respect to release reporting requirements and respond to government agency release reporting requirements as appropriate

3. Review spill incidents; respond to releases as deemed appropriate, up to and including activation of protocols identified in local procedures

Significant Releases of Hazardous Materials or Wastes

Generators of hazardous waste shall:

1. Contact the Environmental Manager

2. Report specifics pertaining to the release, including the location, amount, type, and time of the release

3. Follow protocols identified in local procedures or respond as directed by the Environmental Manager

Environmental manager or designee shall:

1. Assume responsibilities as Incident Commander for the release event

2. Follow protocols identified in the relevant emergency procedures for Hazmat response activities

3. Identify, classify, label, and otherwise manage hazardous waste resultant from the spill response when the release has been containerized or controlled

4. Review and respond to release reporting requirements of governmental agencies related to the hazardous materials incident, including notification of appropriate agencies

Coast Guard Air Station Cape Cod
Procedure 09—Hazardous Wastes and Recycling
(Effective December 5, 2002)

1.0 Purpose:

To detail ASCC's collection of solid wastes, recycling program, and management of household and industrial hazardous wastes.

2.0 Scope:

2.1 This procedure applies to the Massachusetts Military Reservation that is within the USCG's control and/or influence. Both USCG and civilian employees under the jurisdiction of the Massachusetts Military Reservation are bound to this procedure.

2.2 The following materials have been identified as hazardous or universal waste generated by the Reservation and/or identified for recycling:

- Amalgahide (fillings for teeth)

- Developer (from dental lab only)

- Fluorescent light bulbs

- General household waste (propane tanks, gasoline, bleach, paints, and so on)

- Lead (from dental procedures)

- Lithium batteries

- Mercury batteries

- Nickel cadmium batteries

- PCB ballast
- Silver recovery cartridge
- X-rays
- Mixed paper
- Cardboard
- Tires
- Metal
- Lead
- Brass
- Electronics
- Metal (including whiteware)
- Cooking grease
- Food scraps

3.0 Procedure:

3.1 Household curbside collection and disposal of solid waste is contracted out. The waste is incinerated at Seamas's facility where it is converted into energy.

3.2 Collection and composting of food waste is contracted out. Operational activities at the Galley, Activities Center, and Golf Course generate food scraps. These units maintain two separate containers for their waste; one is marked *food waste* the other *solid waste*. The contractor will collect the scraps once a week.

3.3 Universal waste and recyclable material is collected, stored, and managed for disposal/recycling at the Recycling Center (Building 3424). Operating units and residents living in Coast Guard housing are advised as to what material is recyclable and are required to keep those materials separate from solid waste.

3.4 Recyclable material generated by ASCC operational activities, except food scraps, shall be brought to the Recycling Center.

3.5 Residents of Coast Guard housing may bring their recyclable material to the Recycling Center. It is mandatory to recycle cardboard.

3.6   Hazardous waste shall be managed in accord with the Hazardous Waste Management and Contingency Plan.

4.0   Responsibilities:

The Environmental Protection Specialist is responsible for the implementation and application of and compliance with the Hazardous Waste Management and Contingency Plan.

The Recycling Coordinator is responsible for:

- Managing the Recycling Center in accord with the Commonwealth of Massachusetts Transfer Station regulations

- Tracking tonnage volumes/receipts of recycled materials

5.0   Related Documentation:

Hazardous Waste Management Plan

AIRSTAINST 5103 Hazardous Material Communication Program

Procedure 03—Record Keeping and Record Retention

Procedure 10—Hazardous Materials/Waste Storage Inspection

Procedure 12—Manifesting

6.0   Records:

Records generated by this procedure include:

- Hazardous Waste Manifests

13

Emergency Preparedness and Response

Although most environmental management activities address operations and activities that occur on a day-to-day basis, it is important that organizations anticipate the unexpected. Procedures that deal with adverse environmental impacts resulting from abnormal operating conditions or accidental releases are an important element of an environmental management system.

ISO 14001:2004 Text	ISO 14001:1996 Text
4.4.7 Emergency preparedness and response	*4.4.7 Emergency preparedness and response*
The organization shall establish, implement and maintain a procedure(s) to identify potential emergency situations and potential accidents that can have an impact(s) on the environment and how it will respond to them.	The organization shall establish and maintain procedures to identify potential for and respond to accidents and emergency situations, and for preventing and mitigating the environmental impacts that may be associated with them.
The organization shall respond to actual emergency situations and accidents and prevent or mitigate associated adverse environmental impacts.	The organization shall review and revise, where necessary, its emergency preparedness and response procedures, in particular, after the occurrence of accidents or emergency situations.
The organization shall periodically review and, where necessary, revise its emergency preparedness and response	

Continued

Continued

ISO 14001:2004 Text	ISO 14001:1996 Text
procedures, in particular, after the occurrence of accidents or emergency situations. The organization shall also periodically test such procedures where practicable.	The organization shall also periodically test such procedures where practicable.

SIGNIFICANT CHANGES

ISO 14001:2004 sharpens the focus of this clause in two ways. First, it states that organizations are to identify potential incidents that can affect the environment. The original standard referred to accidents and emergency situations without any reference to environmental impact.

Second, it adds language that mandates a response to actual incidents. Although ISO 14001:1996 also intended that organizations respond to incidents, the original language had the unintended consequence of emphasizing written procedures over actual response. As revised, ISO 14001:2004 explicitly states a need for organizations to respond to incidents in a manner that prevents or alleviates associated adverse environmental effects.

Finally, the paragraph related to review and revision of emergency procedures has been clarified. As originally constructed, the paragraph could be interpreted to mean that procedures could be reviewed "as necessary." ISO 14001:2004 states clearly that these procedures are to be reviewed periodically and *revised* as necessary.

INTENT OF ISO 14001:2004

The purpose of this clause is twofold. First, it compels organizations to recognize the causes of possible incidents that could result in environmental harm. Second, it ensures that they will respond appropriately when faced with an accident or other unexpected incident.

Because a thorough assessment of environmental aspects goes beyond normal operational activities and addresses the likelihood of environmental impact under abnormal operating conditions, many organizations find it practical to link the environmental aspects procedure with this requirement. Evaluation of environmental impacts should consider:

- Accidental emissions to the air

- Accidental discharges to water

- Accidental discharges to land

- Specific adverse effects of accidental releases

Information obtained through such an evaluation provides a foundation for procedures that deal with appropriate mitigation and response actions if an incident occurs.

ISO 14001:2004, Appendix A, suggests that an effective emergency response procedure incorporates information about:

- The nature of on-site hazards

- The most likely type and scale of an incident

- The most appropriate methods for responding to an incident

- The actions required to minimize environmental damage

- Evacuation routes and assembly points

- Key personnel and aid agencies

- Sources of assistance from local and other organizations

- Internal and external communication methods

- Post-incident evaluation to determine need for corrective and preventive actions

- Periodic testing of emergency response procedures

The emergency plans that are legally required in many U.S. organizations generally are adequate to fulfill this requirement when an incident occurs as the result of an organization's actions (such as a spill because a hazardous liquid is improperly handled or stored) or a physical deficiency (such as a short circuit that sparks a fire).

A comprehensive emergency plan, however, also takes into account environmental harm that occurs in the wake of natural disasters. Depending on an organization's location, natural occurrences such as earthquakes, hurricanes, blizzards, tornadoes, and floods would be identified as potential emergency situations and appropriate response procedures established.

EXAMPLES

U. S. Steel Gary Works
EMS Procedure 4.4.7—Emergency Preparedness and Response
(Effective October 31, 2005)

1.0 Purpose

    1.1 The purpose of this procedure is to establish and maintain the necessary requirements to identify the potential for and responses to environmental incidents and emergency situations as well as prevent and mitigate the environmental impacts that may occur.

2.0 Scope

    2.1 This procedure applies to all employees and contractor/ suppliers who (1) identify potential and actual environmental incidents, (2) respond to actual environmental incidents, or (3) prevent, reduce, and mitigate environmental impacts associated with environmental incidents.

3.0 References

    3.1 ISO 14001:2004 Standard

    3.2 Environmental Incident Report 70100001 FRM—Exhibit I (page 248)

    3.3 Business Unit Environmental Incident Report 70100007 FRM—Exhibit II

    3.4 Business Unit Formal Fact Finding of Environmental Incident 70100008 FRM—Exhibit III

    3.5 Brochure, *"Integrated Contingency Plan (ICP): An Overview,"* on the Gary Works intranet environmental Web site at: www.xxx

    3.6 ICP manuals are available at various plant locations. For a complete listing of locations, contact the Environmental Control department.

4.0 Definitions

For the purpose of this procedure the following definitions shall apply:

4.1 Integrated Contingency Plan (ICP)—The fully comprehensive manual that contains the detailed requirements to identify the potential for and responses to incidents and emergency situations as well as prevent and mitigate the environmental impacts that may occur.

4.2 *Integrated Contingency Plan: An Overview* (brochure)— Contains summary information from the ICP for the "discoverer" on reporting incidents and for those involved in handling the incident.

4.3 Environmental incident and/or emergency situation—An event that includes: (1) spills or other unpermitted discharges or release of pollutants to the air, water, or land, (2) bypass or malfunction of pollution control equipment, and/or (3) the exceedance of any environmental trigger levels established by or for Gary Complex.

    4.3.1 Exceedance—A violation of a federal, state, or local regulatory limit or condition specified in a permit or consent decree.

4.4 Environmental Incident Reporting System (EIRS)—A database used to record details pertaining to environmental incidents at the Gary Complex. The EIRS includes information used to determine the root cause of the incident and specifies corrective/preventive actions to prevent recurrence of the incident. Each environmental incident at the Gary Complex is assigned a unique EIRS number.

4.5 The Gary Emergency Planning Team consists of Environmental Control, Security and Fire Services, and Safety and Industrial Hygiene.

5.0 Responsibilities

5.1 The following job positions have responsibilities in this procedure:

- Security and Fire Services

- Environmental Control Managers

- Gary Load Dispatchers

- Gary Emergency Planning Team

- Cross-functional teams (CFTs)

- Contractors/suppliers

- All employees

6.0 Procedure

    6.1 Identify Potential Environmental Incidents and Emergency Situations

        6.1.1 The Gary Emergency Planning Team has identified the potential for environmental incidents and emergency situations. These are identified in the ICP.

            6.1.1.1 Input from the cross-functional team's review of environmental aspects may identify additional potential for environmental incidents and emergency situations.

    6.2 Respond to Environmental Incidents and Emergency Situations

        6.2.1 All employees are trained to report environmental incidents and emergency situations to the Gary Works Load Dispatcher. The Load Dispatcher will record details regarding the environmental incident in the Environmental Incident Reporting System and will contact the appropriate Environmental Control Manager on emergency call duty.

            6.2.1.1 If the environmental incident requires a hazardous materials response, the Load Dispatcher will contact the U. S. Steel Security and Fire Services Department.

    6.3 Preventing/Mitigating the Environmental Impacts Associated with Environmental Incidents

        6.3.1 The Gary Complex EMS and Level III Work Instructions are developed, maintained, updated, implemented, and followed to help prevent environmental incidents and emergency situations. They also address the handling of environmental incidents and emergency situations when they do occur.

    6.4 Follow-Up Activities to Environmental Incidents and Emergency Situations

        6.4.1 Environmental Control, Safety and Industrial Hygiene, Security and Fire Services, and/or the involved business unit, staff group, or contractor review the environmental incident and emergency situation and complete the applicable forms in the EIRS.

6.4.1.1 The following forms are used in environmental incidents and emergency situations, where applicable:

- Environmental Incident form (70100001 FRM)

- Business Unit Environmental Incident form (70100007 FRM)

- Business Unit Fact Finding of Environmental Incident (70100008 FRM)

6.4.2 The root cause and corrective/preventive actions are specified in the EIRS report for that incident. Environmental Preventive/Corrective Action Requests (EPCARs) are issued for certain types of environmental incidents (see EMS Procedure 4.5.3—Nonconformity, Corrective Action, and Preventive Action).

6.4.2.1 Environmental Control, Safety and Industrial Hygiene, Security and Fire Services, and/or the involved business unit, staff group, or contractor may take additional actions.

6.4.2.2 Procedures and other documents are reviewed and, when appropriate, revised to ensure that similar environmental incidents and/or emergency situations do not occur.

7.0 Approval

7.1 Approval of this procedure by the Gary Complex Environmental Management System Steering Team is effected by the signature (on the Document Validation Form) of the Manager, Environmental Control that has been designated as the Environmental Management Representative.

7.2 Approved for use.

Manager, Environmental Control and Environmental Management Representative

EMS PROCEDURE 4.4.7—
USS GARY COMPLEX ENVIRONMENTAL INCIDENT REPORT

Incident no._____

Part I: To Be Completed by Load Dispatcher

Received by: _____   Date: _____   Time: _____

Received from: _____   Division: _____   Ext: _____

Date
began:_____   Time: _____   Date
ended:_____   Time: _____

Exact location of incident: _____

Estimated
quantity released:_____   Estimated
area affected: _____

Did material reach plant sewers, GCR, Lake Michigan, other water bodies?_____
If yes, include in description

Description of Incident: *Be specific—include type(s) of material released*

_____
_____
_____
_____

Cause of incident:

_____
_____

What controls and countermeasures have been taken:

_____
_____

Who was contacted: _____   Date: _____   Time: _____

Part II: To Be Completed by Environmental Control

Attach the business unit or contractor Environmental Incident Report

Was verification of business unit or contractor report done? ❑ Yes ❑ No

How? ❑ Field ❑ Phone

Was agency reporting required? ❑ Yes ❑ No *If yes, list agency contact:*

NRC: _____   Date: _____   Time:_____   Incident no. _____

IDEM: _____   Date: _____   Time:_____   Incident no. _____

LERC: _____   Date: _____   Time:_____   Incident no. _____

GAPC:_____   Date: _____   Time:_____   Incident no. _____

Exhibit I   EMS Procedure 4.4.7.   *Continued*

Continued

Cause of incident:

_____

_____

_____

Investigator's   Date of
name and title: _____   investigation: _____

Maintain these records in a permanent file. Attach copies of any related field notes and agency correspondence.

Exhibit I   EMS Procedure 4.4.7.

Delaware North Companies Parks & Resorts

As described in the environmental management system description, emergency response procedures are the responsibility of individual operations.

Coast Guard Air Station Cape Cod
Procedure 17—Training for Spill Response
and Other Incidents
(Effective May 5, 2004)

1.0   Purpose:

To ensure regular scheduled training activities for key personnel identified and required to respond to incidents including, but not limited to, spills, initial onset of fire, and/or a hazardous waste mishap.

2.0   Scope:

2.1   This procedure affects both USCG and civilian employees who are assigned as Satellite Point Managers and/or on the Spill Response Team at ASCC.

3.0   Procedure:

3.1   In each calendar year, Satellite Point Managers shall have at a minimum the following in-house training:

• Annual Hazwaste and Hazwoper training

• Quarterly meetings

3.2 In each calendar year, the Spill Response Team shall have at a minimum the following in-house training:

- Annual Spill Response

- Quarterly spill/emergency response meetings

3.3 Where appropriate (that is, a Satellite Point Manager is also assigned to the Spill Response Team), training may be combined.

3.4 Quarterly meetings are to be held with the intent of ensuring that members are kept appraised of any changes, such as a change in phone numbers, newly assigned member, or new equipment to be used in the response. Meeting may also be used as a "mini" training session, such as in use of a portable fire extinguisher, evacuation procedures, refresher as to locations of fire extinguishers, and so on.

4.0 Responsibilities:

The EH&S Manager, with the support of USCG–ASCC department heads, has the overall responsibility for ensuring that Satellite Point Managers and Spill Response Team Members maintain their qualifications for their assignments.

The Public Safety and Security Officer is responsible for coordinating the annual and quarterly training for Hazwoper and spill response. (Training may be combined where appropriate.)

The Public Safety and Security Officer is also responsible for documenting the annual training and quarterly meetings.

The Fire Safety Technician shall assist the Public Safety Officer in providing practical instructions and updating proper response to varied scenarios.

Individuals assigned as Satellite Point Managers or as Spill Response Team Members are responsible for attending training and quarterly meetings and ensuring that documentation of their attendance is recorded in their training records maintained at the EH&S Department.

5.0 Appendixes:

A. Annual/Quarterly Training/Meetings form

6.0   Related Documentation:

Procedure 03—Record Keeping and Record Retention

Procedure 04—Training Requirements

Procedure 10—Hazardous Materials and Waste Storage Inspection

Procedure 11—Above-Ground Tank Inspection

Procedure 27—Gas Pump Tank Inspection

SPCC Section 14, Training

7.0   Records:

Records generated by this procedure include:

- Annual/Quarterly Training/Meetings form

14

Monitoring and Measurement

It is important for an organization to know whether its environmental management system achieves intended improvements in environmental performance. Recurring evaluation and data collection provide information to confirm the effectiveness of an environmental management system or identify the need for modifications.

ISO 14001:2004 Text	ISO 14001:1996 Text
4.5.1 Monitoring and measurement	*4.5.1 Monitoring and measurement*
The organization shall establish, implement and maintain a procedure(s) to monitor and measure, on a regular basis, the key characteristics of its operations that can have a significant environmental impact. The procedures shall include the documenting of information to monitor performance, applicable operational controls and conformity with the organization's environmental objectives and targets.	The organization shall establish and maintain documented procedures to monitor and measure, on a regular basis, the key characteristics of its operations and activities that can have a significant impact on the environment. This shall include the recording of information to track performance, relevant operational controls and conformance with the organization's objectives and targets.
The organization shall ensure that calibrated or verified monitoring and measurement equipment is used and maintained and shall retain associated records.	Monitoring equipment shall be calibrated and maintained and records of this process shall be retained according to the organization's procedures.

Continued

Continued

ISO 14001:2004 Text	ISO 14001:1996 Text
	The organization shall establish and maintain a documented procedure for periodically evaluating compliance with relevant environmental legislation and regulations.

SIGNIFICANT CHANGES

Two changes to this clause are noteworthy. First, the requirement to document the monitoring and measurement procedure has been removed. It is now up to an organization to decide whether such documentation is necessary. Readers should recall that clause 4.4.4 requires documents that the organization feels are necessary to ensure effective operation and control of processes related to its significant environmental aspects.

Second, the paragraph on evaluating compliance was not retained in the revised clause. ISO 14001:2004 addresses evaluation of compliance in what is now clause 4.5.2.

INTENT OF ISO 14001:2004

As discussed in Chapter 6, ISO 14001:2004 does not require an objective and target for every identified significant aspect. The inability of an organization to address all significant aspects, however, does not diminish its need to be aware of the status of those aspects and their associated impacts.

This clause requires the organization to monitor *all* operational activities that have an actual or potential significant environmental impact, regardless of whether an objective and target have been established for those activities. The resulting data keep the organization informed about its environmental *performance*.

For example, an organization might identify significant impacts that pertain to air and water. It establishes objectives to reduce the impacts on air. By continuing to monitor its impacts on water, however, the organization will discover one of three possible things—impacts on water remain the same, impacts are lessened, or impacts are increased. A change in water quality, whether for better or worse, might be an unforeseen consequence of actions taken to improve air quality. Without regular monitoring, it is likely that such changes would not be noticed.

ISO 14001:2004 defines environmental performance as *measurable* results of an organization's management of its environmental aspects (see section 3.10). *Measurement* can be defined as a deliberate method of designating a numerical value for objects or events. An organization must decide four things for every significant environmental impact:

• *What to measure.* It is important to identify both the tasks that result in adverse environmental impacts and the underlying components of those tasks in order to isolate specific relevant constituents. One or more specific measures can then be established for each relevant component.

An organization that chooses to measure training, for example, could examine resources allocated to training programs, hours of training per employee, percentage of employees involved in training, acquired knowledge by trained employees, and/or reduction in environmental incidents involving trained employees. Acquired knowledge might be an important measure while hours of training per employee is immaterial. An organization must, therefore, employ measures that will provide meaningful information.

• *How to measure.* Four scales of measurement are used in applied statistics. The characteristics of a thing to be measured help determine what kind of measurement scale is appropriate:

– Nominal scales of measurement are used to identify categories of objects or events. The assigned numbers that represent different categories are arbitrary. For example, hazardous waste might be identified by the number "1" and nonhazardous waste by the number "2." Chemicals that result in emissions to air might be classified as "100" while those with discharges to water are "200."

– Ordinal scales reflect values in rank order. Assigned values represent things that are better or worse in comparison to others. Thus, adverse environmental impacts might be labeled "high–medium–low" or rated as "3–2–1." In these examples, "high" and "3" are worse than "medium" and "2" while "low" and "1" are better.

– Interval scales represent equal units of measure. "Pounds (or tons) of hazardous waste" provides one example. The difference between 10 pounds and 11 pounds is exactly the same as the difference between 20 pounds and 21 pounds. One pound always represents exactly the same amount.

- Ratio scales are characterized by equal units of measure and an absolute zero point that is defined as the absence of whatever is being measured. A chemical discharge to water can be measured in parts per million; a measure of zero parts per million means that the chemical has not been discharged.

• *Where to measure.* Some things can be measured at a single point or location in an organization's operation while others require that measures be obtained at multiple points. An effort to measure the amount of hazardous waste generated by different stations in a manufacturing operation might be obtained at a single location because the waste from each station is collected and stored in one designated area. On the other hand, assessing water quality might require sampling at numerous outfalls even though the substance of interest is used at only one area within a facility.

• *When to measure.* An organization must determine whether measures are required continuously (for example, stack emissions over a 24-hour period) or a longer interval is acceptable. Some measures may be taken hourly or daily while others can be collected weekly, monthly, or quarterly. The type of impact and contributing aspects assist in deciding what is appropriate.

Whatever type of measure is selected must be both reliable (it measures consistently) and valid (it accurately measures what it is supposed to). A reliable measure is not necessarily valid; it could consistently measure the wrong thing. A valid measure, however, must be reliable. All measures should be understandable, relevant, and value-neutral.

Once measures are obtained, they can be used to present information in different ways:

- Absolute—raw number without interpretation (for example, total tons of ammonium sulfate discharged per year)

- Relative—information that has been interpreted on the basis of a separate piece of information, such as units of production (for example, tons of ammonium sulfate discharged per ton of product)

- Proportional—information that has been interpreted on the basis of a percentage increase or decrease from a baseline year (for example, percentage decrease in tons of ammonium sulfate discharged during year two compared to tons discharged in year one)

- Aggregated—individual pieces of information that are combined (for example, tons of ammonium sulfate discharged and tons of spent reagent discharged can be combined to describe total tons of pollutants discharged to water).

ISO 14001:2004 also requires the organization to collect information pertaining to operational controls (see Chapter 12) and progress in achieving objectives and targets (see Chapter 6). Operational control requires an understanding of the environmental aspects associated with a particular activity and an established procedure for conducting the activity in an appropriate manner. Data obtained through monitoring and measurement techniques inform an organization whether procedures are being followed and whether they are effective in managing environmental aspects and controlling related environmental impacts.

Specific evaluation criteria should be established for every environmental objective and target. Resulting data help an organization determine whether a proposed course of action yields an anticipated outcome.

Any equipment used for monitoring and measurement must be calibrated or appropriately verified to ensure that any data obtained are accurate.

EXAMPLES

U. S. Steel Gary Works
EMS Procedure 4.5.1—Monitoring and Measurement
(Effective October 26, 2005)

1.0 Purpose

    1.1 This procedure describes the monitoring and measurement of key characteristics of operations and activities associated with significant environmental aspects and impacts.

2.0 Scope

    2.1 This procedure applies to employees who manage and conduct monitoring and measuring functions that are associated with significant environmental aspects.

3.0 References

    3.1 ISO 14001:2004 Standard

    3.2 EMS Procedure 4.3.3—Objectives, Targets, and Programs

4.0 Definitions

    4.1 Key characteristic—A parameter associated with a significant environmental aspect that is monitored and measured on a regular basis to ensure that the parameter falls within limits specified by regulations or operating requirements.

5.0   Responsibilities

   5.1   The following job positions/areas have responsibilities in this procedure:

      • Systems personnel

      • Environmental Control Managers

      • Gary Complex managers

      • Contractors/suppliers

6.0   Procedure

   6.1   Monitoring and Measuring Methods. The monitoring and measuring methods for significant environmental aspects are identified on the ISO 14001 Objectives and Targets page on the Environmental Control intranet Web site. Methods used to monitor the key characteristics of operations associated with significant environmental aspects may include:

      6.1.1   Inspections. Facility and equipment inspections are conducted to ensure that operations are performed in accordance with requirements. The objective of these inspections is to identify and correct situations that could lead to environmental impacts.

      6.1.2   Continuous improvement (CI) projects. The CI process provides planning and progress-tracking tools that enable the identification of and corrective actions for root causes of issues. CI Projects are evaluated for adherence to project-specific goals and objectives in accordance with the implementation schedules established for the project.

      6.1.3   Sampling and analysis programs. Environmental samples and data are collected and analyzed to provide information that determines the environmental perfor-mance at the Gary Complex. Environmental Control and Gary Complex managers are responsible for the coordination of environmental sample and data collection within their areas of responsibility. Environ-mental samples are collected and analyzed in accordance with regulatory and/or Gary Complex methods.

6.1.4   Visible emissions observations. Visible emissions observations are conducted to determine environmental compliance performance at the Gary Complex. These observations are performed by certified Visible Emissions Observers and are conducted in accordance with regulatory and/or Gary Complex methods. The Air Compliance Manager is responsible for visible emissions observations.

6.1.5   Environmental Incident Reporting System/ Environmental Daily Report of Operations (DRO). The Environmental Incident Reporting System and the Environmental DRO are used to record details pertaining to environmental incidents at the Gary Complex. The Environmental Control Department is responsible for the evaluation of conformance with legal and other requirements and for communicating nonconformances through the DRO.

6.2   Monitoring and Measuring Equipment Maintenance

6.2.1   The monitoring and measuring methods listed above may rely on equipment to monitor key characteristics of operations and activities associated with significant environmental aspects. This equipment is maintained by systems personnel in accordance with established procedures or by contractors charged with that responsibility. Activities associated with the maintenance of monitoring and measuring equipment include, but are not limited to, the following:

6.2.1.1   Inspecting and repairing monitoring and measuring equipment.

6.2.1.2   Maintaining documented procedures to control, calibrate, and maintain inspection, measuring, and test equipment.

6.2.1.3   Maintaining and controlling documented procedures, records, and manuals describing equipment test methods, acceptance criteria, and actions to be taken if the equipment is out of calibration.

6.2.1.4 Maintaining calibration information for pertinent monitoring and measuring equipment in an APEX database, Passport database, local records, or in files maintained by the responsible contractor.

6.2.1.5 Maintaining records indicating national or international standards used in test equipment calibration to provide traceability for such calibration. Where there are no nationally or internationally traceable standards, develop and maintain procedures for calibrating equipment.

6.2.1.6 Maintaining inspection, measuring, and equipment calibration records in accordance with the requirements of the U. S. Steel record retention policies.

7.0 Approval

7.1 Approval of this procedure by the Gary Complex Environmental Management System Steering Team is effected by the signature (on the Document Validation Form) of the Manager, Environmental Control that has been designated as the Environmental Management Representative.

7.2 Approved for use.

Manager, Environmental Control and Environmental Management Representative

Delaware North Companies Parks & Resorts P1400.10—Evaluation of Compliance— Monitoring and Measuring
(Effective August 15, 2005)

Policy

Delaware North Companies' GreenPath locations shall maintain documented procedures for evaluating compliance with relevant environmental legislation, regulations, and other requirements, and for monitoring and measuring the performance of the Environmental Management System in regard to its environmental aspects.

Purpose

To describe procedures related to the monitoring and measurement of environmental performance, and the evaluation of compliance with relevant environmental legislation, regulations, and other requirements.

Procedure

Responsibility:

Unit Environmental Managers, or designees, are responsible for establishing procedures to monitor and measure the performance of the Environmental Management System and related activities. The Environmental Managers, or designees, are responsible for implementing and maintaining procedures sufficient to track compliance with relevant environmental legislation, regulations, and other requirements.

Policy:

DNC maintains documented procedures to monitor and measure activities that can have significant impacts on the environment, including performance data, relevant operational controls, conformance with objectives and targets, equipment calibration, compliance with relevant laws and regulations, and/or other requirements.

Process:

Evaluation of Compliance

1. Evaluation of compliance activities are conducted to verify and facilitate improved environmental performance. The purposes of these activities are to:

   - Determine compliance with company environmental policies

   - Determine compliance with applicable laws, regulations, and voluntary obligations

   - Evaluate the effectiveness of environmental management and control systems

   - Evaluate environmental performance

2. Evaluation of compliance may consider environmental matters associated with the facility's activities, including projects, acquisitions and divestments, and activities carried out by contractors.

3. The frequency of these evaluations will be as follows:

- The unit's Environmental Manager will conduct a facilitywide compliance evaluation of all functional areas at least once every three years.

- In each of the two intervening years, limited-scope compliance evaluations may address three of the following eight functional areas:

  1. Hazardous waste

  2. Air pollution control

  3. Solid waste

  4. Water pollution control

  5. Reclamation

  6. Endangered species and other plants and animals

  7. Hazardous materials and substances

  8. Storage tanks

4. Evaluations of compliance may cover selected topics or functional areas. It is not a requirement that all activities be assessed at the same frequency.

5. As soon as possible after completion of compliance-evaluation activities, the Environmental Manager shall prepare a formal report of findings, including the following:

   - Regulatory issues. Any potential violations of laws

   - Company policy. Deficiencies in addressing company policies or procedures

   - Best management practices. Recommendations for improvement in practices, systems, or procedures

   - The report shall be reviewed with facility personnel, as appropriate

   - A copy of the report shall be submitted to the unit's general manager and the Director of Environmental Affairs

6. An action plan to resolve all deficiencies shall be prepared by operating unit and environmental staff.

   - The action plan will then be reviewed and approved by operating unit management

- Corrective actions should begin as soon as possible

- Findings related to regulatory issues should be resolved within three months

- All findings are to be resolved within one year

Monitoring and Measuring

1. Monitoring and measuring are conducted to verify and facilitate improved environmental performance. The purposes of these activities are to:

   - Determine compliance with company environmental policies

   - Determine compliance with applicable voluntary obligations

   - Evaluate the effectiveness of environmental management and control systems

   - Evaluate environmental performance

2. Monitoring and measuring may consider environmental matters associated with the facility's activities, including projects, acquisitions and divestments, and activities carried out by contractors.

3. The frequency of these activities will be determined by the complexity of the issues at the unit. The Environmental Manager will create a list of issues and/or activities that must be subjected to this procedure, including a monitoring and measuring schedule. The issues and/or activities may include:

   - Environmental equipment requiring calibration

   - Environmental objectives, targets, management plans, and related activity logs

   - Utility records and associated reports/charts

   - Waste records and transport manifests

   - Other environmental records

4. As soon as possible after completion of monitoring and measuring activities, the Environmental Manager shall prepare a formal report of findings, including the following:

   - Changes in objectives and targets.

   - Company policy. Deficiencies in addressing company policies or procedures.

- Progress on objectives, targets, and environmental management plans.

- Best management practices. Recommendations for improvement in practices, systems, or procedures.

- The report shall be reviewed with facility personnel, as appropriate.

- A copy of the report shall be submitted to the unit's general manager and the Director of Environmental Affairs.

5. An action plan to resolve all deficiencies shall be prepared by operating unit and environmental staff.

   - The action plan will then be reviewed and approved by operating unit management

   - Corrective actions should begin as soon as possible

   - Findings related to regulatory issues should be resolved within three months

   - All findings are to be resolved within one year

Coast Guard Air Station Cape Cod
Procedure 21—Monitoring Air Emissions
(Effective January 15, 2002)

1.0 Purpose:

The Commonwealth of Massachusetts considers Air Station Cape Cod as an industrial facility, requiring a permit and monitoring of all sources of emissions having the potential to affect air quality. This is to identify permitting and reporting requirements. Since a permit defining the restrictions on air emissions in accord with the Commonwealth of Massachusetts is in place, this procedure specifies the proper reporting requirements and renewal process.

2.0 Scope:

   2.1 This procedure affects ASCC's operations facilities and government housing.

3.0 Procedure:

   3.1 In accord with the Commonwealth of Massachusetts, ASCC has obtained an air emissions permit.

3.2 The permit is to be reviewed annually to ensure that the permit is consistent with current operations. An annual fee and required accompanying report is submitted. (The review, reporting, and payment of fees is prompted by the Commonwealth.) Follow the renewal application instructions.

3.3 Throughout the calendar year, natural gas purchase receipts, bills (or copies thereof), and a log of when and how long the emergency generator was running shall be maintained.

4.0 Responsibilities:

4.1 The EH&S Department Head is responsible for record keeping, ensuring that ASCC operates within the confines of the current permit, and renewing the permit.

4.2 Engineering Facility Engineer is responsible for notifying the EH&S Department Head of when and how long the emergency generator operated and any changes to source equipment.

Procedure 11—Above-Ground Tank Inspection
(Effective June 30, 2003)

1.0 Purpose:

To identify above-ground tank inspections.

2.0 Scope:

2.1 This procedure includes all above-ground tanks at the Massachusetts Military Reservation that are under the ownership or operation of the USCG.

2.2 The locations of the above-ground tanks are noted in the Spill Prevention Control and Contingency Plan, Appendix C.

3.0 Procedure:

3.1 The Satellite Point Manager will inspect the above-ground tanks and surrounding area daily and weekly. The Manager will:

• Look for leaks or signs of corrosion on the tanks

• Look for damage or cracks to the secondary containment area

• Check that proper signs are/remain posted

- Verify that the tank area is secure from accidental ruptures

- Check that drains are clear

- Where applicable, test the alarm

3.2 Upon completion of the daily inspection, the Satellite Manager will complete a CG green logbook, entering the date of inspection, tanks inspected, and comments as necessary.

3.3 The Satellite Manager will complete the inspection log weekly. A copy of the weekly inspection log sheet is provided in Appendix A of this procedure.

3.4 If a deficiency is noted, detail on the deficiency shall be provided as well as corrective action, time period in which the action is to be taken, and any other individual notified of the deficiency.

3.5 Once a week, the Environmental Protection Specialist will review the above-ground tank locations, logbook, and log sheet entries.

3.6 The Environmental Protection Specialist will coordinate with the Satellite Point Manager and the appropriate department head for a review of the deficiency (if any) and implementation of corrective action.

3.7 Any discrepancies noted will be reported to the EH&S Department Head. Action will be taken at the department head level for any discrepancies that persist.

4.0 Responsibilities:

Site Manager is responsible for:

- Maintaining the above-ground tank and surrounding area

- Inspecting the above-ground tank(s) daily and weekly

- At the 3-in-1, inspecting the gas pumps weekly

- Corrective action of any deficiencies noted during inspections

Environmental Protection Specialist is responsible for:

- Auditing log entries

- (Re)inspecting sites as necessary

EH&S Department Head and respective department heads are responsible for the implementation of this procedure.

5.0   Appendixes:

A. Above-Ground Tank Inspection Log

6.0   Related Documentation:

Spill Prevention Control and Countermeasure Plan

Procedure 03—Record Keeping and Record Retention

7.0   Records:

Records generated by this procedure include:

• Above-Ground Tank Inspection Log

15

Evaluation of Compliance

An organization's environmental performance is directly related to its efforts regarding regulatory compliance and fulfillment of requirements associated with voluntary environmental programs and initiatives.

ISO 14001:2004 Text	ISO 14001:1996 Text
4.5.2.1 Consistent with its commitment to compliance, the organization shall establish, implement and maintain a procedure(s) for periodically evaluating compliance with applicable legal requirements.	*4.5.1 Monitoring and measurement [paragraph 3]*
	The organization shall establish and maintain a documented procedure for periodically evaluating compliance with relevant environmental legislation and regulations.
The organization shall keep records of the results of the periodic evaluations.	
4.5.2.2 The organization shall evaluate compliance with other requirements to which it subscribes. The organization may wish to combine this evaluation with the evaluation of legal compliance referred to in 4.5.2.1 or to establish a separate procedure(s).	
The organization shall keep records of the results of the periodic evaluations.	

SIGNIFICANT CHANGES

ISO 14001:2004 begins by stating that the procedure required by this clause is linked to the commitment to compliance that is contained in the environmental policy statement.

The requirement to evaluate compliance with other requirements has been added. ISO 14001:1996 required the environmental policy to contain a commitment to comply with other requirements but made no mention of evaluation.

INTENT OF ISO 14001:2004

Regulatory compliance and compliance with other (voluntary) requirements are referred to in three clauses. Clause 4.2 requires an organization to commit to compliance. Clause 4.3.2 requires an organization to identify all of the applicable legal and other requirements with which it must comply.

This clause says, in essence, that it is not enough to know what legal and other requirements are applicable; an organization must ensure that it actually complies with those requirements. ISO 14001:2004 does not specify that an organization perform a compliance *audit*. Any kind of monitoring activity is acceptable so long as it is executed in a manner that provides information about compliance or lack thereof.

Evaluation of compliance can be incorporated into other evaluation efforts. Many organizations find it efficient to monitor compliance in conjunction with monitoring activities related to significant environmental impacts, operational controls, and environmental objectives and targets (see Chapter 14).

Some organizations choose to combine evaluation of compliance with the environmental management system audit. This approach, however, affects the way in which audit results are handled. Traditionally, compliance audit findings have been protected in two ways:

- Attorney–client privilege permits open discussion between a client and his legal counsel so that the client can obtain effective representation without fear of disclosure. For a compliance audit to be so protected, it must be initiated upon advice of counsel and conducted under the supervision of an attorney.

- Attorney work product privilege protects information such as notes, memoranda, witness statements, and other materials developed by an attorney on behalf of a client. For a compliance audit to be protected under this doctrine, it must be conducted in anticipation

      of litigation and its purpose must be to assist in the client's
legal defense.

Because environmental management system audits are conducted on a planned, ongoing basis, such audits are considered part of normal business activities and, therefore, are not protected. Moreover, audit results typically are shared throughout the audited organization, a practice antithetical to the legal protections described. Thus, the audit is a management tool rather than an activity related to pending litigation. If evaluation of compliance is combined with evaluation of the environmental management system, all findings become part of the system audit and, therefore, are not protected. An organization that wants to protect findings related to regulatory compliance is well advised to keep the two activities separate.

    It is not necessary to keep evaluation of compliance with other requirements to which an organization subscribes separate from an environmental management system audit. Because noncompliance with an industry code of conduct does not carry the same legal liability as regulatory noncompliance, it is unlikely that an organization would seek to shield findings related to compliance with voluntary initiatives.

    For ISO 14001 registration, an organization must provide evidence of:

- A procedure for evaluating legal compliance

- A procedure for evaluating compliance with other requirements to which the organization subscribes

- Implementation of those procedures

- Compliance review by management (required by clause 4.6)

- Corrective action for any noncompliance

In a registration audit, discovery of noncompliance with either a legal requirement or a voluntary requirement to which an organization subscribes does not, in and of itself, mean that the environmental management system shows nonconformance. It can be argued that the environmental management system is performing well because implementation of this required procedure uncovered a problem that might otherwise have gone unnoticed. The commitment to compliance embodied in the environmental policy requires that any identified noncompliance must be addressed by appropriate corrective and preventive actions.

    The registrar audit team will first attempt to determine whether the auditee organization's internal audit team identified the same noncompliance. If it has, the registrar audit team will assess corrective and preventive actions taken. Assuming that such actions are appropriate and timely, the environmental management system will be deemed effective and no system nonconformity report will be generated. If the organization has not responded to the noncompliance, it is likely that a system nonconformity report will be written for failing to fulfill the commitment to compliance (clause 4.2).

If the organization's internal audit has not identified the noncompliance, the registrar audit team will ascertain whether the organization has identified and has access to its legal and other requirements. If it has not identified the requirement for which the noncompliance was detected, a system nonconformity report associated with clause 4.3.2 will be generated.

If the organization has identified the requirement with which it fails to comply, the registrar audit team will question why evaluation of compliance did not reveal this deficiency. It is likely that the system nonconformity report will be associated with clause 4.5.2.

EXAMPLES

U. S. Steel Gary Works
EMS Procedure 4.5.2—Evaluation of Compliance
(Effective October 31, 2005)

1.0 Purpose

    1.1 This procedure describes the methods for the evaluation of environmental compliance at the Gary Complex.

2.0 Scope

    2.1 This procedure applies to employees who are involved in the evaluation of environmental compliance information.

3.0 References

    3.1 ISO 14001:2004 Standard

    3.2 EMS Procedure 4.5.1—Monitoring and Measurement

    3.3 EMS Procedure 4.5.3—Nonconformity, Corrective Action, and Preventive Action

    3.4 EMS Procedure 4.5.5—Internal Audit

4.0 Definitions

    4.1 (None)

5.0 Responsibilities

5.1 The following job positions/areas have responsibilities in this procedure:

- Environmental Control Technical Services Managers

- ISO 14001 Coordinator

- Contractors/suppliers

- U. S. Steel Law Department

- U. S. Steel Audit Department

- U. S. Steel Environmental Affairs

6.0 Procedure

6.1 Environmental Compliance Data Collection

6.1.1 The collection of environmental compliance data and information is described in Section 6.1 of EMS Procedure 4.5.1—Monitoring and Measurement.

6.2 Environmental Compliance Evaluation

6.2.1 Environmental Control Technical Services Managers are responsible for the evaluation of information and data to determine compliance with legal and other requirements at the Gary Complex.

6.2.1.1 The Technical Services Managers may enlist the assistance of U. S. Steel Environmental Affairs and/or U. S. Steel Law Department in the determination of compliance with legal and other requirements.

6.2.2 The ISO 14001 Coordinator is responsible for the scheduling and completion of quarterly audits of objectives and targets and periodic audits of selective environmental compliance issues (see EMS Procedure 4.5.5).

6.2.2.1 An Environmental Preventive and Corrective Action Request (EPCAR) is developed for a noncompliance with legal and other requirements and when a nonconformance is determined by internal EMS audits (see EMS Procedure 4.5.3).

6.2.3 Contractors/suppliers whose activities and services require the establishment and maintenance of on-site operations and equipment are required to participate in periodic reviews of the environmental compliance issues related to their operations. This compliance review includes physical inspections of contractor facilities and a review of required environmental plans and documents. The ISO 14001 Coordinator develops the schedule of contractor environmental compliance reviews as part of the internal audit process. The selection of contractors is based on previous compliance performance, time interval since last review, and the magnitude of the contractor's activities. Deficiencies identified through this inspection process are addressed in accordance with EMS Procedure 4.5.3—Nonconformity, Corrective Action, and Preventive Action.

6.2.4   Periodic corporate environmental compliance audits are conducted to evaluate conformance with relevant environmental regulations, permit conditions, and legal agreements.

6.2.4.1   The U. S. Steel Law Department develops audit plans.

6.2.4.2   The audit teams comprise U. S. Steel representatives from the Law Department, Audit Division, Environmental Affairs, and other U. S. Steel facilities.

6.2.4.3   The U. S. Steel Law Department submits audit reports to the general manager and plant managers.

6.2.4.4   The U. S. Steel Audit Division tracks progress toward closure of exceptions discovered during these audits.

6.2.4.5   All audit documentation, including but not limited to audit results, audit reports, and audit item closure reports, is subject to attorney–client privilege.

6.3   Environmental Compliance Communication

6.3.1   The Environmental Daily Report of Operations (DRO) provides environmental compliance summaries for all business units at the Gary Complex. The DRO includes regulatory and internal exceedances, reportable events, and other classifications of environmental incidents. The DRO is available on the Gary Complex intranet Web site at www.xxx.

6.3.2 Environmental performance charts provide tracking and trending information for each business unit at the Gary Complex. Environmental performance charts are available on the Gary Complex intranet Web site.

6.3.3 Environmental compliance information is also communicated by:

- Plant management meetings

- Area manager meetings

- Corrective/preventive action notifications

- Audit reports

- Telephone/pager alert systems

- Environmental bulletins

7.0 Approval

7.1 Approval of this procedure by the Gary Complex Environmental Management System Steering Team is effected by the signature (on the Document Validation Form) of the Manager, Environmental Control that has been designated as the Environmental Management Representative.

7.2 Approved for use.

Manager, Environmental Control and Environmental Management Representative

Delaware North Companies Parks & Resorts
P1400.10—Evaluation of Compliance—
Monitoring and Measuring
(Effective August 15, 2005)

Policy

Delaware North Companies' GreenPath locations shall maintain documented procedures for evaluating compliance with relevant environmental legislation, regulations, and other requirements, and for monitoring and measuring the performance of the Environmental Management System in regard to its environmental aspects.

Purpose

To describe procedures related to the monitoring and measurement of environmental performance and the evaluation of compliance with relevant environmental legislation, regulations, and other requirements.

Procedure

Responsibility:

Unit Environmental Managers, or designees, are responsible for establishing procedures to monitor and measure the performance of the Environmental Management System and related activities. The Environmental Managers, or designees, are responsible for implementing and maintaining procedures sufficient to track compliance with relevant environmental legislation, regulations, and other requirements.

Policy:

DNC maintains documented procedures to monitor and measure activities that can have significant impacts on the environment, including performance data, relevant operational controls, conformance with objectives and targets, equipment calibration, compliance with relevant laws and regulations, and/or other requirements.

Process:

Evaluation of Compliance

1. Compliance-evaluation activities are conducted to verify and facilitate improved environmental performance. The purposes of these activities are to:

   - Determine compliance with company environmental policies

   - Determine compliance with applicable laws, regulations, and voluntary obligations

   - Evaluate the effectiveness of environmental management and control systems

   - Evaluate environmental performance

2. Evaluation of compliance may consider environmental matters associated with the facility's activities, including projects, acquisitions and divestments, and activities carried out by contractors.

3. The frequency of these evaluations will be as follows:

   • The unit's Environmental Manager will conduct a facilitywide compliance evaluation of all functional areas at least once every three years.

   • In each of the two intervening years, limited-scope compliance evaluations may address three of the following eight functional areas:

     1. Hazardous waste

     2. Air pollution control

     3. Solid waste

     4. Water pollution control

     5. Reclamation

     6. Endangered species and other plants and animals

     7. Hazardous materials and substances

     8. Storage tanks

4. Evaluations of compliance may cover selected topics or functional areas. It is not a requirement that all activities be assessed at the same frequency.

5. As soon as possible after completion of compliance-evaluation activities, the Environmental Manager shall prepare a formal report of findings, including the following:

   • Regulatory issues. Any potential violations of laws.

   • Company policy. Deficiencies in addressing company policies or procedures.

   • Best management practices. Recommendations for improvement in practices, systems, or procedures.

   • The report shall be reviewed with facility personnel, as appropriate.

- A copy of the report shall be submitted to the unit's general manager and the Director of Environmental Affairs.

6. An action plan to resolve all deficiencies shall be prepared by operating unit and environmental staff.

   - The action plan will then be reviewed and approved by operating unit management

   - Corrective actions should begin as soon as possible

   - Findings related to regulatory issues should be resolved within three months

   - All findings are to be resolved within one year

Monitoring and Measuring

1. Monitoring and measuring are conducted to verify and facilitate improved environmental performance. The purposes of these activities are to:

   - Determine compliance with company environmental policies

   - Determine compliance with applicable voluntary obligations

   - Evaluate the effectiveness of environmental management and control systems

   - Evaluate environmental performance

2. Monitoring and measuring may consider environmental matters associated with the facility's activities, including projects, acquisitions and divestments, and activities carried out by contractors.

3. The frequency of these activities will be determined by the complexity of the issues at the unit. The Environmental Manager will create a list of issues and/or activities that must be subjected to this procedure, including a monitoring and measuring schedule. The issues and/or activities may include:

   - Environmental equipment requiring calibration

   - Environmental objectives, targets, management plans, and related activity logs

   - Utility records and associated reports/charts

   - Waste records and transport manifests

   - Other environmental records

4. As soon as possible after completion of monitoring and measuring activities, the Environmental Manager shall prepare a formal report of findings, including the following:

   - Changes in objectives and targets.

   - Company policy. Deficiencies in addressing company policies or procedures.

   - Progress on objectives, targets, and environmental management plans.

   - Best management practices. Recommendations for improvement in practices, systems, or procedures.

   - The report shall be reviewed with facility personnel, as appropriate.

   - A copy of the report shall be submitted to the unit's general manager and the Director of Environmental Affairs.

5. An action plan to resolve all deficiencies shall be prepared by operating unit and environmental staff.

   - The action plan will then be reviewed and approved by operating unit management

   - Corrective actions should begin as soon as possible

   - Findings related to regulatory issues should be resolved within three months

   - All findings are to be resolved within one year

Coast Guard Air Station Cape Cod

Performance Track promotes sustained regulatory compliance through several program components, including compliance self-audits and annual certification that a facility continues to maintain compliance. In response, Air Station Cape Cod has established procedures to address individual regulations. They provide information pertaining to handling and use of the regulated entity and describe how compliance is evaluated.

16

Nonconformity, Corrective Action, and Preventive Action

Failure to correct deficiencies in an environmental management system can render it ineffective over time. Successful systems are characterized by efforts to identify both actual and potential problems and actions to address real and perceived shortcomings.

ISO 14001:2004 Text	ISO 14001:1996 Text
4.5.3 Nonconformity, corrective action and preventive action	*4.5.2 Nonconformance and corrective and preventive action*
The organization shall establish, implement and maintain a procedure(s) for dealing with actual and potential nonconformity(ies) and for taking corrective action and preventive action. The procedure(s) shall define requirements for a) identifying and correcting nonconformity(ies) and taking action(s) to mitigate their environmental impacts, b) investigating nonconformity(ies), determining their cause(s) and taking actions in order to avoid their recurrence,	The organization shall establish and maintain procedures for defining responsibility and authority for handling and investigating nonconformance, taking action to mitigate any impacts caused and for initiating and completing corrective and preventive action. Any corrective or preventive action taken to eliminate the causes of actual and potential nonconformances shall be appropriate to the magnitude of problems and commensurate with the environmental impact encountered.

Continued

Continued

ISO 14001:2004 Text	ISO 14001:1996 Text
c) evaluating the need for action(s) to prevent nonconformity(ies) and implementing appropriate actions designed to avoid their occurrence, d) recording the results of corrective action(s) and preventive action(s) taken, and e) reviewing the effectiveness of corrective action(s) and preventive action(s) taken. Actions taken shall be appropriate to the magnitude of the problems and the environmental impacts encountered. The organization shall ensure that any necessary changes are made to environmental management system documentation.	The organization shall implement and record any changes in the documented procedures resulting from corrective and preventive action.

SIGNIFICANT CHANGES

ISO 14001:2004 presents a more detailed explanation of required actions than was included in the original standard. There is increased emphasis on preventive action. Although ISO 14001:1996 required a procedure for initiating and completing preventive action, this was commonly interpreted to mean preventing the recurrence of an identified nonconformity. ISO 14001:2004 clearly articulates that preventive action must focus on preventing nonconformities from occurring at all.

Measures associated with corrective action also have been clarified. ISO 14001:2004 specifies that the cause of an identified nonconformity must be determined in order to prevent its recurrence. The original standard required "investigation" of nonconformities but did not spell out a need for root cause analysis.

Finally, ISO 14001:2004 requires an organization to review its corrective and preventive actions to determine whether those actions were effective. The original standard contained no similar requirement.

Note that the term *nonconformity* replaces *nonconformance*.

INTENT OF ISO 14001:2004

This clause pertains to any failure to fulfill a requirement imposed by ISO 14001:2004 or an organization's environmental management system documentation. Such failure constitutes an *actual* nonconformity, defined in Section 3.15 as "non-fulfillment of a requirement." It also addresses *potential* nonconformities—weaknesses that do not presently meet the burden of proof of nonconformity but could deteriorate over time.

ISO 14001:2004 defines corrective action (section 3.3) as "action to eliminate the cause of a *detected* nonconformity." Preventive action (section 3.17) is defined as "action to eliminate the cause of a *potential* nonconformity."

Identification of nonconformities tends to be considered in conjunction with environmental management system audits (see Chapter 18). In reality, nonconformities often are identified within the course of daily activities as workers observe actual or potential problems within their individual areas of responsibility.

Regardless of the manner in which actual nonconformities are identified, an organization is expected to correct them. Although it is up to an organization to determine how it will proceed, corrective action commonly focuses on the following measures:

- Taking immediate action to stop the problem

- Initiating analysis of the root cause of the problem

- Implementing a temporary action, if appropriate, until the root cause can be determined

- Based on the results of the root cause analysis, instituting appropriate actions to correct the nonconformity and prevent it from recurring

In addition, an organization must address past problems that occurred as the result of nonconformities. By way of analogy, consider an automobile in which the steering wheel falls off under normal driving conditions. It is not sufficient for the manufacturer to change the design so that the steering wheel remains attached on all newly built cars. Cars already sold also must be fixed. Similarly, corrective action is inadequate if it is solely future-directed. An organization must take action to mitigate environmental harm that already resulted from the nonconformity.

The preventive action response is similar:

- Analyze the root cause of the potential problem

- Based on the results of the root cause analysis, institute appropriate actions to correct the deficiency and prevent it from degenerating to the point of nonconformity

A likely outcome of both corrective and preventive action is change to one or more elements of the environmental management system. Any changes to the system must be made known. Therefore, organizations must incorporate these changes into system documentation (including procedures, operating instructions, and emergency plans), communication efforts, training programs, delineation of responsibility, and allocation of resources, as appropriate.

EXAMPLES

U. S. Steel Gary Works
EMS Procedure 4.5.3—Nonconformity and
Corrective and Preventive Action
(Effective September 19, 2005)

1.0 Purpose

    1.1 The purpose of this procedure is to describe the Gary Complex Environmental Management System (EMS) requirements for the analysis of potential and/or actual environmental nonconformities and the resultant preventive/corrective actions.

2.0 Scope

    2.1 This procedure applies to employees who are involved in the preventive/corrective action process at the Gary Complex.

3.0 References

    3.1 ISO 14001:2004 Standard

    3.2 EMS Procedure 4.5.4—Control of Records

3.3 EMS Procedure 4.5.5—Internal Audits

3.4 EMS Procedure 4.6—Management Review

3.5 Environmental Preventive/Corrective Action Request (EPCAR)—Exhibit I (page 291)

3.6 Example of a completed EPCAR—Exhibit II (page 293)

3.7 EPCAR Log and Jeopardy Report—Exhibit III (page 295)

4.0 Definitions

For the purpose of this procedure the following definitions shall apply:

4.1 Corrective action—Action taken to eliminate the cause of a nonconformity or other undesirable situation in order to prevent recurrence.

4.2 Preventive action—Action taken to eliminate the cause of a potential nonconformity or other undesirable situation.

4.3 Environmental Preventive/Corrective Action Request (EPCAR)—A form (Exhibit I) that is used to request environmental preventive/corrective action and document completion of preventive/corrective action.

4.4 Preventive/Corrective Action Plan—A document (EPCAR) specifying actions to be implemented for preventive/corrective actions with responsibilities and target dates assigned.

4.5 EPCAR Log—A tracking record to monitor progress of the preventive/corrective action system.

4.6 Jeopardy Report—A report used to facilitate timely completion of EPCARs.

4.7 Natural owner—The individual assigned to determine the root cause and who has the authority and responsibility to implement preventive/corrective action.

4.8 Objective evidence—Information that is verifiable and is based on facts obtained through observation, measurement, testing, or other means.

4.9 Systemic environmental issues—Recurring environmental issues with common environmental impacts.

5.0   Responsibilities

   5.1   The following job positions/functions have responsibilities in this procedure:

- Business unit/staff organization managers
- Environmental Management Representative (EMR)
- Gary Complex employees
- ISO 14001 Coordinator
- EPCAR natural owner(s)
- EPCAR verifiers

6.0   Procedure

   6.1   The Gary Complex Environmental Management System may use diagnostic analysis, environmental records, audits, and regulatory reports to highlight the need for preventive and corrective actions.

   6.2   When the general manager, plant managers, business unit/ staff organization managers, the EMR, and/or their management designees determine that environmental preventive/corrective action is needed, an Environmental Preventive/Corrective Action Request (EPCAR) is originated.

      6.2.1   Corrective and preventive action EPCARs may be used to address issues as a result of:

- Notifications from regulatory agencies
- Facility inspections by U. S. Steel or regulatory agencies
- Trigger limit exceedances
- Continuous improvement items from EMS audits and meetings
- Diagnostic analysis or performance results of environmental activities

      6.2.2   EPCARs must be used as identified below when the following conditions occur:

- Serious potential release incidents (75 percent of RQ)

- Release of any quantity of spent pickle liquor, raw coke oven gas, or PCBs ≥ 50 ppm released outside of containment

- Noncompliance with regulatory or consent order limits and conditions

- Third-party audit findings

- Internal Environmental Management System audit findings

6.2.2.1   Issuance of additional EPCARS is not required for nonconformities that are addressed by a previous open EPCAR or for nonconformities where the corrective actions have been implemented.

6.2.3   Corrective Action EPCARs are issued for systemic environmental issues.

6.2.3.1   An established continuous improvement (CI) team in the affected business unit must manage these EPCARs. The Environmental Control Department monitors the effectiveness of corrective actions for these EPCARs under this continuous improvement process. Insufficient progress will require modification of the continuous improvement projects.

6.2.3.2   If the continuous improvement process is not effective in reducing recurring environmental incidents, plant management will develop a program to eliminate the recurring environmental incidents. This program may include but is not limited to focused training activities or work practice audits. Issuance of individual EPCARs for recurring environmental incidents may be withheld while this corrective action program is active.

6.3   Environmental Preventive/Corrective Action Requests (EPCARs)

6.3.1   Initiating an EPCAR

6.3.1.1 The originator describes the problem/nonconformity and attaches any supporting evidence or documents that help clarify or better define the problem.

6.3.1.2 EPCARs may also be generated by providing the necessary information; the ISO 14001 Coordinator or designee prepares the EPCAR.

6.3.2 The ISO 14001 Coordinator may consult with the EMR to determine if the EPCAR is to be processed and if preventive/corrective action is required for the stated problem. If the EPCAR is not processed, the originator is notified and "documentation" is not retained.

6.3.3 Issuing the EPCAR. The originator of the EPCAR determines the appropriate recipient of the EPCAR and completes the "Issued to" field on the EPCAR form.

6.3.4 Assigning natural owner. The "issued to" person or designee assigns a "natural owner" who is automatically notified by e-mail.

6.3.5 Assigning a root cause and establishing a Corrective/Preventive Action Plan and completion schedule. The natural owner evaluates the problem and completes the "Root cause of problem" (section 2) and "Preventive/corrective action taken to eliminate root cause," and "Estimated completion date" (section 3).

6.3.5.1 If appropriate, indicate any interim actions required to prevent further problems if permanent correction cannot be implemented in a timely manner.

6.3.5.2 If appropriate, indicate required procedures and/or work instructions that are being changed to reflect the changes required in the system to prevent recurrence. If necessary, training must be completed on revised procedures and work instructions.

6.3.6 Time limitations. Sections 6.3.4 and 6.3.5 of this procedure must be completed in the EPCAR form within 15 days from the date the EPCAR is issued (section 6.3.3). The only exception to this requirement is when

EPCARs are issued to contractors, and then the time limitation is 30 days.

6.3.7   Completion of EPCAR. When the natural owner has completed all preventive/corrective actions, the "Actual completion date" is then entered (section 3).

6.3.8   Verification of preventive/corrective action. The ISO 14001 Coordinator or designee assigns an independent auditor to verify that the preventive/corrective action has been completed and is effective. Objective evidence and/or observation are required to verify completion. In the event that the preventive/corrective action has not been completed, the natural owner is advised of the need for further action. The person verifying that the preventive/corrective action has been done completes section 4 boxes "Preventive/corrective action verified by," "Date verified," and "Results of verification." The EPCAR and supporting objective evidence (if applicable) are sent to the ISO 14001 Coordinator. In some cases, the ISO 14001 Coordinator or designee may add clarifying comments and/or additions.

6.3.9   Closing the EPCAR. The ISO 14001 Coordinator or designee reviews the objective evidence and/or observations with the auditor, verifying completion of the preventive/corrective action, and closes the EPCAR by completing section 4. In the event that the action has not been completed or is ineffective, the natural owner is contacted with an explanation why the EPCAR was not closed and that further action is required.

6.3.10 A notification of the closed EPCAR will be electronically sent to the originator. If the originator determines that the corrective action plan is incomplete, ineffective, or does not resolve the problem, the ISO 14001 Coordinator is notified and a new EPCAR may be issued.

6.3.11 Copies of closed EPCARs may be electronically sent to other managers who may implement the appropriate actions and controls in their area of responsibility, if applicable (preventive action).

6.3.12 Preventive and corrective actions that are ongoing for business units where operations are suspended or terminated will be assigned a status equivalent to those operations (suspended or terminated). Those preventive and corrective actions will be reinstated within 30 days after operations have resumed.

6.4   EPCAR Log/Jeopardy Report

6.4.1   The ISO 14001 Coordinator or designee is responsible for the EPCAR Log System and Jeopardy Report.

6.4.1.1   The EPCAR Log (Exhibit III, page 295). The ISO 14001 Coordinator or designee will maintain the EPCAR Log System. Several options for sorting information on the EPCAR Log are available. These "sorts" are used to more effectively manage the EPCAR System. Reports are available electronically.

6.4.1.2   The electronic EPCAR Log System issues the Jeopardy Report (Exhibit III, page 295) identifying that the EPCAR is coming due, is due, or is past due. The Jeopardy Report is used by the Environmental Control ISO 14001 Steering Team to facilitate timely completion.

6.5   The preventive/corrective actions taken on a selected number of closed EPCARs will be evaluated for ongoing implementation and effectiveness during internal Environmental Management System audits. Closed EPCARs that have demonstrated ongoing implementation and effectiveness through EMS internal audits require no further action. Closed EPCARs that have not demonstrated ongoing implementation and effectiveness will be addressed through issuance of a new EPCAR.

6.6   If preventive/corrective action cannot be implemented, the originator may discontinue the EPCAR or the EMR may discontinue the EPCAR.

6.7   At least annually, the status, implementation, and effectiveness of this procedure and the EPCAR system are reviewed during Gary Complex EMS Steering Team meetings (EMS Procedure 4.6—Management Review).

7.0 Approval

    7.1 Approval of this procedure by the Gary Complex Environmental Management System Steering Team is effected by the signature (on the Document Validation Form) of the Manager, Environmental Control that has been designated as the Environmental Management Representative.

    7.2 Approved for use.

        Manager, Environmental Control and Environmental Management Representative

Status	EPCAR no.

Section 1—Originator completes

Problem/nonconformity description:	
Type:	Reason:
Originator:	Date written:

Section 2—Issued to and natural owner completes

Issued to:	Issue date:
Natural owner:	Date assigned:
Root cause of problem:	
Business unit formal fact finding of environmental incidents required? Yes ❑ No ❑	

Continued

Exhibit I   EMS Procedure 4.5.3—Environmental Preventive/Corrective Action Request.

Continued

Section 3—Natural owner completes

Preventive/corrective action taken to eliminate root cause:	
Estimated completion date:	Actual completion date:

Section 4—Person verifying preventive/corrective action completes

Verified by:	Date verified:
Results of verification:	
EPCAR closed by:	Date closed:

Section 5

EPCARs issued to other processes/products similar to the ones for which the corrective actions were developed:			
EPCAR no(s).	Description area(s)	Area(s)	Create date:

Exhibit I   EMS Procedure 4.5.3—Environmental Preventive/Corrective Action Request.

Status: Closed	EPCAR no.: 16

Section 1

Problem/nonconformity description:
Gary Works has considered processes for external communication on its significant environmental aspects, but has not recorded its decision, as required by EMS Procedure 4.4.2. The Record of Decision does not appear in either the Level I manual or Level II procedure. Neither document provides a reference to the Record of Decision, and the ISO 14001 Coordinator was unable to provide this record.

Type: Environmental	Reason: Training
Originator: Brown, Donna Jean	Date written: 04/09/2001

Section 2

Issued to: Green, Ken	Issue date: 04/09/2001
Natural owner: Gray, Rick	Date assigned: 04/12/2001

Root cause of problem:
Communications Record of Decision issue was presented to the EMS steering team at a November 3, 2000 management review meeting, but was not decided pending more information on how Clairton Works handled this issue.

Business unit formal fact finding of environmental incidents required? Yes ❑ No ☒

Section 3

Preventive/corrective action taken to eliminate root cause:
Provided necessary information to EMS steering team in December 2000, which included request to electronically respond to recommendation. Record of Decision is an agenda item for the April 30, 2001 management review meeting. Environmental Control will report out on results of the electronic ballot and record decision in the minutes of that meeting.

Estimated completion date: 04/30/2001	Actual completion date: 05/09/2001

Continued

Exhibit II   EMS Procedure 4.5.3—Example of a completed EPCAR.

Continued

Section 4

Verified by: Roth, Glen	Date verified: 05/11/2001

Results of verification:

Reviewed minutes of 04/30/2001 management review meeting (see meeting minutes dated 05/09/2001) and the decision was recorded in the minutes of that meeting.

EPCAR closed by: [ISO 14001 Coordinator]	Date closed: 05/14/2001

Section 5

EPCARs issued to other processes/products similar to the ones for which the corrective actions were developed:

EPCAR no(s).	Description area(s)	Area(s)	Create date

Exhibit II EMS Procedure 4.5.3—Example of a completed EPCAR.

Environmental Preventive/Corrective Action Request (EPCAR) Log and Jeopardy Report—Open EPCARs Past Due or Due within One (1) Week

EPCAR #	Issue date	Description	Issued to	Responsible department	Natural owner	EPCAR reply date	Forecast date	Date status

Exhibit III EMS Procedure 4.5.3—Environmental preventive/corrective action request (EPCAR) log and Jeopardy Report.

Delaware North Companies Parks & Resorts
P1400.06—GreenPath Nonconformance and
Corrective/Preventative Action
(Effective August 1, 2005)

Policy

Delaware North Companies' GreenPath locations shall maintain procedures for defining responsibility and authority for handling and investigating nonconformance with environmental requirements/programs, taking action to mitigate any impacts caused, and for initiating and completing corrective and preventive action.

Purpose

To describe the procedures, responsibilities, and authorities for addressing identified and potential nonconformance with the Environmental Management System (EMS) and conducting corrective and preventive action to correct the nonconformance.

Procedure

Responsibility:

All DNC employees and contractors are responsible for reporting any EMS nonconformances in accordance with this procedure.

The Environmental Manager, or designee, is responsible for addressing and correcting identified nonconformances with the EMS, and initiating action to prevent reoccurrence of the nonconformance.

Policy:

DNC maintains a procedure for defining responsibility and authority for handling and investigating nonconformances, taking action to mitigate any impacts caused, and for initiating and completing corrective and preventive action. Any corrective or preventive action taken to eliminate the nonconformances shall be appropriate to the magnitude of the problems, and commensurate with the environmental impact encountered.

Definitions:

Corrective action—Action taken after an actual nonconformance to prevent recurrence of nonconformity.

Preventive action—A process that identifies and initiates actions to prevent potential nonconformances from occurring.

Process:

Nonconformance Identification

1. Actual and potential nonconformances may be identified by environmental monitoring activities or may be identified due to environmental incidents, deviation from environmental policy, objectives, and targets, or during environmental management system audits and management reviews.

2. Local operations staff and/or the Environmental Manager/designee are responsible for taking immediate corrective action (that is, emergency response), if necessary, when actual nonconformances occur.

3. For all nonconformances, operations personnel or the Environmental Manager/designee is responsible for completing section I of the Nonconformance Investigation form, titled "Summary of the Observation, Nonconformance, or Incident."

Nonconformance Investigation and Root Cause Determination

1. The Environmental Manager/designee is responsible for investigation of the reported nonconformance and documenting the results of the investigation in section II of the EMS Nonconformance Investigation form, titled "Investigation/Comments." This investigation may include facilities inspections, personnel interviews, review of inspection log sheets and forms, accident reports, audit reports, and other relevant documents.

2. Based on the investigation, the Environmental Manager/designee will identify the root cause of the nonconformance, if possible, and document this finding in section III of the EMS Nonconformance Investigation form, titled "Root Cause Determined (if possible)."

Corrective/Preventive Action

1. The Environmental Manager/designee has the authority to determine whether corrective action and/or preventive action are required

2. Input from DNC staff shall be solicited, when applicable

3. The determination will be documented in section IV of the EMS Nonconformance Investigation form, titled "Corrective/Preventive Action"

4. Corrective action can be a very involved and complex process, or it may be minor, perhaps involving only identification and implementation of specific training

5. Preventive action may involve changes to EMS documentation, including the addition of objectives and targets

Closure

1. The Environmental Manager/designee is responsible for verifying that the required corrective or preventive actions have been taken and that successful implementation is obtained. Verification should be done as soon as possible after the actions have been taken, and may use the same information as was used during nonconformance investigation. If the actions are not successfully implemented, the Environmental Manager/designee will discuss the situation with the affected operating personnel and take appropriate action.

2. After successful implementation is achieved, the Environmental Manager/designee will stop the nonconformance investigation and close the nonconformance.

3. The decision of the Environmental Manager/designee to close the nonconformance will be documented in section V of the EMS Nonconformance Investigation form titled "Closure."

4. When corrective or preventive action is taken, the Environmental Manager/designee will review the action at an appropriate time to determine the results of the action. This review will include an examination of the effectiveness of the corrective/preventive action. This review will be recorded/documented in memorandum form by the Environmental Manager/designee, and, if necessary, follow-up action will be taken until all issues are resolved.

Required Documentation:

- EMS Nonconformance Investigation form

Coast Guard Air Station Cape Cod

Air Station Cape Cod has not established a separate procedure for addressing nonconformities and associated corrective and preventive actions. Existing operating procedures were reviewed and corrective/preventive action sections were incorporated where appropriate. A corrective/preventive action section is included when a new operating procedure is created.

17

Control of Records

Records provide information that confirms the occurrence of activities or verifies performance relative to a fixed or recommended standard. They are, therefore, important in evaluating actions taken and results achieved by an environmental management system.

ISO 14001:2004 Text	ISO 14001:1996 Text
4.5.4 Control of records	*4.5.3 Records*
The organization shall establish and maintain records as necessary to demonstrate conformity to the requirements of its environmental management system and of this International Standard, and the results achieved.	The organization shall establish and maintain procedures for the identification, maintenance and disposition of environmental records. These records shall include training records and the results of audits and reviews.
The organization shall establish, implement and maintain a procedure(s) for the identification, storage, protection, retrieval, retention and disposal of records.	Environmental records shall be legible, identifiable and traceable to the activity, product or service involved. Environmental records shall be stored and maintained in such a way that they are readily retrievable and protected against damage, deterioration or loss. Their retention times shall be established and recorded.
Records shall be and remain legible, identifiable and traceable.	
	Records shall be maintained, as appropriate to the system and to the organization, to demonstrate conformance to the requirements of this International Standard.

SIGNIFICANT CHANGES

The paragraphs have been reordered. What had been the last paragraph in the original standard is now the first paragraph. This places more emphasis on the purpose of records.

The objective of the records procedure has been expanded. Originally, the procedure addressed identification, maintenance, and disposition. The revised standard continues to require attention to identification and disposal of records. However, *maintenance* of records has been clarified to mean storage, protection, retrieval, and retention.

INTENT OF ISO 14001:2004

ISO 14001:2004 defines a record (section 3.20) as a "document stating results achieved or providing evidence of activities performed." This clause requires that an organization collect information for two distinct purposes. First, it must provide evidence of conformity to environmental management system requirements. This information is the proof that specific activities have been implemented. Second, it must stay informed about the results of system-related activities. This information becomes part of the decision-making process associated with activities such as establishing objectives and targets, management review, and continual improvement. Five clauses in ISO 14001:2004 state explicitly that records must be kept:

- 4.4.2 Competence, training and awareness. Several kinds of records are required: those that demonstrate worker competence, those that identify training needs, and those that confirm that identified training needs have been addressed.

- 4.5.1 Monitoring and measurement. Requires two kinds of records. One set of records, described in the first paragraph, must include information sufficient to monitor an organization's environmental performance. This includes significant environmental impacts resulting from its operations and progress in achieving environmental objectives and targets. The other set concerns the calibration, verification, and maintenance of monitoring and measuring equipment.

- 4.5.2 Evaluation of compliance. Results of evaluations of compliance with applicable legal requirements must be recorded. For those organizations that voluntarily subscribe to other (nonregulatory) requirements, records also must be kept of evaluations of compliance with those other requirements.

- 4.5.5 Internal audit. The results of internal audits of the environmental management system must be recorded.

- 4.6 Management review. Reviews of the environmental management system must be recorded and retained.

In addition, several clauses implicitly require records by stating that activities must be documented:

- 4.3.1 Environmental aspects. Requires that information that identifies environmental aspects and determines those aspects that have an actual or potential significant impact must be documented.

- 4.3.3 Objectives, targets and program(s). States that environmental objectives and targets must be documented. Such a record demonstrates that an organization established environmental objectives and targets, as required by ISO 14001:2004. The records required by clause 4.5.1 demonstrate progress in achieving objectives and targets.

- 4.4.1 Resources, roles, responsibility and authority. Requires that roles and responsibilities be defined and documented. The documentation serves as a record that definitions were established.

- 4.4.3 Communication. The decision whether to communicate externally about significant environmental aspects must be documented. Relevant communication received from external interested parties also must be documented.

An organization can handle its records in any manner it chooses as long as they are stored in a way that protects them from harm and can be retrieved when needed. ISO 14001:2004 also requires an organization to specify how long records will be retained. Unlike other types of records for which retention times can be defined solely by the organization that creates them, environmental records often have retention periods specified by laws or regulations. Therefore, record retention should take into account an organization's legal requirements.

An organization also is required to ensure that its records are:

- *Legible.* Many types of records require workers to enter information by hand onto a form rather than typing it and storing it electronically. It is important that workers write clearly so that data can be read by others. Records should be in ink, rather than pencil, to prevent smudging or erasure.

- *Identifiable*. Records should be labeled so that their purpose is apparent. A record titled "Manifests" is somewhat ambiguous; however, records titled "Hazardous Waste Manifests" and "Nonhazardous Materials Manifests" distinguish between the two categories and make clear what kind of information is contained in a particular record.

- *Traceable*. The linkage between an activity and an associated record should be clear. Procedures and work instructions should identify the records that are to be generated in conjunction with activities and operations. A record should contain information sufficient to distinguish the sequence of events from which the record is derived.

EXAMPLES

U. S. Steel Gary Works
EMS Procedure 4.5.4—Control of Records
(Effective September 19, 2005)

1.0 Purpose

   1.1 The purpose of this procedure is to establish and maintain a uniform system for the identification, storage, protection, retrieval, retention, and disposal (as applicable) of environmental records at the Gary Complex.

2.0 Scope

   2.1 This procedure applies to environmental records that demonstrate conformance to the requirements of the Gary Complex Environmental Management System and the ISO 14001 Standard.

3.0 References

   3.1 ISO 14001:2004 Standard

   3.2 Environmental Records Retention Schedule 70100052TBL— Exhibit II (page 305)

4.0 Definitions

   For the purpose of this procedure, the following definitions shall apply:

4.1 Environmental record—Any record, electronic or hard copy, identified on the Environmental Records Retention Schedule (Exhibit II) that demonstrates conformance with the Gary Complex Environmental Management System (EMS) and legal and other requirements.

4.2 Environmental Records Retention Schedule (Exhibit II)—A schedule that represents the Gary Complex Environmental Management System record retention requirements.

5.0 Responsibilities

5.1 The following job positions have responsibilities in this procedure:

- Business unit or staff management

- Environmental Record Control Custodians

- ISO 14001 Coordinator

- Business unit cross-functional teams (CFT)

- Law Department

- Accounting Department

6.0 Procedure

6.1 Identification of Environmental Records

6.1.1 Business unit or staff management appoints an Environmental Record Control Custodian. The APEX Document Custodian may perform this function, if delegated by business unit or staff management.

6.1.2 The business unit/staff Environmental Record Control Custodians, along with their Environmental Compliance Managers and cross-functional teams (CFT), use the Environmental Records Retention Schedule (Exhibit II) to determine if existing environmental records are adequately identified and satisfy the record retention requirements.

6.1.3 ISO 14001 Coordinator incorporates new and/or revised records information into the Environmental Record Retention Schedule, which is made available on the Gary Works intranet.

6.1.4 The business unit/staff Environmental Record Control Custodians also enter new and/or revised records information into the Record Retention List—Exhibit I (page 305).

6.2 Storage of Environmental Records

6.2.1 The Environmental Record Control Custodian determines the filing status of environmental records and processes the records per the requirements listed below in 6.3.1 through 6.3.3.

6.2.2 Environmental records that remain in an active status are filed per area work instructions.

6.2.3 Environmental records that are inactive and are stored locally are packaged and labeled to prevent damage, loss, or deterioration per area work instructions.

6.3 Destruction of Environmental Records

6.3.1 The business unit/staff Environmental Record Control Custodian uses the Records Retention List (Exhibit I) to determine if it is time to destroy an environmental record (also see area work instructions).

6.3.2 Records that have not reached the expiration date require no action.

6.3.3 Requests to hold environmental records beyond their expiration date must be submitted in writing to the USS Records Management Administrator, 600 Grant Street, Pittsburgh, PA 15219-4776. Such a request must state the reason for the request and specify the additional length of time that the location wishes to hold the records. Once approval is received, the Environmental Records Control Custodian must maintain the accompanying documents.

7.0 Approval

7.1 Approval of this procedure by the Gary Complex Environmental Management System Steering Team is effected by the signature (on the Document Validation Form) of the Manager, Environmental Control that has been designated as the Environmental Management Representative.

7.2   Approved for use.

Manager, Environmental Control and Environmental Management Representative

Document no. Description	Active filing location	Inactive		Time
		Short term	Long term	
9610F123 Mixed steel log	J. Smith (117)	NA	NA	5 years
0000M424 EMS meeting minutes	T. Jones (114)	NA	NA	2 years

Exhibit I   EMS Procedure 4.5.4—Records retention list.*
* List contains numerous pages; these two entries provided for illustration.

Business unit or staff group responsible for record	Description of record	Retention period (years)	Remarks
Environmental Control	Environmental air compliance tests	10	After date of test report
ISO 14001 Coordinator	EMS meeting minutes	2	

Exhibit II   EMS Procedure 4.5.4—Environmental records retention schedule.*
* Schedule contains seven pages; these two entries provided for illustration.

Delaware North Companies Parks & Resorts
P1400.09—GreenPath Records Management
(Effective September 1, 2005)

Policy

Delaware North Companies' GreenPath locations shall establish, implement, and maintain procedures for the identification, maintenance, storage, retrieval, protection, retention, and disposition of environmental records.

Purpose

To provide guidelines for the identification, maintenance, and disposition of environmental records.

Procedure

Responsibility:

The Director of Environmental Affairs is responsible for the creation, retention, and ultimate disposition of records associated with the corporate Environmental Management System (EMS).

The Environmental Manager, or designee, is responsible for the creation, retention, and ultimate disposition of records associated with the EMS at the operating location.

Policy:

DNC maintains procedures for the identification, maintenance, and disposition of environmental records. Records are maintained as legible, identifiable, traceable to their related activities, and readily retrievable. Records are retained to demonstrate conformance with the Environmental Management System Standard of the International Organization for Standardization (ISO) 14001.

Each GreenPath operating location is authorized to maintain a records retention schedule for locally managed records.

Process:

Records Retention

Director of Environmental Affairs (corporate) or Environmental Manager/ designee (operating location):

1. Maintains EMS Records Management Matrix

2. Modifies the Records Management Matrix in the electronic EMS Manual and in the environmental filing system, as required

Records Transmittal to Long-Term Storage.

Director of Environmental Affairs (corporate) or Environmental Manager/ designee (operating location):

1. Annually reviews records stored and the Records Management Matrix to identify inactive records to be forwarded to long-term storage or destroyed.

2. Arranges for transfer of inactive records to long-term storage

3. Retains information detailing the types and locations of inactive records forwarded to long-term storage

Records Retrieval from Long-Term Storage

Director of Environmental Affairs (corporate) or Environmental Manager/
designee (operating location):

1. Effects retrieval of requested containers from long-term storage

2. Updates environmental files to reflect the retrieval of records
   from long-term storage

Destruction of Records in Long-Term Storage

Director of Environmental Affairs (corporate) or Environmental Manager/
designee (operating location):

1. Annually reviews records in long-term storage. Identifies records
   to be destroyed.

2. Arranges for destruction of records in long-term storage,
   as required.

3. Updates departmental files to reflect the destruction of records.

Destruction of Records in On-Site Environmental Files

Director of Environmental Affairs (corporate) or Environmental Manager/
designee (operating location):

1. Annually reviews the Records Management Matrix to identify
   records to be destroyed

2. Arranges for destruction of records in the environmental files,
   as appropriate

3. Updates departmental files to reflect the destruction of records

Required Documentation:

- Current copy of the Records Management Matrix

Coast Guard Air Station Cape Cod
Procedure 03—Record Keeping
(Effective February 1, 2001)

1.0 Purpose:

To establish ASCC's record-keeping requirements and
retention period.

2.0 Scope:

    2.1 This procedure applies to ASCC's EMS exclusively. Examples of records include, but are not limited to, the policy, procedures, worksheets, training records, and audits.

    2.2 Both USCG and civilian employees are bound by this procedure.

3.0 Procedure:

    3.1 Records shall be legible, identifiable, and maintained so that they are readily retrievable. The required retention period for environmental documents is outlined below.

Record Retention Requirements

Training records	
for current personnel:	Until closure of the facility
for former employees:	At least three years from the date the employee last worked at the facility
Obsolete procedures*	One master copy archived until closure of the facility; all other controlled copies removed and destroyed
Audits	Until the closure of the facility
Worksheets/checklists	5 years
Aspects, objectives, targets	Until the closure of the facility
Environmental permits	5 years
Hazardous waste manifests	3 years
Chemical analysis testing	3 years
Waste sample manifests	3 years
Reports of spills, releases of hazardous substances	1 year
Waste analysis and other data required from large quantity generator	5 years

* Obsolete documents retained for legal and/or knowledge preservation purposes are to be suitably identified as such.

All retention periods are extended automatically during the course of any enforcement or judicial action as directed by the EH&S department head.

4.0   Responsibilities:

Any record created per a procedure (documented or otherwise related to the EMS) shall be maintained by the individual identified within the procedure. If an individual is not identified as responsible for record keeping, the individual responsible for the procedure shall maintain the record.

5.0   Related Documentation:

SPCC section 13, Record Keeping

18

Internal Environmental Management System Audit

An environmental management system audit serves two functions—it tells an organization whether all requirements are being met and helps management identify opportunities for improvement.

ISO 14001:2004 Text	ISO 14001:1996 Text
4.5.5 Internal audit The organization shall ensure that internal audits of the environmental management system are conducted at planned intervals to a) determine whether the environmental management system 1) conforms to planned arrangements for environmental management including the requirements of this International Standard, and 2) has been properly implemented and is maintained, and	*4.5.4 Environmental management system audit* The organization shall establish and maintain (a) program(s) and procedures for periodic environmental management system audits to be carried out, in order to a) determine whether the environmental management system 1) conforms to planned arrangements for environmental management including the requirements of this International Standard, and 2) has been properly implemented and is maintained, and

Continued

Continued

ISO 14001:2004 Text	ISO 14001:1996 Text
b) provide information on the results of audits to management. Audit program(s) shall be planned, established, implemented and maintained by the organization, taking into consideration the environmental importance of the operation(s) concerned and the results of previous audits. Audit procedure(s) shall be established, implemented and maintained that address • the responsibilities and requirements for planning and conducting audits, reporting results and retaining associated records. • the determination of audit criteria, scope, frequency and methods. Selection of auditors and conduct of audits shall ensure objectivity and the impartiality of the audit process.	b) provide information on the results of audits to management. The organization's audit program, including any schedule, shall be based on the environmental importance of the activity concerned and the results of previous audits. In order to be comprehensive, the audit procedures shall cover the audit scope, frequency and methodologies, as well as the responsibilities and requirements for conducting audits and reporting results.

SIGNIFICANT CHANGES

Most of the changes to this clause reflect an effort at clarification:

- Language indicating that audits are conducted at *planned intervals* replaces the requirements for *periodic* audits

- Reference to the audit program has been expanded to specify that audit programs must be planned, established, implemented, and maintained

- The term *operation* replaces *activity*

- Responsibilities and requirements for planning audits and retaining associated records have been added
- Audit criteria must be determined in addition to scope, frequency, and methods

Unlike the original version, ISO 14001:2004 specifies that audits must be conducted in a manner that ensures objectivity and impartiality. Section 3.14 defines an *internal audit* as a "systematic, independent and documented process for obtaining audit evidence and evaluating it objectively to determine the extent to which the environmental management system audit criteria set by the organization are fulfilled." A note following this definition explains that auditor independence can be demonstrated by the absence of responsibility for the activity being audited. An *auditor* is a "person with the competence to conduct an audit" (section 3.1).

INTENT OF ISO 14001:2004

Internal audits are intended to ensure that the environmental management system conforms to all requirements of ISO 14001:2004 and those imposed by an organization's policies, procedures, instructions, and other guiding documents. Audit results are intended to provide managers and decision-makers with a thorough understanding of an environmental management system's strengths and weaknesses.

Perhaps the greatest challenge in conducting an environmental management system audit is understanding clearly the parameters that bound audit activities. An environmental management system audit is neither an environmental performance audit nor a regulatory compliance audit. This distinction is confirmed by clauses 4.5.1 and 4.5.2. The former addresses evaluation of environmental performance through monitoring of significant environmental impacts, operational controls, and progress in achieving objectives and targets; the latter requires periodic evaluation of regulatory compliance.

Therefore, an environmental management system audit does not evaluate environmental performance. It determines whether an organization has established monitoring and measuring procedures and implements them to track performance. Similarly, the system audit does not evaluate regulatory compliance. It ascertains whether an organization has established and implemented a procedure for evaluating regulatory compliance. An environmental management system audit verifies that appropriate procedures are in place and functioning to ensure conformity with both ISO 14001:2004 and an organization's documentation.

The internal audit procedure must address:

• *Responsibilities.* Qualifications to perform the tasks required of a lead auditor or audit team member must be established and individuals deemed competent to participate in environmental management system audits identified. As required by clause 4.4.1, audit responsibility must be defined, documented, and communicated to relevant workers.

• *Audit criteria.* The documents that contain requirements to which an environmental management system must conform make up the audit criteria. Typically, ISO 14001:2004 and an organization's environmental policy, system description, and procedures constitute audit criteria for a full environmental management system audit. Criteria for a surveillance audit would include only those ISO 14001:2004 clauses and associated descriptions and procedures selected for the audit.

• *Scope.* Identifies facilities and departments as well as processes and operational activities to be audited.

• *Frequency.* The scope, environmental impacts, and past performance of an environmental management system are key considerations in determining how often audits are conducted. Organizations that are small, have few significant adverse environmental impacts, or have a history of conformity are likely to audit less often than organizations that are large, have many significant adverse environmental impacts, or have a history of nonconformities.

At a minimum, most organizations establish a three-year audit schedule that reflects the frequency with which their respective registrars conduct audits—typically an initial, full-system audit, five surveillance audits every six months thereafter, a full-system audit at the beginning of the next three-year cycle, and so on. Areas with identified nonconformities are included in subsequent audits regardless of their place on the schedule.

• *Methods.* An organization can employ any method it chooses. Accepted audit practices are described in ISO 19011, *Guidelines for quality and/or environmental management systems auditing.* Four sections of that standard address principles of auditing, managing an audit program, audit activities (including preparation, collecting data, preparing an audit report, and follow-up), and competence and evaluation of auditors.

Although an organization's audit of its environmental management system is often thought of as an *internal* audit, ISO 14001:2004 does not require an organization's employees to serve as auditors. An organization can use outside auditors to fulfill this requirement. The most common practices entail using outside auditors from:

• *Corporate headquarters.* Organizations with numerous facilities may find it financially advantageous to train and support a small team of environmental management system auditors as a corporate function. The team travels to, and conducts audits for, each facility as needed.

• *Sister facilities.* Smaller organizations may be unable to dedicate the resources required for a sufficient number of auditors. In such a circumstance, an organization might borrow auditors from sister facilities and lend its auditor to their teams.

• *Consortia.* Individual enterprises can pool their expertise by creating a pool of qualified auditors who come from the membership of a consortium. The team audits the system of any consortium member organization.

• *Consulting firms.* An organization can hire a consultant to conduct an audit on its behalf.

In each of these cases, the environmental management system audit can be used to fulfill the requirement that an organization audit its system.

EXAMPLES

U. S. Steel Gary Works
EMS Procedure 4.5.5—Internal Audit
(Effective October 26, 2005)

1.0   Purpose

   1.1   The purpose of this procedure is to establish the requirements for the Gary Complex internal Environmental Management System (EMS) audits, which are used to verify that the EMS is properly implemented and maintained.

2.0   Scope

   2.1   This procedure applies to employees involved in internal EMS audits at the Gary Complex.

3.0   References

   3.1   ISO 14001:2004 Standard

   3.2   EMS Procedure 4.5.3—Nonconformity, Corrective Action, and Preventive Action

   3.3   EMS Procedure 4.5.4—Control of Records

3.4   EMS Procedure 4.6—Management Review

4.0   Definitions

4.1   Objective evidence—Information that is verifiable and is based on facts obtained through observation, measurement, testing, or other means.

4.2   Nonconformance—A nonconformance finding is appropriate when an area fails to implement a required element of the EMS. Any item that is classified as a nonconformance must have corrective action taken and verified.

4.3   Conformance—A conformance finding is appropriate when an area demonstrates implementation of a required element of the Environmental Management System.

5.0   Responsibilities

5.1   The following positions have responsibilities in this EMS Procedure:

- ISO 14001 Coordinator

- Environmental Control ISO 14001 Steering Team

- Gary Complex managers

- Contractors/suppliers

- Internal EMS auditors

6.0   Procedure

6.1   Qualification and Requirements for Environmental System Lead Auditors and Auditors

6.1.1   Environmental System Lead Auditor

6.1.1.1   The ISO 14001 Coordinator serves as the lead auditor.

6.1.1.2   The minimum qualification requirements for lead auditor are:

6.1.1.2.1   Attend, at a minimum, an ISO 14001 lead auditor training class with a certificate of completion (or other suitable paperwork) documenting the training.

6.1.1.2.2 One year of environmental experience at the Gary Complex, including a minimum of 40 hours of specific environmental education, and assignment as a manager in Environmental Control.

6.1.2 Auditors:

6.1.2.1 The minimum qualification requirements for auditors are:

6.1.2.1.1 Attend, at a minimum, an ISO 14001 internal auditor training class with a certificate (or other suitable paperwork) documenting the training.

6.1.2.1.2 Participate as an observer in at least two Environmental Management System audits.

6.1.2.1.3 Receive training on the Gary Complex EMS Level II System.

6.1.2.2 The ISO Coordinator maintains the list of qualified auditors.

6.2 Environmental Management System Audits

6.2.1 The ISO 14001 Coordinator develops a schedule for EMS Audits. The audit schedule is reviewed, revised, and approved by the Environmental Control ISO 14001 Steering Team. The schedule includes the audit focus and areas to be audited. The schedule is designed considering the status and importance of the activities being audited.

6.2.2 Auditor workshops are conducted with EMS internal auditors to review the scope, criteria, and methods for the scheduled audits. Auditor assignments are conducted during these workshops. Auditors are not assigned to conduct audits within their business unit.

6.2.3 The ISO 14001 Coordinator notifies the organization being audited of the upcoming audit (at a minimum, one week prior to the audit).

6.2.4 On the day of the audit an opening meeting may be held to review the scope of the audit, introduce the audit team, and answer any unresolved issues/questions.

6.2.5 The audit team conducts the audit using the prepared checklist of questions. The audit checklists provide descriptions of audit criteria, audit scope, and audit methods. Additional questions may be asked to fully evaluate conformance or nonconformance. Objective evidence will be examined to confirm implementation (conformance).

6.2.6 After conducting the audit, a closing meeting may be held to review the results of the audit.

6.2.7 The ISO 14001 Coordinator prepares and publishes the completed audit checklists identifying conformances and nonconformances. Copies of the completed audit checklists are distributed to the business unit, staff, and/or contractor that was the subject of the audit. Other key personnel (as appropriate) receive a copy of the audit checklists.

   6.2.7.1 An EPCAR will be issued on all audit nonconformances in accordance with EMS Procedure 4.5.3.

6.3 Audit Results Reported During Management Review

6.3.1 During the Gary Complex EMS Steering Team management review meeting, the EMR or designee summarizes the results of the EMS audits, although specific audit issues (findings, and so on) may be discussed.

7.0 Approval

7.1 Approval of this procedure by the Gary Complex Environmental Management System Steering Team is effected by the signature (on the Document Validation Form) of the Manager, Environmental Control that has been designated as the Environmental Management Representative.

7.2 Approved for use.

Manager, Environmental Control and Environmental Management Representative

Delaware North Companies Parks & Resorts P1400.11—GreenPath Environmental Management System Audits
(Effective September 1, 2005)

Policy

Delaware North Companies (DNC) maintains procedures for periodic EMS audits of DNC GreenPath operating locations. Audits are conducted to evaluate the EMS conformance with the Environmental Management System Standard of the International Organization for Standardization (ISO) 14001, and to report the status of the EMS to management.

Purpose

This procedure outlines the process to be used to conduct planned audits of the Environmental Management System (EMS) to determine if it conforms to planned arrangements and has been properly implemented and maintained, and to inform management of the results of the audits.

Procedure

The Director of Environmental Affairs is responsible for the audit schedule and protocols. Audits will be conducted by qualified internal auditors.

Definitions:

Environmental management system—That part of the overall management system that includes organizational structure, planning activities, responsibilities, practices, procedures, processes, and resources for developing, implementing, achieving, reviewing, and maintaining the environmental policy.

Environmental management system audit—A systematic and documented verification process of objectively obtaining and evaluating audit evidence to determine whether an organization's environmental management system conforms to the environmental management system audit criteria set by the organization, and for communication of the results of this process to management.

Environmental management system audit criteria—Policies, practices, procedures, or requirements, including ISO 14001 standards, and, if applicable, any additional EMS requirements against which the auditor compares collected audit evidence about the organization's environmental management system.

Process:

1. Environmental management system audits are performed to ensure that the system is functioning as planned and is facilitating achievement of the environmental objectives and targets

2. Qualified DNC personnel will conduct EMS audits

3. EMS audits will be completed at planned intervals according to the schedule at the end of this procedure

4. Approximately 20 percent of the effort allocated for audits within a given year may be reallocated to different topics by the Director of Environmental Affairs and Environmental Managers, or designees, based on the results of previous audits

Responsibility	Task
Director of Environmental Affairs	1. Plans and schedules EMS audits
	2. Selects qualified auditors as appropriate to audit the various functions
EMS auditor(s)	3. Conducts EMS audit
	4. Records audit findings using notes and the Internal EMS Audit Report and Internal EMS Audit Worksheet forms, as appropriate
Director of Environmental Affairs and/or Environmental Managers/designees	5. Reviews audit findings and implements response actions within two weeks of their submittal
	6. Determines which findings will be referred to the formal corrective action review system
	7. Summarizes and presents the results of the Internal EMS Audit Report to management on an annual basis

EMS Audit Schedule*

Location	J	F	M	A	M	J	J	A	S	O	N	D
Asilomar										X		
Balsams					X							
Denver Mint				X								
DNC HQ				X								
Fresno											X	
Geneva			X									
Grand Canyon												
Harrison Hot Springs					X							
Jones Beach				X								
Kennedy Space Center				X								
Niagara Falls				X								
Philadelphia Mint		X										
San Diego	X											
Sequoia												
Tenaya Lodge										X		
Wheeling Island					X							
Yellowstone							X					
Yosemite											X	

* This is a tentative schedule designed to ensure that the EMS at all locations will be audited at a minimum of once per year. Audits may be conducted at other times of the year, and those audits may substitute for the scheduled audits. The complexity of operations, the environmental importance of operations, or the condition of EMS management may necessitate additional audits.

Required Documentation:

- Internal EMS Audit Reports

Coast Guard Air Station Cape Cod

Internal audits are conducted annually. In addition, the environmental management system cross-functional team meets monthly to discuss the system and related environmental issues.

19

Management Review

Periodic assessment of an environmental management system and the resulting recommendations fulfill the environmental policy commitment to continual improvement.

ISO 14001:2004 Text	ISO 14001:1996 Text
4.6 Management review	*4.6 Management review*
Top management shall review the organization's environmental management system, at planned intervals, to ensure its continuing suitability, adequacy, and effectiveness. Reviews shall include assessing opportunities for improvement and the need for changes to the environmental management system, including the environmental policy and environmental objectives and targets. Records of the management reviews shall be retained. Input to management reviews shall include a) results of internal audits and evaluations of compliance with legal requirements and with other requirements to which the organization subscribes,	The organization's top management shall, at intervals that it determines, review the environmental management system, to ensure its continuing suitability, adequacy and effectiveness. The management review process shall ensure that the necessary information is collected to allow management to carry out this evaluation. This review shall be documented. The management review shall address the possible need for changes to policy, objectives and elements of the environmental management system, in light of environmental management system audit results, changing circumstances and the commitment to continual improvement.

Continued

Continued

ISO 14001:2004 Text	
b) communication(s) from external interested parties, including complaints, c) the environmental performance of the organization, d) the extent to which objectives and targets have been met, e) status of corrective and preventive actions, f) follow-up actions from previous management reviews, g) changing circumstances, including developments in legal and other requirements related to its environmental aspects, and h) recommendations for improvement. The outputs from management reviews shall include any decisions and actions related to possible changes to environmental policy, objectives, targets and other elements of the environmental management system, consistent with the commitment to continual improvement.	

SIGNIFICANT CHANGES

Three changes are significant: Although continual improvement of the environmental management system was intended as a key consideration of management review in the original standard, the language used to describe the purpose of management review was somewhat ambiguous. ISO 14001:2004 states explicitly that management review includes assessing opportunities for improvement.

Unlike ISO 14001:1996, which stated only that "necessary information" be considered, the revision lists eight specific categories of information that must be included as inputs to the management review process.

Finally, ISO 14001:2004 requires that decisions about the environmental management system must be reflected in specific actions. In other words, recommending a particular change to the system is insufficient; an organization must follow through and implement recommendations in order to fulfill the commitment to continual improvement that is contained in the environmental policy.

INTENT OF ISO 14001:2004

As an environmental management system is designed, it reflects an organization's conviction that it is:

- *Suitable*. Appropriate to fulfill the requirements imposed by ISO 14001:2004

- *Adequate*. Sufficient resources are available to accomplish planned outcomes

- *Effective*. Capable of producing a desired result

Over time, top management must consider whether the environmental management system *continues* to be suitable, adequate, and effective. In other words, if the system were being designed now, would it be identical to the system that is in place or would some elements and activities be addressed differently?

The inclusion of *changing circumstances* on the list of inputs to the review is intended to encompass variations such as modified or new products, activities or services of an organization, scientific and technological advances related to an organization's operations, evolving views and concerns of external parties, newly applicable or changes to previously applicable regulatory requirements.

Unlike the environmental management system audit, which is tactical in nature, management review should be viewed as strategic. The purpose of the management review is to identify opportunities for improving the environmental management system. This activity determines the degree to which an organization lives up to its commitment to continual improvement that is articulated in the environmental policy.

Section 3.2 defines continual improvement as a "recurring process of enhancing the environmental management system in order to achieve improvements in overall environmental performance consistent with the organization's environmental policy." In other words, an organization must improve its system in a manner that, ultimately, improves its environmental performance.

Despite the fact that ISO 14001:2004 describes the system review as a top management activity, it is not limited to top management. The standard requires that top management must participate. However, additional parties can also be included. Contributors to the management review process typically are:

- *Executives.* Decision-makers who provide the authority and resources to address recommended improvements

- *Managers.* Overseers of operations with identified significant environmental aspects and functions associated with elements of the environmental management system such as training and communication

- *Employees.* Workers and staff who are knowledgeable about discrete components of the environmental management system and associated environmental performance

These participants provide the information that serves as inputs to the review, evaluate that information, recommend improvements to the environmental management system, and authorize action.

The requirement to retain records of management reviews can be met in whatever fashion is acceptable to an organization. Such records often take the form of meeting minutes or reports. Information contained in a management review record typically includes the agenda, names, and titles of participants, copies of the various records and documents presented for consideration during the review, and conclusions and recommendations of those involved in the review.

EXAMPLES

U. S. Steel Gary Works
EMS Procedure 4.6—Management Review
(Effective October 26, 2005)

1.0 Purpose

    1.1 The purpose of this procedure is to describe the management review process for the Gary Complex Environmental Management System (EMS).

2.0 Scope

    2.1 This procedure applies to members of the Gary Complex EMS Steering Team (top management) who review elements of the EMS to ensure its continuing suitability, adequacy, and effectiveness.

3.0 References

    3.1 ISO 14001:2004 Standard

    3.2 EMS Procedures 4.2 through 4.5.5

4.0 Definitions

    4.1 Management review is a comprehensive evaluation of the Gary Complex EMS by the Environmental Management System Steering Team.

        4.1.1 Steering Team members include the Gary Complex general manager (chairman of the team), plant managers, business unit and staff managers, the plant management (APEX) representative, and the EMR.

    4.2 The Environmental Policy is defined as the intentions and principles of the Gary Complex as they relate to overall environmental performance (including objectives and targets) as formally expressed by top management.

5.0 Responsibilities

    5.1 The following job positions have responsibilities in this procedure:

- Gary Complex EMS Steering Team members

- Environmental Management Representative (EMR)

- ISO 14001 Coordinator

6.0 Procedure

    6.1 Management Review Meeting Overview

        6.1.1 The Gary Complex EMS Steering Team meets at least annually to ensure ongoing suitability, adequacy, and effectiveness of the EMS. Relevant information, performance data, and results presented during the meeting allow the Steering Team to thoroughly complete their evaluation of the EMS. Based on the information presented in the meeting, changes to the EMS will be made, if necessary. Meeting minutes will be documented and provided to Steering Team members. Other personnel attend the Steering Team meeting by invitation.

6.2 Preparing for the Management Review Meeting

6.2.1 The EMR, or designee, prepares an agenda by reviewing the previous meeting minutes and by receiving input from the Steering Team members or other interested employees/organizations.

6.2.2 A selection of topics for discussion might include the following:

- Follow-up actions from previous management review meetings

- Results of internal audits and evaluations of compliance with legal and other requirements

- Communications from outside interested parties

- Environmental performance

- The extent to which objectives and targets have or have not been met

- The status of corrective and preventive actions

- Changing circumstances

- Recommendations for improvement

6.2.3 The EMR, or designee, establishes the date and time, publishes the agenda items, and distributes them to the Steering Team members for their review and preparation for the meeting.

6.3 Holding a Management Review Meeting

6.3.1 The EMR, or designee, conducts the meeting based on the agenda items. Any changes to previously published agendas are announced. (Note: the agenda and any handouts are provided to the attendees.)

6.3.2 The meeting attendance sheets are completed and become part of the meeting minutes.

6.3.3 A designated representative takes the meeting minutes. The meeting minutes record decisions made and action items taken or that will be taken.

6.3.4 The meeting agenda items are presented, reviewed, and discussed by Steering Team members.

6.4 Follow-Up Activities from the Management Review Meeting

6.4.1 The EMR, or designee, reviews the meeting minutes to ensure their accuracy, makes any necessary changes, and updates accordingly. The EMR signs the meeting minutes and distributes them to the Steering Team members. A copy of the meeting minutes along with the accompanying agenda and attendance sheets are retained per EMS Procedure 4.5.3—Control of Records.

6.4.2 The ISO 14001 Coordinator follows up on action items that need to be addressed. If EPCARs are issued, the EPCAR system is used to track progress. Other action items are assigned completion dates and responsibilities and are tracked to ensure timely completion.

7.0 Approval

7.1 Approval of this procedure by the Gary Complex Environmental Management System Steering Team is effected by the signature (on the Document Validation Form) of the Manager, Environmental Control that has been designated as the Environmental Management Representative.

7.2 Approved for use.

Manager, Environmental Control and Environmental Management Representative

Delaware North Companies Parks & Resorts
P1400.12—GreenPath Management Review
(Effective September 9, 2005)

Policy

The Environmental Managers will annually conduct a review of the EMS to ensure its continued suitability, adequacy, and effectiveness. The review will include the Operations Executive.

Purpose

To outline the process operating location management will use to regularly review the effectiveness and viability of the Environmental Management System (EMS).

To assign responsibility for scheduling, conducting, and documenting management reviews.

Procedure

Responsibility:

The Director of Environmental Affairs has the responsibility and authority to assure that the requirements of the EMS are met and to follow this procedure.

The Operations Executive assumes the responsibility and authority to assure that the requirements of the EMS are met within the operating location and to follow this procedure. The Operations Executive may delegate this responsibility and authority to another person.

Process:

1. The local Environmental Manager will schedule an annual review of the EMS with the unit's top manager and, if appropriate, other operating location staff

2. The management review will be conducted during the first quarter of the calendar year

3. The agenda for management review meetings *will* address, at a minimum, the following:

   Changing circumstances:

   - Assessment of the continuing suitability of the EMS

   - Annual review of the Environmental Policy Statement

   - Effectiveness of the environmental procedures in carrying out the Environmental Policy

   - Changes in legislation, technology, and plant operations

   Commitment to continual improvement:

   - The continual improvement process

   - Progress on objectives and targets

   - Status of significant-impact items

- Recommendations for improvement to EMS management and environmental performance

EMS audit results:

- Review of third-party environmental audits

- The results of internal environmental audits

- Evaluation of compliance, legal, and other requirements

- Effectiveness of corrective action

- Status of corrective/preventive action and nonconformances

Actions and issues:

- Communication with external parties

- A review of previous management reviews to determine if decisions and recommendations have been acted on

- May include a variety of topics related to the effective management of the EMS

4. Other topics that *may* be included at management review meetings are:

- Audits of waste management practices

- Solutions to environmental problems and review of environmental indices and trends

- Supplier performance

- Recommendations for continual improvement

- Effluent and emission test results and inventories

5. The Environmental Manager has the responsibility to keep the minutes of management review meetings

6. Follow-up actions and decisions made during the management review shall be documented in the minutes of management review meetings

7. The Environmental Manager has the responsibility to distribute minutes to all appropriate staff members

8. The minutes, together with other internal documents pertaining to the meetings, are confidential and shall be made available to non-DNC personnel only on approval of the Director of Environmental Affairs

Required Documentation:

- Management review meeting minutes

Coast Guard Air Station Cape Cod

Although ISO 14001:2004 requires management review, it does not mandate a formal procedure. Air Station Cape Cod requires an annual management review and additional meetings are conducted when top management identifies a need.

Meetings are documented in the form of minutes, as illustrated in the example below.

COAST GUARD AIR STATION CAPE COD
Senior Management Review
Performance Track and Environmental Management System

March 15, 2005

Commanding Officer
Executive Officer
Environmental Health and Safety Manager

1. Reviewed status of Performance Track commitments/EMS target and objectives

    A. Reduce generation of, and improve the management of, ASCC nonhazardous waste. Reduce disposal, increase recycling of nonhazardous waste. Base year (2003)—890 tons (740 tons incinerated, 150 tons reused/recycled); performance commitment—by 2006 reduce to 870 tons. Two numbers are measured: 1. incineration/disposal, 2. recycling. Two goals: 1. reduce generation of nonhazardous waste, 2. reduce disposal, increase recycling.

        i. Reviewing our performance data: ASCC waste being disposed has increased, while recycling has decreased. Baseline year (2003)—disposed of 740 tons, recycled 150 tons; 2004—disposed of 754 tons, recycled 118 tons.

        ii. Top management concluded:

Continued

Continued

a. Personnel change is needed to aggressively promote ASCC recycling program

b. Expand Recycling Center hours: open Center on Saturdays

c. Promote household recycling with community residents

d. Expand materials to be recycled

e. Partner with town of Bourne to improve efficiency

B. Reduce greenhouse gas emissions by five percent

   i. Base year 2003—conducted emissions inventory which included electrical and natural gas usage and mobile source fuel consumption.

   ii. Top management was informed that our GHG emission reduction commitment was on track. Although mobile source fuel usage increased as a result of operational tempo, electricity purchased from the utility provider decreased as a result of installing a fuel cell.

   iii. Top management is pleased with progress but instructed the following: commence the implementation of an energy program:

     a. Track utility usage on a monthly basis

     b. Look into the possibility of installing meters for the larger facilities; track usage/trends in real time

     c. Start to investigate renewable/sustainable energy sources

     d. Continue to procure Energy Star appliances for both operational facilities and housing

     e. Increase procurement of recycled-content products

       • Base year 2003—12,000 lbs.; commitment of 15,000 lbs. by 2006

       • 2004—purchased 15,640 lbs. of recycled-content products; met goal in first year

       • Top management instructed an increase beyond the original commitment

Continued

2. Reviewed internal audit findings; verified documented corrective actions

3. Approved last review (Feb 2005) of environmental aspects

4. Concerns/issues, external communication

   A. Through public meetings and other forums on and off the MMR, ASCC has been able to communicate with external public. However, ASCC Web site has not been revised, which is essential for conformance with our external communication requirement.

   B. Top management will create a new department responsible for information management, which includes Web site management.

5. Next formal top management meeting—November 2005.

20

The Future of Environmental Management

With more than 90,000 ISO 14001 certificates in 127 countries, it is clear that environmental management has been embraced by organizations worldwide. Environmental concern is becoming as important in the global marketplace as product quality, cost, and service.

Mechanisms for responding to concerns about environmental issues have advanced along a continuum from command-and-control regulations, to risk management, to international protocols to address global degradation and sustainable development, to environmental management. That progression will continue.

THE ISO 9001 MODEL

The advent of ISO 9001, initially published in 1987, provides a basis for comparison with the progress of ISO 14001. At the end of 2004, the last year for which data are available, ISO 14001 was eight years old. Examination of data at the eight-year mark for ISO 9001 (1995) reveals some interesting contrasts (Table 20.1).

ISO 14001 certification lags behind certification to ISO 9001. This may be due to the fact that more industry sectors mandated implementation of quality systems throughout the supply chain than has been the case for environmental management systems.

Additionally, ISO 14001 explicitly states that organizations can self-declare conformity to the standard. The number of organizations that choose to self-declare rather than pursue registration is not reflected in the data. (ISO 9001:1994 made no mention of self-declaration. However, ISO 9001:2000 states that it can be used by internal parties to assess an organization's ability to meet customer, regulatory, and organizational requirements, thereby suggesting that self-declaration is now an option.)

Table 20.1 Comparison of ISO 9001 certificates and ISO 14001 certificates worldwide eight years after publication.

Region	ISO 9001 (1995)		ISO 14001 (2004)	
	Number	%	Number	%
Africa/West Asia	3,378	2.65	3,007	3.32
Australia/New Zealand	10,526	8.27	2,092	2.31
Central and South America	1,220	0.95	2,955	3.26
Europe	92,611	72.72	39,812	43.96
East Asia	9,240	7.26	35,960	39.70
North America	10,374	8.15	6,743	7.45
Total	127,349	100.00	90,569	100.00

Sources: For ISO 9001 data, *The ISO Survey of ISO 9000 and ISO 14000 Certificates, Tenth Cycle* (2001); for ISO 14001 data, *The ISO Survey of Certifications 2004* (Sept. 15, 2005).

The dispersion of ISO 9001 certificates differs from ISO 14001. Australia/New Zealand and Europe have a far greater proportion of quality system certificates (81 percent) than environmental management system certificates (46 percent). Countries in East Asia account for relatively few quality certificates (seven percent) but more than one-third of environmental management certificates (nearly 40 percent). Within North America, differences are less extreme (Table 20.2).

Extending evaluation of the similarities and differences between the two standards to its logical conclusion requires forecasting the likely status of ISO 14001 in 2013 in comparison to 2004 data for ISO 9001 (Table 20.3)—the years in which each can claim a 17-year history.

In the next nine years, it is unlikely that ISO 14001 certificates will increase from their 2004 level of 90,569 (see Chapter 1) at a rate that will equal the gains seen in quality certification over a 17-year history. A focus on numbers alone, however, ignores the characteristics that will define growth in environmental management.

Two issues will be at the forefront of environmental management in coming years—increased and expanded implementation of integrated management systems among large organizations and growing acceptance and implementation of environmental management systems among small and medium-sized enterprises (SMEs).

Table 20.2 Comparison of ISO 9001 certificates and ISO 14001 certificates in North America eight years after publication.

Country	ISO 9001 (1995)		ISO 14001 (2004)	
	Number	**%**	**Number**	**%**
United States	8,762	84.46	4,759	70.58
Canada	1,397	13.47	1,492	22.13
Mexico	215	2.1	492	7.30
Total	10,374	100.00	6,743	100.00

Sources: For ISO 9001 data, *The ISO Survey of ISO 9000 and ISO 14000 Certificates, Tenth Cycle* (2001); for ISO 14001 data, *The ISO Survey of Certifications 2004* (Sept. 15, 2005).

Table 20.3 ISO 9001 certificates worldwide, 2004.

Region	ISO 9001 (2004)	
	Number	**%**
Africa/West Asia	31,309	4.67
Australia/New Zealand	19,997	2.98
Central and South America	17,016	2.54
Europe	326,895	48.76
East Asia	225,220	33.60
North America	49,962	7.45
Total	670,399	100.00

Source: For ISO 14001 data, *The ISO Survey of Certifications 2004* (Sept. 15, 2005).

INTEGRATION OF MANAGEMENT SYSTEMS

The majority of organizations that have chosen to implement an environmental management system already had in place a quality management system. Worldwide there were 90,569 ISO 14001 certificates at the end of 2004, compared to 670,399 ISO 9001:2000 certificates. Additional certificates for quality management system standards in the auto industry and medical device sector increase the total to 683,523. An increasing number of these quality-registered organizations will implement an environmental management system in coming years.

Lack of familiarity with environmental management coupled with apprehension that an environmental nonconformity would jeopardize a quality certificate persuaded organizations to separate their quality and environmental management systems. As these organizations became more comfortable with their environmental issues, knowledgeable about the similarities between ISO 9001 and ISO 14001 requirements, and aware of redundancies, many opted to integrate both sets of requirements into one management system.

The value of integration was reinforced by the revision efforts that culminated in the third edition of ISO 9001:2000 and the second edition of ISO 14001:2004. Among the stated goals for these revisions was to make each standard *more compatible* with the other. Enhanced compatibility, in turn, makes it easier for organizations to establish an integrated system.

Environmental Management and Occupational Health and Safety

A small number of organizations have gone one step further. They have implemented expanded systems that address occupational health and safety in addition to quality and environment.

To date, ISO has no plans to develop an occupational health and safety (OHS) management system standard. Although such a standard was considered in 1996, an international workshop on the need for such a document garnered little support. This issue was reconsidered in 2000 and ISO again decided not to pursue development of management system standards for OHS.

In 1999, the British Standards Institution (BSI) published OHSAS 18001:1999, *Occupational Health and Safety Management Systems Specifications*, an internationally accepted standard for implementing an occupational health and safety management system. It is compatible with ISO 9001 and ISO 14001 (Table 20.4)

In the United States, the American National Standards Institute (ANSI) and the American Industrial Hygiene Association (AIHA) published ANSI/AIHA Standard Z10, *Occupational and Safety Management Systems*. It provides a framework for continual improvement of an organization's health and safety performance. As with OHSAS 18001, Z10 is compatible with ISO 9001 and ISO 14001 and can be integrated with them. In addition, Z10 is compatible with occupational health and safety management approaches

Table 20.4   Comparison of clauses in ISO 14001:2004 and OHSAS 18001:1999.

ISO 14001:2004	OHSAS 18001:1999
Introduction	—
1 Scope	1 Scope
2 Normative references	2 Reference publications
3 Terms and definitions	3 Definitions
4 Environmental management system requirements	4 OH&S management system elements
4.1 General requirements	4.1 General requirements
4.2 Environmental policy	4.2 OH&S policy
4.3 Planning	4.3 Planning
4.3.1 Environmental aspects identification, risk assessment	4.3.1 Planning for hazard and risk control
4.3.2 Legal and other requirements	4.3.2 Legal and other requirements
4.3.3 Objectives, targets and programs	4.3.3 Objectives
4.3.4 OH&S management programs	
4.4 Implementation and operation	4.4 Implementation and operation
4.4.1 Resources, roles, responsibility and authority	4.4.1 Structure and responsibility
4.4.2 Competence, training and awareness	4.4.2 Training, awareness and competence
4.4.3 Communication	4.4.3 Consultation and communication
4.4.4 Documentation	4.4.4 Documentation
4.4.5 Control of documents	4.4.5 Document and data control
4.4.6 Operational control	4.4.6 Operational control
4.4.7 Emergency preparedness and response	4.4.7 Emergency preparedness and response
4.5 Checking	4.5 Checking and corrective action

Continued

Continued

ISO 14001:2004	OHSAS 18001:1999
4.5.1 Monitoring and measurement	4.5.1 Performance measurement and monitoring
4.5.2 Evaluation of compliance	—
4.5.3 Nonconformity, corrective action and preventive action	4.5.2 Accidents, incidents, nonconformance and corrective and preventive action
4.5.4 Control of records	4.5.3 Records and records management
4.5.5 Internal audit	4.5.4 Audit
4.6 Management review	4.6 Management review

used in the U.S., including the Voluntary Protection Programs (VPP) promulgated by the Occupational Safety & Health Administration (OSHA), U.S. Department of Labor.

Environmental Management and Social Responsibility

If occupational health and safety issues offer an integration opportunity in the short term, social responsibility suggests a long-term focus. ISO has begun work on a guidance standard, with publication anticipated in 2009.

Although still in the early stage of development, ISO 26000 is likely to include many of the concepts embedded in Social Accountability (SA) 8000. Published in 1997, SA8000 contains criteria related to child labor, forced labor, health and safety, unions and collective bargaining, discrimination, disciplinary practices, working hours, and compensation.

A ninth criterion, management systems, addresses policy, management review, training, corrective action, and communication, among other issues. These requirements were crafted for compatibility with ISO 9001 and ISO 14001 and therefore lend themselves to integration with quality and environmental management efforts.

While SA8000 was fashioned as an auditable standard for third-party verification and certification, ISO plans to offer ISO 26000 as a guidance document. The decision to publish ISO 26000 as an informative (non-auditable) standard rather than as a normative (auditable) standard reflects the position taken by many business leaders that social responsibility is a political and cultural issue rather than a technical or scientific matter. As such, the topic is subject to widely divergent views that are difficult to standardize.

An organization that integrates occupational health and safety issues into an environmental management system is most likely to extend its efforts to include social responsibility. Although the populations of interest and specific associated requirements differ, the overarching objective of occupational health and safety and social responsibility is the same—safe and appropriate working conditions and personal well-being of those who work for or on an organization's behalf.

IMPLEMENTATION BY SMEs

Although the introduction to ISO 14001 states that it is intended to apply to all types and *sizes* of organization, most organizations that implemented environmental management systems in conformity with ISO 14001:1996 were large organizations (Table 20.5). The lack of participation by small and medium-sized enterprises persuaded ISO to revise ISO 14001 in a manner that made it easier for such organizations to use. Despite that effort, representatives of the small business community in Europe expressed concern that the second edition of ISO 14001 was not sufficiently different from its predecessor. ISO/TC 207 Subcommittee 1, which was responsible for both initial development of ISO 14001 and its revision, responded by establishing the Strategic SME Group.

Table 20.5 Definitions of small and medium-sized businesses.

EU (European Union)—Fewer than 50 employees is small; fewer than 250 employees is medium.

INEM (International Network for Environmental Management)—Fewer than 500 employees.

ISO (International Organization for Standardization)—Does not formally define business size.

- *ISO/TC 207*—An April, 1997, meeting arranged by Subcommittee 1 on problems specific to SMEs and ISO 14001 was based on analysis of companies with fewer than 200 employees.
- *Strategic SME Group*—Fewer than 100 employees.

SBA (U.S. Small Business Administration)—500 employees for most manufacturing and mining industries; 100 employees for wholesale trade industries.

Experience with ISO 14001:1996

In early 2005, the Strategic SME Group surveyed more than 1500 SMEs from 71 countries in an effort to identify incentives for and barriers to implementing an environmental management system. Because the second edition of ISO 14001 was published only two months prior (in November, 2004), survey results[1] reflect SME experience with and attitudes about ISO 14001:1996.

Perhaps the most surprising finding was the number of SMEs positively disposed toward environmental management. Despite rhetoric to the contrary, 46 percent of SMEs reported having an environmental management system and another 14 percent were in the process of developing one. Fewer than half (40 percent) did not have an environmental management system.

ISO 14001 is the environmental management system standard of choice for 86 percent of SMEs. Another five percent use ISO 14001 in conjunction with the Eco-Management and Audit Scheme (EMAS), one percent use EMAS alone, and eight percent use some other system.

The top three reasons given by SMEs for implementing ISO 14001 are customer requirements, continuous improvement of environmental performance, and improved regulatory compliance. However, when asked about the top three benefits that resulted from implementation, improved environmental compliance moved from third position to first. Customer requirements dropped from first place to second. The third benefit cited was improved employee commitment.

The three greatest obstacles cited by SMEs that implemented an environmental management system were lack of time, insufficient staff resources, and lack of ISO 14001 expertise in the organization.

Particularly notable is the finding that more than two-thirds (69 percent) of SMEs that implemented ISO 14001 also implemented other management systems. Of that group, the majority (81 percent) successfully integrated their environmental management system with a quality management system and approximately one-quarter (28 percent) with an occupational health and safety management system.

A number of concerns regarding certification surfaced. The primary disadvantages mentioned by certified SMEs are increased paper burden, costs outweigh benefits, and productivity is unaffected. Despite these perceived shortcomings, only one percent of the SMEs surveyed said they plan to drop their certification.

Outlook for Medium-Sized Businesses

While the SME Group survey results provide valuable insight into the perceptions and experiences of SMEs regarding environmental management, it would be a mistake to rely on them too heavily in projecting the future of ISO 14001.

First, the survey was limited to organizations that were familiar with ISO 14001. Thus, there is no way to know how the concept of environmental management is viewed by SMEs that lack such familiarity.

Estimates suggest that SMEs account for more than 90 percent of business worldwide and therefore are significant contributors to depletion of natural resources and pollution. It is important, however, to distinguish between medium-sized organizations and those that are small. The smallest organizations, those with one to five employees, are sometimes referred to as microenterprises.

Although there is a tendency to think of SMEs as one group, what is true for medium-sized businesses is not necessarily reflected in the small business community. Small organizations often do not have formal management systems. Additionally, the majority of small businesses do not feel that they have any adverse environmental impacts. Many of these organizations, in fact, are unaware of their environmental legal obligations. Any expectation that they will evince interest in activities designed to improve environmental performance beyond the levels imposed by laws and regulations is ill-conceived.

Implementation of ISO 14001 by SMEs will increase in coming years, with much of the growth in medium-sized entities within selected industry sectors. For example:

- *Automotive.* The automotive industry has required ISO 14001 registration of its Tier 1 suppliers for the past few years. Expect Tier 1 suppliers to begin requiring evidence of effective environmental management from lower-tier suppliers

- *Chemical.* The American Chemistry Council (ACC) has created RC-14001, a management system for chemical companies that combines the requirements of ISO 14001 and the six codes of management practice known as Responsible Care. Implementation is mandatory for all ACC members.

Expect additional sectors to adopt similar requirements.

THE CHALLENGE AHEAD

ISO 14001 has become the standard of choice for organizations with an interest in environmental management. Its popularity reflects the juxtaposition of a structured approach comprising universal principles and the flexibility to apply those principles in a manner that reflects the realities of the legal requirements, existing infrastructure, available resources, and cultural norms in individual settings.

Organizations implement ISO 14001 for a variety of reasons. For some, the tangible benefits are paramount—improved environmental performance, better compliance record, reduced environmental risks, and, therefore, reduced associated costs, keeping or acquiring customers. For others, the benefits are less concrete—for example, an image of environmental leadership or recognition of an organization as "world-class."

Regardless of an organization's motivation, there is no doubt that ISO 14001 has transformed the business landscape. Environmental management has become an integral part of business, a circumstance that was unimaginable on the first Earth Day in 1970.

Organizations have come to recognize that environmental management results in a win–win situation for all stakeholders—it protects the environment by reducing an organization's adverse environmental impacts, it increases shareholder value through innovation and cost savings, it improves employee morale, and it forges stronger relationships with regulators, members of the community, and environmental groups. ISO 14001:2004 provides an effective framework for environmental management and improved environmental performance.

ENDNOTE

1. *The Global Use of Environmental Management System*[sic] *by Small and Medium Enterprises.* Executive Report from ISO/TC 207/SC1 Strategic SME Group. May 2005.

Glossary

auditor—Person with the competence to conduct an audit.

auditor independence—Freedom from responsibility for the activity being audited.

boundaries, functional—Operations, processes, activities, products, and services encompassed by an environmental management system.

boundaries, physical—Locations at an organization's site that are included within an environmental management system.

certification—Written assurance, based on third-party evaluation, that an environmental management system conforms to all requirements; often used synonymously with registration.

competence—Effective execution of required actions.

continual improvement—Recurring process of enhancing the environmental management system in order to achieve improvements in overall environmental performance consistent with an organization's environmental policy.

contractor—Organization or person that provides a service to another organization.

corrective action—Action to eliminate the cause of a detected nonconformity.

define—To provide a distinct, clear explanation of characteristics and attributes.

Design for the Environment—EPA program that provides industry-specific information about environmental impacts associated with the design or redesign of products and processes.

document—Information and its supporting medium, such as paper, magnetic, electronic or optical computer disc, photograph, or master sample.

environment—Surroundings in which an organization operates, including air, water, land, natural resources, flora, fauna, and humans.

environmental aspect—Element of an organization's activities, products, or services that can interact with the environment.

environmental impact—Any adverse or beneficial change to the environment resulting wholly or in part from an environmental aspect.

environmental management system—Organizational structure, planning activities, responsibilities, practices, procedures, processes, and resources used to develop and implement an environmental policy and manage environmental aspects.

environmental objective—Overall environmental goal, consistent with the environmental policy, that an organization sets itself to achieve.

environmental performance—Measurable results of an organization's management of its environmental aspects.

environmental policy—Overall intentions and direction of an organization related to its environmental performance as formally expressed by top management.

environmental target—Detailed performance requirement that arises from an environmental objective.

establish—Create; bring into existence.

function—Group of related actions that contribute to a larger accomplishment.

implement—Carry out or accomplish by concrete measures.

informative—Describes an ISO guideline; does not have auditable requirements.

interested party—Person or group concerned with or affected by the environmental performance of an organization.

internal audit—Systematic, independent, and documented process for obtaining audit evidence and evaluating it objectively to determine the extent to which environmental management system requirements are fulfilled.

level—Position of rank with assigned control and authority.

lifecycle assessment—Compilation and evaluation of the inputs, outputs, and potential environmental impacts of a product system throughout its lifecycle.

maintain—Keep in an intended state; prevent failure or decline.

nonconformity—Failure to fulfill a stated requirement.

normative—Describes an ISO specification; having auditable requirements.

operation—Functions and supporting processes performed by workers on behalf of an organization.

organization—Company, corporation, firm, enterprise, authority, institution, or other entity with a defined function and autonomous management structure.

PDCA cycle—*See* Shewhart cycle.

pollution prevention—Waste management hierarchy defined by the Pollution Prevention Act of 1990 as:

- *Prevention*—prevent or reduce pollution at the source whenever feasible

- *Recycling*—where pollution cannot be prevented, it should be recycled in an environmentally safe manner whenever feasible

- *Treatment*—in the absence of feasible prevention and recycling, pollution should be treated in accordance with applicable standards prior to releases or transfers

- *Disposal*—the least desirable alternative

prevention of pollution—Use of processes, practices, techniques, materials, products, services, or energy (separately or in combination) to avoid, reduce, or control the creation, emission, or discharge of any type of pollutant or waste.

preventive action—Action to eliminate the cause of a potential nonconformity.

procedure—Specified way to carry out an activity or process.

record—Document stating results achieved or providing evidence of activities performed.

registration—Written assurance, based on third-party evaluation, that an environmental management system conforms to all requirements; often used synonymously with certification.

risk—Probability that life, health, property, and/or the environment will be harmed as a result of a given hazard.

risk management—Evaluation and implementation of practices designed to reduce risk.

scope, audit—Facilities, departments, operational activities, and processes to be audited.

scope, environmental management system—Physical and functional boundaries.

self-declaration—Assertion by an organization based on its own evaluation that it conforms to all ISO 14001 requirements.

Shewhart cycle—A four-part model for improving processes that involves planning (identifying problems and developing solutions), doing (implementing proposed solutions), checking (determining what actually happened), and acting (incorporating successful solutions into day-to-day operations); also referred to as the PDCA cycle.

significant—Meaningful.

supplier—Organization or person that provides a product to another organization.

top management—Individuals with executive responsibility and authority for the organization to which an environmental management system is applied.

Bibliography

Bendavid-Val, A., and N. P. Cheremisinoff. *Achieving Environmental Excellence: Integrating P2 and EMS to Increase Profits.* Lanham, MD: Government Institutes, 2003.

Block, M. R. *Identifying Environmental Aspects and Impacts.* Milwaukee: ASQ Quality Press, 1999.

Block, M. R., and I. R. Marash. *Integrating ISO 14001 into a Quality Management System,* 2nd ed. Milwaukee: ASQ Quality Press, 2002.

Cheremisinoff, N. P., and A. Bendavid-Val. *Green Profits: The Manager's Handbook for ISO 14001 and Pollution Prevention.* Burlington, MA: Butterworth-Heinemann, 2001.

Edwards, A. J. *ISO 14001 Environmental Certification Step by Step,* revised edition. Burlington, MA: Butterworth-Heinemann, 2004.

ISO/TC207/SC1 Strategic SME Group. *The Global Use of Environmental Management System by Small and Medium Enterprises.* Geneva: International Organization for Standardization, 2005.

Kinsella, J., and A. D. McCully. *Handbook for Implementing an ISO 14000 Environmental Management System,* 3rd ed. Bothell, WA: Shaw Environmental, 2005.

O'Brien, T. *Ford and ISO 14001: The Synergy Between Preserving the Environment and Rewarding Shareholders.* New York: McGraw-Hill, 2001.

Schoffman, A., and A. M. Tordini. *ISO 14001: A Practical Approach.* New York: Oxford University Press, 2000.

von Zharen, W. M. *ISO 14001: Positioning Your Organization for Environmental Success.* Lanham, MD: Government Institutes, 2001.

Whitelaw, K. *ISO 14001 Environmental Systems Handbook,* 2nd ed. Oxford, England: Elsevier Butterworth-Heinemann, 2004.

Zackrisson, M., G. Bengtsson, C. Astrand, and C. Norberg. *Measuring Your Company's Environmental Impact: Templates and Tools for a Complete ISO 14001 Initial Review.* London: Earthscan, 2004.

Index

A

ANSI/AIHA Standard Z10,
*Occupational and Safety
Management Systems,* 338–40
audit findings, protected status of,
270–71
audits, environmental management
system, 270–71
internal, 312–15
authority, versus responsibility, 101
awareness training, 124–25, 126

B

boundaries, functional, 21–22
boundaries, physical, 21
Business Charter for Sustainable
Development, 3
Business Council for Sustainable
Development, 3

C

Carson, Rachel, 1
certification, versus registration, 14
Code of Environment Management
Principles (CEMP), 11
communication

approaches and tools, other,
152–53
approaches and tools, verbal,
146–51
approaches and tools, written,
143–45
as defined under ISO 14001:2004,
140
of environmental policy, 27
external, 141–42
internal, 140–41
comparison, of ISO 14001 and ISO
9001 certifications, 335–37
competence, worker, 124–25
competency training, 125–26
compliance, regulatory, evaluation of,
270–72
continual improvement
as defined under ISO 14001:2004,
21
in environmental management, 7
in environmental policy, 25
and management review, 325–26
contractor, versus supplier, 216
corrective action, 282–84

D

Delaware North Companies Parks &
Resorts

background, xviii–xx
EMS procedure, examples
environmental policy, 31–32
P1400.01—GreenPath
Introduction and
Summary, 181–88
P1400.02—GreenPath
Environmental Aspects,
48–51
P1400.03—GreenPath Legal
and Other Requirements,
69–71
P1400.04—GreenPath
Environmental
Responsibility, 105–11,
129–32
P1400.05—GreenPath
Hazardous Waste
Management, 228–37
P1400.06—GreenPath
Nonconformance and
Corrective/Preventive
Action, 296–98
P1400.07—GreenPath
Communications,
158–61
P1400.08—GreenPath
Document Control,
208–11
P1400.09—GreenPath Records
Management, 305–7
P1400.10—Evaluation
of Compliance—
Monitoring and
Measuring, 260–64,
275–79
P1400.11—GreenPath
Environmental
Management System
Audits, 319–21
P1400.12—GreenPath
Management Review,
329–332
P1400.13—Sustainable
Development, 92–94
Design for the Environment (DfE), 4
document, as defined under ISO
14001:2004, 20–21, 199
documentation

requirements under ISO
14001:2004, 164–65
documents
control of, 198–200
internal versus external, 200
versus records, 199
types of media, 199

E

Earth Day, 1
Earth Summit, 3
emergency preparedness and
response, 242–43
employee involvement, in
environmental management, 7
environmental aspects
associated with contractors and
suppliers, 218
as defined under ISO 14001:2004,
37
in emergency preparedness,
242–43
identifying, 37–38
significant, 39–40
environmental impacts
as defined under ISO 14001:2004,
37
in emergency preparedness,
242–43
identifying, 38–39
monitoring, 254–55
significant, 39–40
environmental management
future of, 335–44
history of, 1–6
and occupational health and safety,
338–40
in the private sector, 10
in the public sector, 10–12
purpose of, 6–8
and social responsibility, 340–41
environmental management system
audits, 270–71
internal, 312–15
environmental performance, 10, 254–
55, 313
environmental policy, 23

designing, 26–27
Environmental Protection Agency
(EPA)
history, 2
National Environmental
Performance Track, 11–12,
279
ethics, environmental, 7
Executive Order 12856, 10
Executive Order 13148, 11
external communication, 141–42

F

*Framework Convention on Climate
Change,* 3

G

general awareness training, 125–26
*Greening the Government Through
Leadership in Environmental
Management,* 11
GreenPath environmental
management system,
background, xviii–xx

H

hazardous waste shipping/disposal
guidance, U. S. Steel Gary
Works EMS procedure
example, 223–28

I

information, types of, 256
integration of ISO 14001 with
other management systems,
337–41
interested party, definition, 87
internal communication, 140–41
International Chamber of Commerce
(ICC), 3
interval scales, of measurement, 255

ISO 9001 certifications, compared
to ISO 14001 certifications,
335–37
ISO 9001:2000 *Quality management
systems—Requirements*
compatibility with ISO
14001:2004, 12
integration with ISO 14001 EMS,
337–41
ISO 14001 certifications
compared to ISO 9001
certifications, 335–37
worldwide statistics, 8–10
ISO 14001:1996, *Environmental
management systems—
Specification with guidance
for use*
experience of SMEs with, 342
revision of, 12
ISO 14001:2004, *Environmental
management systems—
Specification with guidance
for use*
compatibility with ISO 9001:2000,
12
implementation by SMEs, 341–43
integration with ISO 9001 quality
management system,
337–41
intent of
4.1 General requirements,
20–22
4.2 Environmental policy,
25–28
4.3.1 Environmental aspects,
37–40
4.3.2 Legal and other
requirements, 62–64
4.3.3 Objectives, targets and
programs, 85–88
4.4.1 Resources, roles,
responsibility and
authority, 100–102
4.4.2 Competence, training and
awareness, 125–26
4.4.3 Communication, 140–42
4.4.4 Documentation, 164–66
4.4.5 Control of documents,
199–200

4.4.6 Operational control,
216–18
4.4.7 Emergency preparedness
and response, 242–43
4.5.1 Monitoring and
measurement, 254–57,
270–72
4.5.3 Nonconformity,
corrective action and
preventive action,
283–84
4.5.4 Control of records,
300–302
4.5.5 Internal audit, 313–15
4.6 Management review,
325–26
organization of, 12–16
scope of, 21–22
significant changes from ISO
14001:1996
4.1 General requirements,
19–20
4.2 Environmental policy,
24–25
4.3.1 Environmental aspects,
36–37
4.3.2 Legal and other
requirements, 62
4.3.3 Objectives, targets and
programs, 84–85
4.4.1 Resources, roles,
responsibility and
authority, 100
4.4.2 Competence, training and
awareness, 124–25
4.4.3 Communication, 140
4.4.4 Documentation, 164
4.4.5 Control of documents,
198
4.4.6 Operational control, 216
4.4.7 Emergency preparedness
and response, 242
4.5.1 Monitoring and
measurement, 254, 270
4.5.3 Nonconformity,
corrective action and
preventive action,
282–83

4.5.4 Control of records, 300
4.5.5 Internal audit, 312–13
4.6 Management review,
324–25
ISO 14004:1996, *Environmental
management systems—
General guidelines on
principles, systems and support
techniques,* 16
ISO 19011, *Guidelines for quality
and/or environmental
management systems auditing,*
314
ISO 26000 (social responsibility)
guidance document, 340–41

K

Kyoto Protocol, 3

L

legal requirements
compliance with, in environmental
policy, 25–26
identifying, 63–64
lifecycle assessment (LCA), 4

M

management commitment
in environmental management, 7
top, under ISO 14001:2004, 22
management representative, 101–2
management review, 324–26
management systems, integration of
quality and environmental,
337–41
measurement, of environmental
performance, 255–57
medium-sized enterprise, versus small
business, 343
monitoring and measurement,
254–57
Montreal Protocol, 3

N

National Environmental Performance
    Track, 11–12, 279
National Environmental Policy Act
    (NEPA), 1
nominal scales, of measurement, 255
nonconformity, 282–84
    actual versus potential, 283

O

objectives and targets
    establishing, 85
    programs for achieving, 86–87
occupational health and safety, and
    environmental management,
    338–40
OHSAS 18001:1999, *Occupational
    Health and Safety Management
    System Specifications,* 338–40
operational control, 216–18
ordinal scales, of measurement, 255
organization, as defined under ISO
    14001:2004, 20
other requirements
    examples, 62–63
    compliance with, evaluation of,
        270–72
    compliance with, in environmental
        policy, 26

P

plan–do–check–act (PDCA) cycle,
    15–16
pollution prevention (P2), 4, 25
    versus prevention of pollution, 6,
        25
Pollution Prevention Act of 1990
    (PPA), 4
prevention of pollution
    in environmental policy, 25
    versus pollution prevention, 6, 25
preventive action, 282–84
procedures, definition, 165

programs, for achieving objectives
    and targets, components, 87–88
protection, of audit findings, 270–71
public access, to environmental
    policy, 27–28

R

ratio scales, of measurement, 256
records
    control of, 300–302
    as defined under ISO 14001:2004,
        300
    versus documents, 199
    requirements under ISO
        14001:2004, 300–302
    retention period, 301
    training, 126
*Reducing Risk: Setting Priorities and
    Strategies for Environmental
    Protection,* 2
registration, versus certification, 14
regulatory compliance, evaluation of,
    270–72
reliability, versus validity, 256
Reorganization Plan No. 3, 2
resources, requirements under ISO
    14001:2004, 100–101
responsibility, versus authority, 101
risk, 2
risk management, 2

S

SA8000 (Social Accountability)
    Standard, 340–41
self-declaration, versus certification,
    14
Shewhart cycle, 15–16
Silent Spring, 1
skills training, 125–26
small and medium-sized enterprises
    (SMEs), and ISO 14001
    implementation, 341–44
small business, versus medium-sized
    enterprise, 343

social responsibility, and
environmental management,
340–41
Strategic Advisory Group on the
Environment (SAGE), 3–4
supplier, versus contractor, 216
system description, document, 165

T

targets, degree of difficulty, 85–86
Technical Committee (TC) 207, 4
top management obligations, under
ISO 14001:2004, 22
training
identifying needs, 125–26
records, 126

U

*Unfinished Business: A Comparative
Assessment of Environmental
Problems,* 2
United Nations Conference on
Environment and Development
(UNCED), 3
United States Steel Corporation
background, xv–xviii
Gary Complex Level I System
Manual, 175–81
Gary Works EMS procedure,
examples
4.2—Environmental Policy,
28–31
4.3.1—Environmental Aspects,
40–47
4.3.2—Legal and Other
Requirements, 64–69
4.3.3—Objectives, Targets, and
Programs, 88–92
4.4.1—Resources, Roles,
Responsibility, and
Authority, 102–4
4.4.2—Competence, Training,
and Awareness, 127–29

4.4.3—Communication,
154–57
4.4.4—EMS Documentation,
166–74
4.4.5—Document Control,
201–7
4.4.6—Operational Control,
218–28
4.4.7—Emergency
Preparedness and
Response, 244–49
4.5.1—Monitoring and
Measurement,
257–60
4.5.2—Evaluation of
Compliance, 272–75
4.5.3—Nonconformity
and Corrective and
Preventive Action,
284–95
4.5.4—Control of Records,
302–5
4.5.5—Internal Audit,
315–18
4.6—Management Review,
326–29
U.S. Coast Guard Air Station Cape
Cod
background, xx–xxi
communication activities, 161–62
corrective/preventive action, 298
EMS procedure, examples
01—Environmental Aspects
Review Procedure,
51–60
02—Legal Requirements,
71–81
03—Record Keeping,
307–9
04—Training Procedure,
133–35
06—Objectives and Targets,
94–97
07—Document Control
Procedure, 212–14
09—Hazardous Wastes and
Recycling, 237–39

11—Above-Ground Tank
Inspection, 265–67
17—Training for Spill
Response and Other
Incidents, 249–51
18—New Arrivals/Check-In,
135–37
21—Monitoring Air Emissions,
264–65
Environmental Management
System, 189–95
environmental policy, 32–33
organizational structure
and responsibilities,
112–22
internal audits, 321
management review, 332–34

V

validity, versus reliability, 256
verbal communications, approaches
and tools, 146–51

W

waste characterization and
classification guidance,
U. S. Steel Gary Works EMS
procedure example, 220–23
work instructions, definition, 165
worker competence, 124–25
written communications, approaches
and tools, 143–45